Published by Times Books
An imprint of HarperCollins Publishers
1 Robroyston Gate, Glasgow G33 1JN
www.harpercollins.co.uk

HarperCollins Publishers
Macken House, 39/40 Mayor Street Upper
Dublin 1, D01 C9W8, Ireland

First published 2025

© Times Media Limited 2025
Text © Julian Holland 2025
Photographs © see credits page 224
The Times® is a registered trademark of Times Media Ltd

All rights reserved. No part of this publication may be reproduced, stored in a retrieval system, or transmitted, in any form or by any means, electronic, mechanical, photocopying, recording or otherwise without the prior permission in writing of the publisher and copyright owners.

Without limiting the exclusive rights of any author, contributor or the publisher of this publication, any unauthorised use of this publication to train generative artificial intelligence (AI) technologies is expressly prohibited. HarperCollins also exercise their rights under Article 4(3) of the Digital Single Market Directive 2019/790 and expressly reserve this publication from the text and data mining exception.

HarperCollins does not warrant that any website mentioned in this title will be provided uninterrupted, that any website will be error free, that defects will be corrected, or that the website or the server that makes it available are free of viruses or bugs. For full terms and conditions please refer to the site terms provided on the website.

A catalogue record for this book is available from the British Library

ISBN 978 0 00 875861 5

10 9 8 7 6 5 4 3 2 1

Printed in India

If you would like to comment on any aspect of this book,
please contact us at the above address or online.
email: times.books@harpercollins.co.uk

www.timesbooks.co.uk

This book contains FSC™ certified paper and other controlled
sources to ensure responsible forest management.

For more information visit: www.harpercollins.co.uk/green

THE TIMES

BRITISH RAILWAYS

An illustrated history: 1948–1994

JULIAN HOLLAND

Skirting the North Sea, Class '91' 25kV AC electric locomotive No 91022 at speed with an East Coast Main Line express from Kings Cross to Edinburgh on 28 May 1993

Contents

Introduction	6
The birth of British Railways	8
British Railways regions	12
Early line closures	16
The continuation of 'Big Four' locomotive construction	20
Railway hotels	28
Railway works	32
British Railways standard steam locomotives	42
Motive power depots	50
Locomotive exchanges	58
Early diesel, gas turbine and electric locomotives	62
Diesel shunters	68
The 1955 'Modernisation Plan'	74
First-generation diesel-electric locomotives	80
Diesel and gas turbine locomotive prototypes	88
Railway unions and labour disputes	92
Diesel multiple units	94
Blue Pullmans	100
Diesel-hydraulic locomotives	102
Diesel engine sheds	108
Post-war electrification	110
Electric locomotives and multiple units	116
Marshalling yards and freight services	122
British Railways Mark 1 carriages	126
Named trains	130
British Railways ferries	134
Sleeping car trains	136
Motorail	138
Rural branch lines	140
Seaside branch lines	144
Camping coaches	148
Travelling Post Office	150
Railway accidents	154
Trainspotting	158
British Railways corporate design and publicity	164
The 'Beeching Report'	168
Mass railway closures	172
A new identity	178
InterCity	180
The end of steam haulage	184
Second-generation diesel-electric locomotives	190
High-speed trains	196
Electrification	200
Passenger and freight sectorisation	204
Railway preservation	208
The death of British Rail	214
Index	220
Acknowledgements	224

Introduction

In 2024 the newly elected Labour Government announced plans to re-nationalise Britain's railway passenger services. However, we have already been there before, 77 years ago, though that time it was the entirety of the country's railways (with a few minor exceptions) that was nationalised.

Following the post-war Labour Government's decision to nationalise much of Britain's transport undertakings, mining and heavy industry, British Railways (BR) was born on 1 January 1948. Soon to be loathed and loved in equal measure by the country's hard-pressed travelling public (most of whom did not own a car), the new state-controlled railway system was saddled with an archaic and worn-out network, and decrepit motive power and rolling stock brought on by six years of wartime hardship and a lack of maintenance and investment.

However, by the early 1950s the tide had slowly started to turn, with a gradual return to profitability and the introduction of new standardised classes of steam locomotives and rolling stock. At the same time the Branch Lines Committee axed several thousand miles of unprofitable rural lines across Britain. Sadly, the optimism was short-lived as militant rail unions were already rolling up their sleeves for a confrontation with the Government – there followed several years of disputes which culminated in the infamous national rail strike of 1955. This seventeen-day walkout ended with irreversible damage to the railways, especially on the freight side where already dwindling traffic was permanently lost to road transport.

Nonetheless, development continued. In 1955 the Manchester to Sheffield route via Woodhead Tunnel was opened to electric traction, and BR published what is known as its 'Modernisation Plan', *Modernisation and Re-Equipment of British Railways*. The latter foresaw the hurried introduction of diesel haulage and the eradication of steam motive power by the 1960s. Meanwhile, in 1955 BR also posted its first loss, which only increased in the subsequent years, reaching £67.7 million per year by 1960. As a result of the mounting losses, *The Reshaping of British Railways* (or the 'Beeching Report' as it is commonly known) was published in 1963. This led to the closure of

The 'unicycling lion' was the first British Railways' logo that was applied to steam locomotives or their tenders.

a further 4,500 route miles of railway by the 1970s, along with 2,300 stations and the loss of 68,000 railway jobs. British Railways had, sadly, reached its nadir.

The end for British Railways came at the beginning of 1965 when it rebranded its public image as British Rail and went on to introduce the highly successful InterCity brand of passenger trains, High Speed Trains and freight sectorisation. In this form, British Rail survived until 1993, when mounting debt led to the passing of the Railways Act by Parliament, ushering in a new era of privatisation.

This book is the story of the life and times of this equally much-loved and much-despised national institution from its birth in 1948 to its demise in 1994.

Seen here at Oxford on a Paddington to Worcester service in the early 1960s, one of the former GWR locomotives built by British Railways, 'Castle' Class 4-6-0 No 7008 Swansea Castle was completed at Swindon Works in May 1948 and withdrawn from Old Oak Common shed (81A) in September 1964.

The birth of British Railways

'Railway mania' was sweeping across Britain by the mid-19th century. Vast profits were being made by speculators investing in newly established railway companies at a time when new railway lines were spreading, seemingly uncontrollably, across the land. As a snapshot, in the short time between 1845 and 1847, Parliament authorised the construction of around 8,000 miles of railway line, and about 270 independent railway companies received government approval during that period. Substantial profits were enjoyed by those investors who had struck it rich by backing the more successful ventures. Conversely, some hapless investors lost a fortune as many enterprises faltered, their proposals incorporated into flourishing ongoing schemes of the larger and more aggressive companies – many companies were simply just wound up and their schemes abandoned. There was limited structure in the early development of Britain's railways, with some companies running on relatively short, sometimes rural routes, and doomed to failure from the outset. However, some of the more lucrative ventures were eventually incorporated into the grander and more successful companies that had already been created and were thriving, such as the Great Western Railway and the London & North Western Railway.

By the outbreak of the First World War in 1914, Britain's railways comprised around 20,000 route miles of track owned by 120 separate companies. For strategic reasons the railways were placed under government control and were relentlessly worked around the clock in support of the war effort. When hostilities came to an end they were seriously run-down and in need of huge investment. Furthermore, the country was unable to support so many diverse and, in some cases,

LMS Stanier Class '5MT' 4-6-0 No 5047 trundles through Dumfries with a down mixed goods train, c.1946.

coexisting companies, and drastic measures were urgently required to secure the future of rail transport. As a result, in 1920 Sir Eric Geddes, the Minister of Transport, submitted a proposal to Parliament for the nationalisation of Britain's railways, but this plan came at the time of a post-war coalition government and insufficient support was forthcoming. On the back of the proposal, however, the 1921 Railways Act was introduced, and those 120 railway companies were consequently incorporated in 1923 into what became known as the 'Big Four' – Great Western Railway (GWR), London Midland & Scottish Railway (LMS), London & North Eastern Railway (LNER) and Southern Railway (SR).

The GWR, LMS and LNER benefitted from high volumes of freight traffic, including vast tonnages of coal, as well as from long-distance passenger traffic. In contrast, the predominantly passenger-focused SR carried more than a quarter of the total UK passenger traffic over much shorter routes in some of the most densely populated parts of the country, and its early electrification policy responded to its particular needs. The four companies cooperated on significant railway industry matters, despite being nominally in competition with each other, and during the Second World War their management boards were once again united under the direction of the Railway Executive Committee. Upon election of a Labour government in 1945, with its landslide majority, the opportunity was finally seized to nationalise Britain's railway system.

The Second World War left Britain's railway infrastructure war-torn yet again, and to all intents and purposes entirely bankrupt through lack of investment and maintenance, with many of its locomotive and rolling stock fleets either destroyed or damaged. The 'Big Four' group of companies that had been brought about in the aftermath of the First World War had similarly taken over a run-down railway system, in what was then deemed to be a better alternative to nationalisation. Within a decade they went on to turn it into one of the best in the world. Sadly this progress was quite literally stopped in its tracks while back under government control, specifically that of the Railway Executive Committee, between August 1939 and December 1947.

Most of the transport and heavy industry interests in Britain were nationalised under the post-war Labour Government. The Transport Act was given royal assent in August 1947, and the following year the railways and virtually all public transport systems came under the control of the new British Transport Commission (BTC), which was responsible to the Ministry of Transport, overseeing the systems' modernisation and integration. Each form of transport was controlled by an executive committee, the Railway Executive being duly created to administer all but a few minor railways. Thus, on 1 January 1948, British Railways was born.

LEFT: *The 1947 Transport Act was the Act of Parliament under which the Labour Government nationalised Britain's railways.*

OVERLEAF: *Reaching every corner of Britain, British Railways' network in 1949.*

British Railways regions

Under the newly nationalised service, the railway network was divided into six operating regions: Southern, Western, London Midland, Eastern, North Eastern and Scottish. They were loosely based on the old 'Big Four' companies' systems but with the separate region for Scotland. (Military and industrial railways did not come under the umbrella of BR, neither did the London Transport railway system, which was taken over by the London Transport Executive.) Despite some central control, the regions were afforded an appreciable degree of autonomy and inter-regional rivalry continued as before, particularly on the Western Region.

BR's Regional Managers were responsible to the Railway Executive for day-to-day operations; after the Railway Executive was abolished in 1952, they then reported to the British Transport Commission (BTC) at their offices in Marylebone Road, London. From 1955, under BR's Modernisation Plan, they were granted greater autonomy for the overall management of their regions. Matters common to more than one BR region were managed by the Railways Division, which mainly consisted of the headquarters staff of the former Railway Executive, forming an integral part of the BTC's head office. In 1963, the BTC itself was abolished and replaced by the British Railways Board (BRB). The six BR regions then acted as statutory boards subordinate to the BRB, with its Regional Managers reporting to the Board in accordance with the provisions of the Transport Act 1962.

The regions (see map overleaf) were structured as follows:

Southern Region

The Southern Region (SR) was largely based upon the former Southern Railway area, which had been the smallest of the 'Big Four'. Relatively self-contained, it was operated largely by electric traction. It covered south London, southern England and the south coast, encompassing the busy commuter belt areas in Kent, Sussex and Surrey, with some services also extending into Berkshire, Wiltshire, Dorset and even as far as Devon and northeastern Cornwall, which latterly became colloquially named 'The Withered Arm'. The SR also operated services on the Isle of Wight as well as assuming operating responsibility for the former Somerset & Dorset Joint Railway route, with locomotive traction provision being undertaken by the London Midland Region. The SR had three operating divisions – Eastern, Central and Western – all administered from offices at London Waterloo station.

Seen here in the early 1950s, BR-built 'Castle' Class 4-6-0 No 7012 Barry Castle being oiled around by the fireman prior to departure from Swansea (High Street) station for London Paddington.

Western Region

The Western Region (WR) initially consisted of the former Great Western Railway, with the addition of some minor railways and joint lines. Its regional boundaries were controversially adjusted several times during the 1950s, most notably taking in some Southern and Western Region lines, but also certain lines west of Birmingham which, in 1963, were transferred to the London Midland Region. Administered from offices at London Paddington station, the WR continued in very much the same vein as its predecessor, the GWR, which dated back to its original formation in 1833 and was the only company of the 'Big Four' to retain its name.

London Midland Region

The area covered by London Midland Region (LMR) principally included former LMS lines in England and Wales. It was the largest of the 'Big Four' by area, consisting of the West Coast Main Line, the Midland Main Line south of Carlisle and the ex-Midland cross-country route from Bristol to Leeds. The London, Tilbury and Southend line, a peculiar anomaly completely isolated from other LMR routes, was in 1949 transferred to the Eastern Region. In 1958 there was a major redrawing of boundaries, with LMR lines in South Wales and southwest of Birmingham being transferred to the Western Region. Additionally, lines in South Yorkshire and Lincolnshire passed to the Eastern Region, but in return the LMR took control of the former Great Central Railway lines outside of those counties. Additionally, LMR lines in North and West Yorkshire passed to the North Eastern Region in 1958. The LMR was initially managed from offices adjacent to London Euston station, then later from Stanier House in Birmingham.

Eastern Region

The Eastern Region (ER), together with the North Eastern Region (NER) which it absorbed in 1967, covered most lines of the former London & North Eastern Railway, except in Scotland. Over time the ER was geographically organised rather than being based upon pre-Nationalisation ownership, with the aforementioned boundary changes with the LMR taking place in 1949 and 1958. In the 1960s the ER became one of the regions most affected by the Beeching 'Axe' (see pages 168–171), losing route miles in every county that it served. The ER lines were managed as the Great Northern (London King's Cross services) and the Great Eastern (London Liverpool Street and Fenchurch Street services), administered from offices at Liverpool Street station. Following the merger with the NER, the ER's main headquarters were relocated to York.

North Eastern Region

The North Eastern Region was a near direct post-Nationalisation descendent of the pre-Grouping North Eastern Railway and was managed from offices at York. The NER's trunk routes comprised the northernmost section of the East Coast Main Line in England between Doncaster and just north of Berwick, the line between Hull and Leeds, the Tyne Valley line between Newcastle and Carlisle, and other connecting lines in Northumberland, Durham, and the East and North Ridings of Yorkshire. Rural branch lines in Northumberland, Durham and the Yorkshire Dales and Moors also fell within the region, which subsequently bore the brunt of Beeching closures. In addition, the NER also covered the heavily industrialised conurbations of Teesside, Wearside and Tyneside, with its suburban passenger services and coal, steel and chemicals freight traffic. Although it gained former LMS lines from the re-drawing of the boundary with the LMR in 1963, the NER was disbanded in 1967 when it was merged with the ER, thereafter reflecting the LNER of the 'Big Four' period.

Scottish Region

Scotland's railways were brought under unified management for the first time through the creation of BR's Scottish Region, its two main constituents comprising the former LMS and LNER lines in Scotland, and, initially, a variety of shipping lines. The Scottish Region, consisting of 3,625 route miles, was almost the same size as the WR and represented 19% of BR's entire mileage. It was managed from offices at Buchanan Street in Glasgow. Its network was greatly reduced in the 1960s under the Beeching 'Axe', and cutbacks even continued following the doctor's resignation in June 1965, such as Glasgow's Princes Street and Buchanan Street stations in September 1965 and November 1966 respectively, and the controversial closure of the Waverley Line between Carlisle and Edinburgh in January 1969.

OVERLEAF: *The six geographical regions of British Railways after nationalisation.*

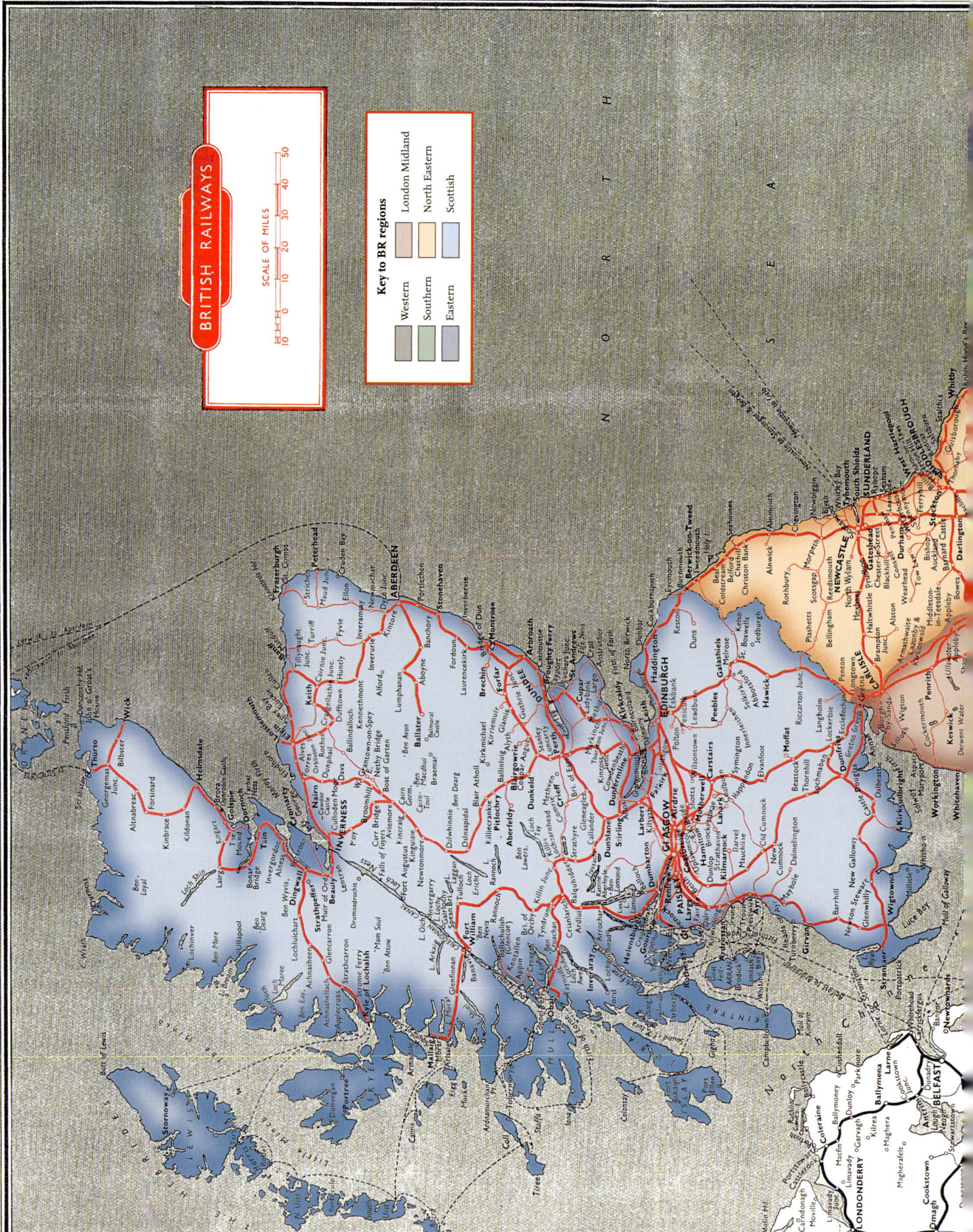

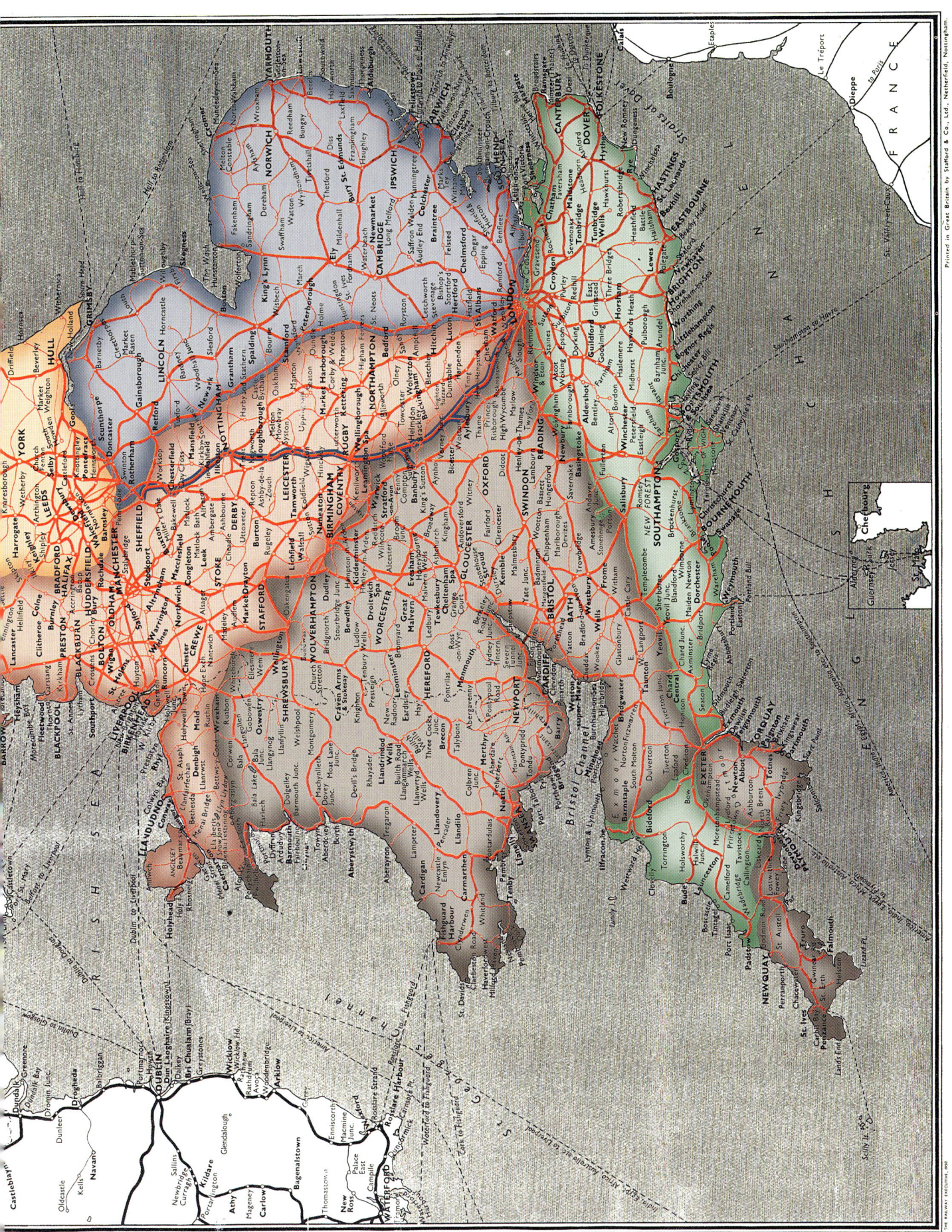

Early line closures: the Branch Lines Committee

At the end of hostilities in 1945 the 'Big Four' railway companies were in a severely run-down state. When Nationalisation followed in 1948 the newly formed British Transport Commission (BTC) wasted no time in seeking to reduce mounting losses on lightly used rural lines. Years before Dr Richard Beeching came onto the scene (see page 168–171), the BTC's Branch Lines Committee was formed. It was a national committee of Railway Executive members, with one representative from each BR region, and its remit was to investigate the commercial standing of every branch line. Consideration was also given to the potential replacement of steam-hauled passenger services with lightweight diesel railcars.

BR, with some optimism, had taken over a substantial network of around 20,000 route miles of railway, with some duplication of routes which had historically evolved during the railway companies' competitive pre-Grouping years of the late 19th century. Together with many loss-making rural branch lines, this all combined to cause a significant drain on BR's finances. The Branch Lines Committee was tasked with closing the least-used lines. Setting the course for the two decades that followed, its legacy continued after it was disbanded in 1953 and the BR regions took up the mantle.

In terms of making closure decisions, the London Midland Region was far from proactive; in contrast, the Western Region embraced the culling process, especially in the West Country where it closed lines such as the Princetown branch in 1956 and the branch from Totnes to Ashburton (for passengers in 1958 and goods traffic in 1962) – the route of today's heritage railway to Buckfastleigh.

Overall, the closure of uneconomic railways gathered pace. Between 1948 and 1962, over 230 routes were closed, totalling around 3,300 route miles. The railway community was decimated, with staff numbers being reduced by more than a quarter. Every geographical region of the country was

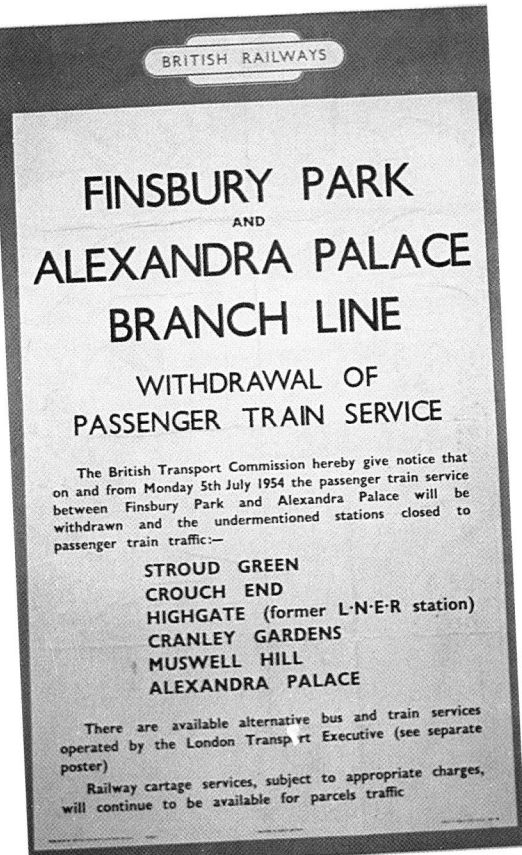

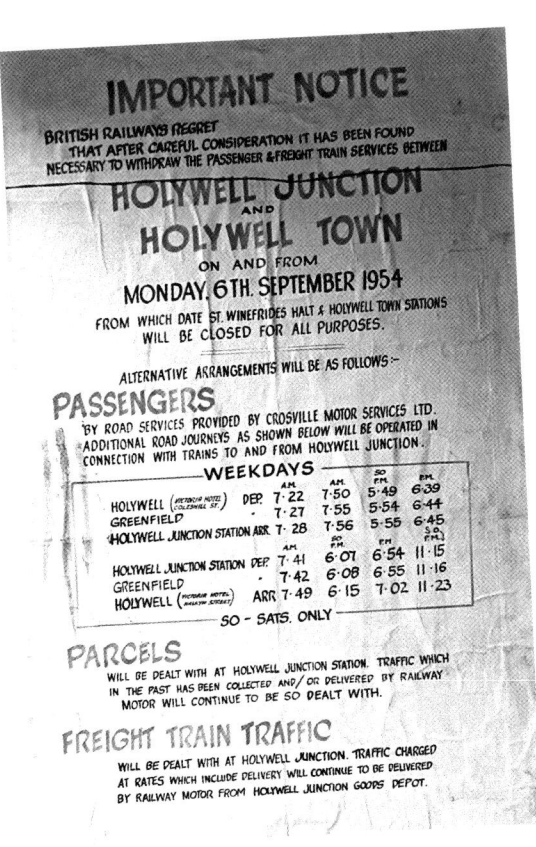

TOP: The 1½-mile branch line from Holywell Junction on the North Wales mainline to Holywell Town closed on 6 September 1954.
BOTTOM: The 3-mile Finsbury Park to Alexandra Palace line closed to passengers on 3 July 1954.

TOP: *LNER Class 'N1' 0-6-2T No 4587 is seen at Alexandra Palace with a train for King's Cross c.1947.*
BOTTOM: *Ivatt Class '2MT' 2-6-2T No 41276 is seen at Holywell Town on the last day of services, 4 September 1954.*

A 'foreigner' from the Western Region, BR-built Class '1600' 0-6-0PT No 1646 approaches Skelbo station with a mixed train for Dornoch on 3 June 1960. This 7¾-mile branch line from The Mound closed just 10 days later.

Ex-GWR '2251' Class 0-6-0 No 2240 at Winchester Chesil station with a 'last' train on 5 March 1960. Located on the Didcot, Newbury & Southampton Railway, this line closed two days later. However, it was reopened for holiday traffic between June and September that year and also in the summer 1961, closing completely on 9 September 1961.

impacted. The numbers of line closures per region were as follows:

Southwest England – 14
Southern England – 23
Eastern England – 20
Central England – 51
Wales – 35
Northern England – 47
Scotland – 42
TOTAL – 232 line closures

Of particular note was the closure of the Midland & Great Northern Joint Railway in East Anglia on 28 February 1959, the closure of the Midland & South Western Junction Railway between Cheltenham and Andover on 9 September 1961, and the trans-Pennine line between Barnard Castle and Penrith on 20 January 1962.

The cull of branch lines during the 1950s did not deliver the desired results; some studies even found that it would have been far more cost effective to subsidise some of them, notwithstanding the social benefits that could have been derived by their retention. This fact was reinforced by the views of several protest movements that had emerged. BR's finances continued to haemorrhage and in 1955 it recorded its first operating loss, with much freight traffic being lost to more flexible and competitively priced road transport. The national rail strikes of the 1950s only compounded this situation, and car and lorry mileage was soaring year upon year, having been fuelled by the lifting of petrol rationing.

A radical solution was needed from the Government to resolve the railway's dire commercial standing. Consequently, from 1 January 1963 the BTC was abolished under the 1962 Transport Act and replaced by the British Railways Board. The Act included provisions to limit the powers of local Transport Consultative Committees holding inquiries into any closure proposals, thereby removing any obligation to consider strategic and social factors.

Britain's railways had been an ongoing burden on the taxpayer since Nationalisation in 1948 – but so had the Armed Forces, the Police and the NHS, which are never expected to make a profit but to operate within a budget. Although the 1955 Modernisation Plan had attempted to bring the railways into the 20th century, the steady loss of passengers and freight to road transport, coupled with a worn-out system, out-of-date working practices, over-manning and strike action had, by 1961, brought about a staggering £87 million annual working deficit for British Railways (£1.65 billion at today's figures), and the Government had to stem these ever-increasing losses to the public purse. More drastic action was necessary.

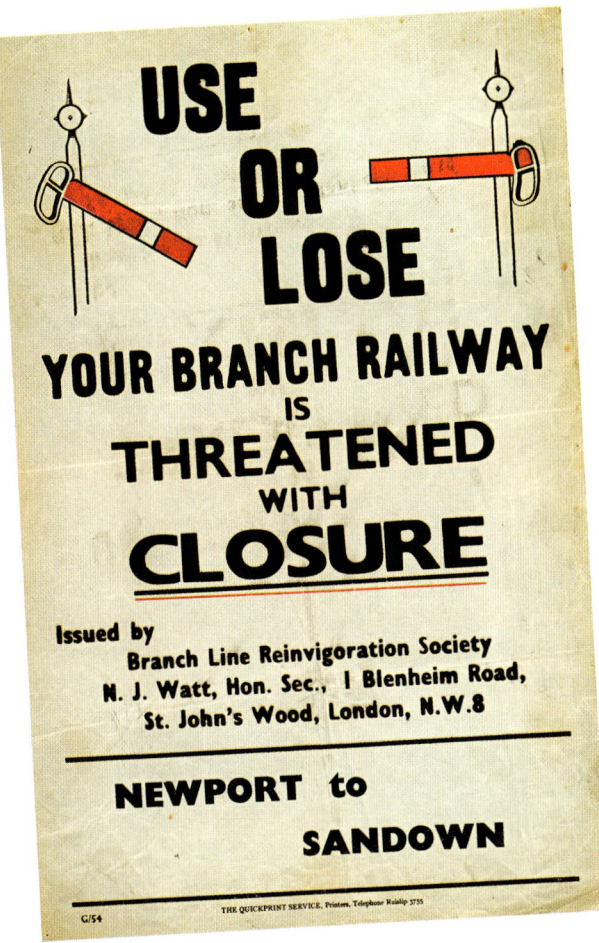

This 'Use it or lose it' poster was displayed at stations on the Newport to Sandown branch line on the Isle of Wight. The message obviously fell on deaf ears as the line closed on 6 February 1956.

Ivatt Class '4MT' 2-6-0 No 43145 at Peterborough North station with a last train for Wisbech North on 28 February 1959. The Midland & Great Northern Joint Railway line from Peterborough North to Wisbech North closed two days later.

The continuation of 'Big Four' locomotive construction

One of the challenges facing British Railways after its inception was the diversity and age of its rolling stock. The majority of its steam locomotive fleet had seen between 50 and 75 years' service, including working through two world wars. The development of mainline diesel traction had only just begun, and while a limited number of modest, although robust and extremely reliable, six-coupled diesel shunting locomotives had been introduced by the 'Big Four' companies before Nationalisation, it would be another decade before sufficient numbers of well-proven 'thoroughbred' diesel locomotives could be regularly called upon for work around the network for passenger and freight diagrams. For the time being, the reliable but nevertheless labour-intensive steam locomotive was still very much in favour.

Great strides had been made in the 1930s by the 'Big Four' companies in the development of the steam locomotive – with engines such as the renowned Gresley and Bulleid Pacifics, Stanier's Pacifics and mixed traffic 4-6-0s, and the Collett 4-6-0s – but the onset of the Second World War saw any further progress immediately stymied. However, after the cessation of hostilities some of the most successful of the 'Big Four' steam locomotive designs were perpetuated on the basis that they were already well proven and there was no further development work necessary. Furthermore, they could be quickly introduced into traffic to replace locomotives lost during the war. Notable among these were Stanier's ubiquitous 'Black Five' 4-6-0s, Collett's 'Castle' Class 4-6-0s, Hawksworth's 'County' Class 4-6-0s and Arthur Peppercorn's Class 'A1' 4-6-2s. Also of note were the extremely innovative 'Merchant Navy' and the 'West Country'/'Battle of Britain' light Pacifics designed by Oliver Bulleid, some, in fact, having been introduced during wartime since they were officially classified as mixed traffic locomotives.

Western Region

'Manor' Class 4-6-0 Nos 7820-7829 Collett's 'Manor' Class 4-6-0 was the GWR's late-1930s lighter version design of the 'Grange' Class, for use on lines with restricted route availability. However, the outbreak of the Second World War saw just twenty being built. A further batch of ten locomotives (numbered 7820-7829) was subsequently constructed by BR at Swindon Works in 1950. Their light axle loading enabled them to work into Cornwall and over the Cambrian lines extending along the Welsh west coast and across to Shrewsbury. No 7829, along with No 7808 from the original batch, remained in service at Gloucester until the end of Western Region steam in December 1965. Remarkably, nine of the thirty built have survived into preservation, five being BR-built examples.

'Castle' Class 4-6-0 Nos 7008-7037 (▶) The culmination of this famous class was the production of the '70XX' series at Swindon Works between 1946 and 1950, Nos 7008-7037 being built following Nationalisation in 1948. It is remarkable that a design that first appeared in 1923 and which was a development of Churchward's 'Star' Class of 1906 should have still been in production during the BR era. The final 'Castles' embodied several refinements including the fitting of double chimneys, larger superheaters and re-profiled outside steam pipes, enhancing their capabilities further and providing a capacity for high-speed running. The rapid dieselisation of the Western Region saw the final 'Castle', No 7029 *Clun Castle*, taken out of service at Gloucester depot in December 1965.

BR-built 'Castle' Class 4-6-0 No 7026 Tenby Castle *in ex-works condition outside Swindon Works on 14 February 1954. Built at Swindon in 1949 this fine locomotive was withdrawn from Tyseley shed (2A) in October 1964.*

'Modified Hall' Class 4-6-0 Nos 6991–6999, 7900–7929
These 4-6-0s were a radical development by Hawksworth of the earlier Collett '4900' 'Hall' Class, with 61 being built at Swindon Works from 1944, and BR continuing their construction until 1950. The original 'Hall' design was so successful that a total of 330 locomotives of both classes were built, although nearly everything about the Hawksworth 'Modified Hall' was different to the Collett design. Hawksworth subsequently made further improvements to some of the locomotives due to the declining quality of coal, including a larger three-row superheater and improved draughting and hopper ashpans. Some were fitted with the flat, high-sided Hawksworth tender.

'2251' Class 0-6-0 Nos 3218–3219 Designed by Charles Collett, the GWR '2251' Class 0-6-0 was first introduced in 1930, with 120 examples constructed at Swindon Works, the last design of 0-6-0 tender locomotive to be built in Britain. Designed for mixed traffic work and equipped with the same boiler as the '9400' heavy pannier tanks built from the 1940s and into the 1950s, they were particularly well suited to the steeply graded branch lines in Mid and North Wales. Two were built under BR auspices, No 3218 being the first BR locomotive to be built at Swindon Works, in 1948, finally being taken out of service from Templecombe depot in May 1965.

'1500' Class 0-6-0PT Nos 1500–1509 The Hawksworth heavy-duty '1500' Class 0-6-0PT first appeared from Swindon Works with outside cylinders and Walschaerts valve gear in 1949. It was originally intended as a new BR Western Region standard class shunter, but in the event only ten were built. Most were employed on empty coaching stock movements between Old Oak Common carriage sidings and London Paddington station, while others worked in the Newport area. Their route availability and short wheelbase limited their usefulness, and they proved to be short-lived, with BR No 1509 being withdrawn in August

Brand new BR-built '1600' Class 0-6-0PT No 1662 outside Swindon Works on 13 March 1955. Only three days old when pictured here, this locomotive was withdrawn from Hereford shed (85C) at the end of 1963.

1959 and the last three from Old Oak Common in 1963. Three passed into industrial service with the National Coal Board, and resultantly No 1501 survived into preservation.

'5700' Class 0-6-0PT Nos 6760–6779, 9662–9682 Collett's '5700' Class 0-6-0PT was the standard GWR locomotive design for shunting and light-goods work when it was introduced in 1929, but also proved versatile for use on branch line passenger duties. No fewer than 837 were built between Swindon Works and five private locomotive builders, intended as replacements for older GWR saddle and pannier tank locomotives, some dating back to the 1880s. Nos 6750–6779 were built at Swindon Works between 1947 and 1950, and Nos 9662–9682 built entirely under BR ownership at Swindon Works in 1948–49. Locomotives numbered in the 67XX series were used exclusively for shunting duties, not being vacuum brake-fitted nor with automatic train control.

'1600' Class 0-6-0PT Nos 1600–1669 (▲) Designed by Frederick Hawksworth, this class was built for light branch lines, short-distance freight transfers and shunting duties.

Nearing the end of its short life, BR-built 'Modified Hall' Class 4-6-0 No 6999 Capel Dewi Hall is seen here at Oxford shed in the summer of 1965. Built at Swindon Works early in 1949 this locomotive was withdrawn from Oxford shed (81F) at the end of 1965.

A pure GWR design based on William Dean's '2021' Class of 1897, all 70 were built by BR at Swindon Works between 1949 and 1955. This was the eleventh hour for BR steam locomotive construction and consequently withdrawals began early – No 1652, built in December 1954, was withdrawn from Swansea East Dock shed in January 1960. The last three to remain in BR service were withdrawn from Croes Newydd shed during 1966 and one of these, No 1638, has survived into preservation.

'9400' Class 0-6-0PT Nos 3400–3409, 8400–8499, 9410–9499 This Hawksworth class was a development of the '5700' Class designed for heavy shunting, short-distance freight, and passenger and empty stock duties, but many had a short life due to the onset of dieselisation. The first ten locomotives, Nos 9400–9409, were built at the GWR Swindon Works and were superheated. A further 200 non-superheated locomotives appeared after Nationalisation, built variously between 1949 and 1956 and subcontracted to the Hunslet Engine Company, Robert Stephenson & Hawthorns, W. G. Bagnall and the Yorkshire Engine Company. Nos 8400–8406 were used at Bromsgrove on banking duties.

Southern Region

'West Country' and 'Battle of Britain' Class 4-6-2 Nos 34071–34110 Bulleid's lightweight 4-6-2 locomotives were named after either West Country locations or wartime RAF air squadrons, fighters and personalities. Unlike the 'Merchant Navy' Class, just 60 'Light Pacifics' were rebuilt. Whilst most of the class emerged from Brighton Works between 1945–49, BR Eastleigh Works built the final batch of ten, and these were taken into service between February 1950 and January 1951. The end of Southern Region steam services in July 1967 saw most remaining members being scrapped, but thanks to Dai Woodham's scrapyard at Barry, twenty passed into preservation.

'Merchant Navy' Class 4-6-2 Nos 35021–35030 (▼) Designed by Oliver Bulleid, this class was the first Pacific-type to run on the Southern Railway, and was introduced during the Second World War in 1941. This radical locomotive design, with its clean lines using air-smoothed casing, elevated motive power into the modern age. The first two batches of ten were delivered from Eastleigh Works during 1941–42 and 1944–45. A further order for ten was fulfilled by BR Eastleigh Works between 1948–49, with boilers and tenders constructed at Brighton and their frames at Ashford Works. During the 1950s their air-smoothed casing was removed and chain-driven valve gear replaced with Walschaerts valve gear.

'Leader' Class 0-6-0+0-6-0T No 36001 (▼) Bulleid's experimental articulated 0-6-0+0-6-0T aimed to extend the life of steam traction, eliminating the operational drawbacks of conventional steam locomotives. Developed between 1946–49, the unique design with an offset boiler fired from a central cabin, driving cabs at each end, and two chain-driven bogies, each powered by three cylinders, resulted in a diesel-like appearance. One locomotive was completed at Brighton Works and underwent trials based around Brighton. A further four were begun, but design problems, indifferent performance and high development costs led to 36001 being withdrawn in November 1950. Both 36001 and the other incomplete locomotives were quietly scrapped during 1951.

Rebuilt BR-built 'Merchant Navy' Class 4-6-2 No 35022 Holland America Line *on the turntable at Exmouth Junction shed (72A) on 12 September 1965. Built at Eastleigh Works in 1948 this powerful locomotive was withdrawn from Weymouth Radipole shed (70G) in May 1966.*

Oliver Bulleid's 'Leader' Class 0-6-0+0-6-0T No 36001 at Eastleigh on 21 October 1950. Completed at Brighton Works in June 1949 this unusual and unsuccessful locomotive was withdrawn in November 1950.

London Midland Region

BR-built 'Coronation' Class 4-6-2 No 46257 City of Salford waits to depart from Euston station in May 1956. Built at Crewe Works in 1948 this locomotive was withdrawn from Carlisle Kingmoor shed (12A) in September 1964.

Fairburn Class '4MT' 2-6-4T Nos 42050–42186, 42190–42199 Built between 1945–51 to a design that Charles Fairburn based on the earlier 1935 Stanier 2-6-4T, itself derived from Henry Fowler's 1927 design. It was distinguishable from Stanier's engines by a gap in the running plate ahead of the cylinders and it had a shorter wheelbase. The modified design subsequently formed the basis for the later BR Standard Class '4MT' tank built from 1951. Intended mainly for suburban passenger services, most of the locomotives were constructed at Derby Works, with Nos 42066–42106 built at Brighton Works. The class was withdrawn between 1961 and 1967 and two have survived in preservation.

Ivatt Class '4MT' 2-6-0 Nos 43003–43161 The first three locomotives of this class emerged from Horwich Works in 1947, the remaining 159 being built following Nationalisation. With motion and pipework well exposed, the design incorporated high running plates for ease of maintenance. Together with the double chimneys originally fitted to Nos 43000–43049, but later replaced, they were considered by many to be the ugliest LMS-designed locomotives to ever appear. Their construction was divided between Horwich, Doncaster, and Darlington Works. Robert Riddles closely based his BR Standard Class '4MT' 2-6-0 on this design. Darlington Works-built No 43106, the last to be withdrawn, in June 1968, immediately passed into preservation from BR.

Ivatt Class '2MT' 2-6-2T Nos 41210–41329 Designed by Henry George Ivatt as a light, mixed traffic locomotive to replace various elderly LMS tank locomotive classes. Built between 1946–52, just ten emerged from Crewe Works before Nationalisation. All members of the class were constructed at Crewe Works apart from the final batch of ten, which were built at Derby Works. They incorporated labour-saving devices such as self-emptying ashpans and rocking grates. Although primarily London Midland Region locomotives, the final 30 built at Crewe, Nos 41290–41319, were allocated to the Southern Region from new, with a small number sent to the Western Region's Bristol Bath Road depot.

Stanier Class '5MT' 4-6-0 Nos 44658–44757 Designed by William Stanier, the successful 'Black Fives' were built between 1934–51, 842 in total being constructed. Following Nationalisation, locomotives Nos 44658–44757 entered service between May 1949 and May 1951, although not in a numerical sequence, having been built by BR Crewe Works (Nos 44658–44667 and 44718–44757) and Horwich Works (Nos 44668–44717). Although some of the BR-built class members survived in service during the last months of steam traction, surprisingly not one single BR-built example has been preserved from the 100 built, although eighteen locomotives built prior to Nationalisation have been preserved, twelve having passed directly following BR service.

Ivatt 'Coronation' Class 4-6-2 No 46257 (▲) The Stanier LMS 'Coronation' Class were some of the most powerful steam locomotives ever used in Britain, a total of 38 being built at Crewe Works between 1937–48. The final two 'Coronation' Class locomotives were constructed to H. G. Ivatt's modified design at the outset, without streamlined casing and fitted with smoke deflectors to prevent drifting exhaust from obscuring the crew's forward vision. Also fitted were roller bearings, a redesigned cab-side and rear frame, and a cast steel trailing truck, as well as a hopper ashpan and rocking grate. The final class member, No 46257 *City of Salford*, was designed by H. G. Ivatt and emerged from Crewe Works with BR numbering in May 1948. It was withdrawn in September 1964.

Ivatt Class '2MT' 2-6-0 Nos 46420–46527 (▼) Designed by H. G. Ivatt, this lightweight class was built for cross country and branch line services. It was introduced two years before Nationalisation. Offering a greater range, it was essentially a tender version of the Class '2MT' 2-6-2T. Just twenty of the class were built before Nationalisation, with the rest built between 1948 and 1953. Nos 46420–46464 were built at Crewe, 46465–46502 at Darlington, and 46503–46527 at Swindon Works. Allocated to all regions except the Southern, most were based on the London Midland Region. The last members were withdrawn in 1966 and seven, all BR-built examples, passed into preservation. The design was later adopted as the basis for the BR Standard Class '2MT'.

BR-built Ivatt Class '2MT' 2-6-0 No 46459 at Whitehaven Bransty in 1954. Built at Crewe Works in 1950 this locomotive was withdrawn from Nuneaton shed (5E) in September 1965.

Eastern and North Eastern Regions

Peppercorn Class 'A1' 4-6-2 Nos 60114–60162 (▶) Designed by Arthur Peppercorn for the LNER, this class was a further development of a design by Edward Thompson, in turn based on Nigel Gresley's original 'A1' (later rebuilt as 'A3') Class locomotive. Designed for the heaviest passenger trains on the East Coast Main Line (ECML), during the austere post-war years their reliability and ease of maintenance proved their worth. BR Darlington Works built Nos 60130–60152, the remainder being built at Doncaster Works. By the early 1960s advancing dieselisation sadly saw their days numbered and withdrawals took place between 1962–66. None survived into preservation, although the

Peppercorn Class 'A1' 4-6-2 No 60123 H. A. Ivatt at Croxdale, south of Durham, on 12 May 1950. Built at Doncaster Works in 1949 this locomotive was withdrawn from Ardsley shed (56B) in October 1962.

Class 'K1' 2-6-0 No 62021 at work at Peth Lane, Blaydon, on 26 April 1959. Built by the North British Locomotive Company in 1949 this versatile locomotive was withdrawn from Tyne Dock shed (52H) in October 1966.

A1 Steam Locomotive Trust's famous North Road Darlington Works-built No 60163 *Tornado* has deservedly filled this void.

Peppercorn Class 'A2' 4-6-2 Nos 60526–60539 The 'A2' Class was a mixed traffic locomotive based on an original Thompson design, the first locomotive emerging in December 1947 from Doncaster Works on the eve of Nationalisation. Originally 30 were ordered but just a further fourteen were built at BR Doncaster Works in 1948, incorporating several design modifications. The final 'A2' built, No 60539 *Bronzino*, entered traffic at Heaton shed in August 1948. Employed on a variety of passenger and parcels services, the 'A2's allocated to depots in England were withdrawn between 1962–63, and the three remaining Scottish class members were taken out of service in 1966, No 60532 *Blue Peter* then being acquired for preservation.

Thompson Class 'B1' 4-6-0 Nos 61274–61409 The LNER Class 'B1' was the most successful of Edward Thompson's designs, a total of 410 being built between 1942–52. Initially built at Darlington Works, the 136 members of the class built following Nationalisation were jointly constructed by the North British Locomotive Company (Nos 61274–61399), with just the final ten built at BR's Darlington Works (Nos 61400–61409). As a general mixed traffic workhorse, the LNER/BR 'B1' Class could be compared with the LMS 'Black Five' and the GWR 'Hall' classes and were popular with crews, working all over the former LNER system and occasionally beyond. Withdrawals took place between 1961–67 and two passed into preservation, one built under BR auspices.

Worsdell Class 'J72' 0-6-0T Nos 69001–69028 These shunting locomotives were designed by Wilson Worsdell and first introduced in 1898. They were built over a period of 54 years by three different railway companies, the original twenty emerging from the North Eastern Railway (NER) Darlington Works in 1899. Further class members with slight modifications and totalling 55 were built between 1914–23. Nigel Gresley reclassified them as the LNER 'J72' (from NER 'E1') and proceeded to have a further ten built in 1925. Remarkably, a further 28 were built at BR Darlington Works between 1949–51. Just two remained by 1964 and were taken into departmental stock temporarily until the end of BR steam on the North Eastern Region, one passing into preservation.

Peppercorn Class 'K1' 2-6-0 Nos 62001–62070 (▲) Peppercorn's Class 'K1' were the last steam locomotives built to an LNER design, although all were delivered following Nationalisation, entering service between May 1949 and March 1950. They were built by North British Locomotive Company in Glasgow. Employed throughout the former LNER network, they proved to be highly versatile locomotives, working modest coal trains through to express passenger services, and they also performed well on West Highland Line services. During their final years of service, they were exclusively used on North Eastern Region coal trains. All were withdrawn between 1962–67, with the final surviving class member, No 62005, narrowly making it into preservation.

Ivatt Class '2MT' 2-6-2T No 41287 on a Horsham line service at Guildford station in 1964. Built at Crewe Works in 1950 this locomotive was withdrawn from Eastleigh shed (70D) in July 1966.

The grand St Pancras Renaissance London Hotel at St Pancras station. Designed by George Gilbert Scott it was opened as the Midland Grand Hotel in 1873 by the Midland Railway.

Railway hotels

The first railway hotels were opened in the late 1830s, almost at the inception of long-distance rail travel, and were situated at key stations such as London Euston and Birmingham Curzon Street. Most other companies then followed the example set by the London and Birmingham Railway, and by 1913 there were no fewer than 93 hotels owned by various railway companies, with the majority adjoining the station that they served. Notable examples were the Great Western Royal Hotel at London's Paddington, the Royal Victoria Hotel in Sheffield, Glasgow's Central Hotel, and the Caledonian Hotel adjoining Edinburgh's Princes Street station. The Midland Hotel in Manchester is arguably one of the most famous of the railway hotels. Built next to the company's Central station and opened in 1903, it was frequented by visiting American cotton traders. The company's 1873-built Midland Grand Hotel at London St Pancras station was not such a long-term success, though. Although prospering until after the First World War, when it was taken over by the LMS, it was closed in 1935 and its premises were then used as railway offices. However, many other hotels established by the early railway companies during the Victorian era have survived and continue to prosper today.

The individual policies of the 'Big Four' railway companies differed, with the LNER and LMS being the most enthusiastic in their provision. Upon nationalisation of transport and the establishment of the British Transport Commission, just 49 hotels were by that time remaining in railway ownership. Following the Second World War many hotels were in a sadly neglected state and, along with railway catering, were subsequently brought under the control of the BTC's Railway Executive. This provision proved to be short-lived, for on 1 July 1948 the hotels were transferred from direct railway control and placed

Opened in 1841, the Midland Hotel at Derby is the world's oldest surviving railway hotel.

Seen here on 8 September 1976, the Great Eastern Hotel at London's Liverpool Street station. The hotel was built in 1884 by the Great Eastern Railway on the site of Bethlehem Royal Hospital.

The art deco Midland Hotel at Morecambe was built by the London, Midland & Scottish Railway in 1933. The architect was Oliver Hill and the hotel contains sculpture by Eric Gill.

under BTC's Hotels Executive, chaired by Lord Inman, who was later succeeded by Sir Harry Methven. By this stage the Hotels Executive had under its control some 55 hotels and 400 station refreshment rooms, as well as various golf courses, tennis courts, laundries, wine cellars and bottling facilities. Prestigious hotels in the portfolio included those at London Paddington (Great Western Royal Hotel opened in 1854), London Charing Cross (Charing Cross Hotel opened in 1865), London Liverpool Street (Great Eastern Hotel opened in 1884), London Marylebone (Hotel Great Central opened in 1899), and in Edinburgh (North British Station Hotel opened in 1902).

Following the abolition of the BTC in 1962, further change came about with the transfer of its rail businesses to the newly established British Railways Board (BRB). British Transport Hotels Ltd (BTH) was then founded to manage the hotels despite the BRB chairman, Richard Beeching, arguing for their retention within the BRB's portfolio. It was the intention to give BTH a high degree of autonomy, with the aim of attracting outside expertise into the business. Consequently, the British Railways Act 1968 empowered BTH to expand its business beyond the railway estate and the company contemplated opening several new hotels but, in the event, only one such hotel was opened, the Old Course Hotel at St Andrews in 1968. However, under the Conservative Government in 1970 the BTH estate was rationalised, and its portfolio of 34 hotels was initially reduced to 29 by 1979. Further pressure placed on nationalised industries by the Conservatives to consider asset disposal led to its hotels being sold off by open tender. By 1984, the disposal was complete, and the history of BTH was at an end. Many of the hotels have since been refurbished and restored to their former glory, some with a new name, such as the Hilton London Paddington and the Balmoral Hotel in Edinburgh. One of the most famous of the railway hotels, the art deco Midland Hotel at Morecambe, has reopened its doors following years of neglect and a subsequent major restoration.

With Edinburgh's North British Railway Hotel overlooking proceedings, ex-LMS 'Jubilee' Class 4-6-0 No 45727 Inflexible *waits to depart from Waverley station on 1 June 1957. The hotel was opened in 1902 and is now known as the Balmoral Hotel. The locomotive was built at Crewe Works in 1936 and withdrawn from Corkerhill shed (67A) in December 1962.*

Railway works

Most large railway companies in Britain established their own workshops, not only for the construction of their locomotives, passenger vehicles and freight wagons, but also for the ongoing heavy repairs and maintenance of their fleets. Entire towns sprang up around these sometimes large, self-sufficient establishments. Indeed, today's major towns of Swindon, Crewe, Doncaster, Derby and Eastleigh owe their origins to the pre-Grouping railway companies, but they will arguably always be more associated with the 'Big Four'. A total of 21 main workshops subsequently passed into BR ownership, with just six surviving at privatisation in 1994.

A 1950s British Railways' leaflet for Ashford Works. The works were established by the South Eastern Railway in 1847 and closed in 1982.

ENGLAND

Ashford Works

Along with Brighton and Eastleigh, Ashford had been one of the three main workshops of the Southern Railway, concentrating mainly on locomotive and wagon construction and repair, which continued into the BR era. During its long history Ashford Works built or rebuilt nearly 1,000 locomotives, including many famous classes that survived to see service on British Railways such as 'N', 'N1' and 'U' Class 2-6-0s and 'W' Class 2-6-4 tanks. Under Southern Railway and later BR management, the works turned out 30 diesel shunters (the 152XX, later BR Class '12'), twenty of Bulleid's 'Q1' Class 0-6-0s, fourteen Stanier '8F' 2-8-0s, and the first two of the SR mainline diesel-electrics, Nos 10201 and 10202 – the latter was the last locomotive to be built at Ashford when it was rolled out in the autumn of 1951. All locomotive production and repairs were moved to Eastleigh in 1962 and the works finally closed in 1982.

Brighton Works

Brighton Railway Works was one of the earliest railway-owned locomotive repair facilities and was established by the London, Brighton & South Coast Railway. Constructing and maintaining both locomotives and carriages, between 1852 and 1957 more than 1,200 steam locomotives were built there. After the Second World War and then Nationalisation, locomotive construction and maintenance work continued, and Brighton Works was responsible for both the design work and the construction of several of the new BR Standard class locomotives as well as building one of the three prototype diesel-electric locomotives, No 10203, in 1954. As a consequence of the 1955 Modernisation Plan, locomotive construction ceased during 1957 and locomotive repairs the following year. From then, some of the site continued in railway use for the stabling of electric multiple units.

Crewe Works

The original 'Old Works' at Crewe was built in 1840 by the Grand Junction Railway. As the London & North

Crewe Works on 22 September 1979. Receiving attention were diesel-electric locomotives Class '37' No 37001, Class '40' No 40044, Class '47' No 47267 and Class '37' No 37183.

Hot work inside Crewe Works!

BRITISH RAILWAYS

Western Railway's demand grew for new locomotives, further works buildings were constructed adjacent to the Crewe–Chester line. The Old Works was then used for repairing locomotive boilers until the demise of steam traction. At its height under LMS ownership, over 20,000 workers were employed, and notable locomotives such as Stanier's 'Princess Royal', 'Princess Coronation', 'Jubilee' and Class '5' were constructed there. Following Nationalisation the works built the BR Standard 'Britannia' and 'Clan' Pacifics, and some of the '9F' Class 2-10-0s. The works had built over 7,300 locomotives by the time its last, '9F' No 92250, was completed in 1958. Diesel production had already commenced in 1959, with some shunters (Class '08') and many Sulzer Type 2s (Class '24'), 'Peaks' (Class '45'), 'Westerns' (Class '52'), Brush Type 4s (Class '47') and Class '56' locomotives built there. The Class '87', '90' and '91' electric locos also emerged from Crewe after the works had been set up as part of British Rail Engineering Ltd (BREL). In the mid-1980s much of the site was cleared and sold for major non-railway development.

Darlington Works

Darlington Works was established by the Stockton & Darlington Railway in 1863 and by 1875 had built over 100 locomotives, the first North Eastern Railway designs appearing in 1877. Between 1913 and 1921 a total of 120 of the NER Raven Class 'T2' (LNER Class 'Q6') 0-8-0 freight locomotives had been built there as well as in 1914 ten Bo-Bo 1,500V DC (No 265XX) electric locomotives to run between Shildon and Newport. After the 1923 Grouping one new locomotive per week rolled off the LNER production line, with Gresley's 'K3' Class 2-6-0 first appearing in 1924. Both the Gresley 'V' 2-6-2 and 'A1' 4-6-2s were also built there. Following Nationalisation, both steam and diesel locomotives were built at Darlington including BR's Standard Class '2' 2-6-0s between 1952 and 1956, and 85 Sulzer Type 2s (Classes '24' and '25') between 1960 and 1961. A large order of 385 350-hp Class '08' diesel-electric shunters were constructed between 1953 and 1962. Following rationalisation by BREL the works was run down and closed in 1966.

Derby Litchurch Lane

The Midland Railway's Derby Carriage and Wagon Works opened in 1873 and continued to build rolling stock under the ownership of the LMS. Following Nationalisation by British Railways it was the principal rolling stock works of the London Midland Region, and was where the BR Mark 1 carriage was developed from the early 1950s, the 'Derby Lightweight' aluminium-body Diesel Multiple Units (DMUs) from 1953, the all-steel 'Derby Heavyweight' DMUs from 1956 and, from 1958, new Class '108' 'Derby Lightweights', with Class '107' DMUs built in 1960. Upon transfer of ownership in 1970 to BREL, it was renamed Litchurch Lane Works. In the late 1970s a major reorganisation saw wagon building and repairs cease. Still under the auspices of BR in the mid-1980s, around 150 of Class '140' 'Pacer' units were produced before BREL was privatised and became wholly owned by Asea Brown Boveri (ABB). Its future has since been reassured with further rolling stock orders for Britain being won.

Derby Works

First opened around 1840, Derby Works comprised several locomotive design and construction facilities which in 1873 developed into the Midland Railway Locomotive Works. Post-Grouping, the works at Derby and Crewe were the two locomotive construction and repair facilities of the LMS. Derby Works produced its first 0-6-0 diesel shunter in 1934 and during the Second World War built Stanier Class '5' 4-6-0s and Fairburn 2-6-4Ts, and in 1947–48 the first mainline diesel-electric locomotives, Nos 10000 and 10001. Under BR ownership it produced Standard Class '4' 2-6-4Ts and Class '5' 4-6-0s, 'Peaks' (Classes '44', '45' and '46'), most of the Sulzer Type 2 (Classes '24' and '25') and many Class '08' shunters. When the final Sulzer Type 2 emerged from Derby Works in May 1967 over 1,000 locomotives had been built there. Production ceased in 1966 when under BREL ownership. BREL was privatised in 1989, after which Derby Works concentrated on supplying locomotive bogies and components until closure finally came about in 1990.

Doncaster Works

Doncaster Works, also referred to as 'The Plant', was established by the Great Northern Railway in 1853. Initially building carriages, by the late 19th century locomotive construction had begun. Among the locomotives the works has produced are the 'Stirling Singles', the 'Ivatt Atlantics' and Gresley's Pacifics,

Class '56' diesel locomotive No 56084 under construction at Doncaster Works on 27 July 1980. Completed in October of that year this powerful locomotive was withdrawn in September 2008.

including his world-famous No 4472 (BR 60103) *Flying Scotsman* and 'A4' Pacific *Mallard*. Over 2,000 steam locomotives were constructed at Doncaster, the last being a BR Standard Class '4' 2-6-0 for the Scottish Region. From 1958, after modernisation of the works, 68 of the Class '03' 204-hp 0-6-0DM shunters were built at Doncaster as well as several Class '08' shunters. For the West Coast Main Line (WCML) electrification, the Class '85' and '86' electric locomotives were built, and also the Class '71' dual third rail/overhead electrics for the Southern Region. From 1976 until 1987, some of the Class '56' and all the Class '58' diesel-electrics were constructed. The works remains open today but the owners, Wabtec, have announced its closure in 2028.

Eastleigh Works

A carriage and wagon works was first opened at Eastleigh in Hampshire by the London & South Western Railway in 1891. Locomotive construction, previously undertaken at Nine Elms in London, was transferred to new workshops in 1910 and it became the principal works for the Southern Region in 1923. Prior to Nationalisation, locomotives constructed there included Robert Urie's 'H15', 'S15', and 'King Arthur'

Class and 'Lord Nelson' 4-6-0s, 'Schools' 4-4-0s, 'U1' 2-6-0s, 'W' 2-6-4Ts and 'Q' Class 0-6-0s. After 1937, Eastleigh constructed all of Bulleid's 30 'Merchant Navy' and six 'West Country' Pacifics as well as 23 of the LMS '8F' 2-8-0s. Following Nationalisation, steam locomotive construction ceased at Eastleigh, although from thereon between 1956 and 1961 it was heavily occupied in rebuilding over 90 of the Bulleid 4-6-2 classes. During the 1960s the works evolved from

BR Standard Class '5MT' 4-6-0 No 73171 receives attention in Eastleigh Works in 1965. Built at Doncaster Works in 1957 this short-lived locomotive was withdrawn from Eastleigh shed (70D) in October 1966.

repairing steam locomotives to diesel locomotive and carriage and electric multiple unit repairs, and built the first six electro-diesel (Class '73') locomotives. Following privatisation, the works was acquired from BREL by a management buyout and after several changes of ownership it still undertakes rail vehicle maintenance under the auspices of Arlington Fleet Services Ltd.

Gorton Locomotive Works

A locomotive works was first built at Gorton in southeast Manchester in 1849 for the Manchester, Sheffield & Lincolnshire Railway. Under the Great Central Railway, Gorton became the main works for the construction and repair of its locomotives and rolling stock, the latter being undertaken elsewhere from 1907. Under LNER ownership most new locomotive design and construction was moved to the company's larger Doncaster and Darlington Works, although from 1930 and beyond Nationalisation Gorton continued to carry out some construction and heavy locomotive overhauls, also producing new boilers and all castings. The last steam locomotive completed at Gorton was the 'B1' Class 4-6-0 No 61349 in 1949. Between 1950 and 1954 the works went on to build the 64 'EM1' Class (later Class '76') and 'EM2' Class (later Class '77') locomotives for the Woodhead electrified line between Sheffield and Manchester. Following a reorganisation of BR's railway workshops, all work was transferred from Gorton to Doncaster and the works was closed in 1963.

Horwich Works

Locomotive work began at Horwich, near Bolton, in 1886, initially repairing Lancashire & Yorkshire locomotives, then building its first locomotive in 1889. The works is recognised for the design of the successful LMS 'Crab' Class 2-6-0, of which 70 were built at Horwich. Locomotive construction continued there until 1931, when it was suspended due to the economic depression, but was resumed in 1944. Between 1945 and 1950 it built several LMS Stanier 'Black Five' 4-6-0s, LMS Ivatt Class '4' 2-6-0s and BR Standard Class '4' 2-6-0s, the last, No 76099, being outshopped from the works in 1957. The works went on to build 170 Class '08' shunters between 1958 and 1962, after which work was concentrated on locomotive repairs and finally wagon maintenance. Closure came in 1983 under the management of British Rail Engineering Ltd.

Lancing Carriage Works

Insufficient space at Brighton Works forced the London, Brighton & South Coast Railway to establish their carriage and wagon works to the west at Lancing, where wagon production commenced in 1909, followed by carriage construction in 1912. Under Southern Railway it concentrated its carriage construction at Lancing, closing the carriage works at Ashford. Although the works continued to operate after Nationalisation, rationalisation of BR's works saw the closure of Lancing in 1965, when all work was transferred to Eastleigh.

Stratford Works

Stratford Works undertook locomotive building for the Great Eastern Railway (GER), its predecessor, the Eastern Counties Railway, having established a works there in 1847. Following the 1923 Grouping, locomotive production ceased at Stratford, but locomotive maintenance continued. Workshop capacity was rationalised after Nationalisation although Stratford continued to maintain steam and, later, diesel locomotives. The original works site ceased operations in 1963, with most of the work then being transferred to Doncaster. The 1915-built building subsequently became a diesel locomotive repair shop referred to as 'The Factory'. This diesel repair shop was finally closed in March 1991 and the site was then developed into Stratford International station on the high-speed line (HS1) between St Pancras and the Channel Tunnel.

Swindon Works

Swindon Works, first opened in 1843, was the principal locomotive, carriage and wagon works for the Great Western Railway and, from 1948, the Western Region of British Railways. Following Nationalisation, Swindon built many of the BR Standard Class locos including 45 Class '3' 2-6-2 tanks, 80 Class '4' 4-6-0s, 20 Class '3' 2-6-0s and 53 Class '9F' 2-10-0s, including the last steam locomotive built for BR, No 92220 *Evening Star*. The ill-thought-out 1955 Modernisation Plan brought more work for Swindon, including the building of 38 of the 'Warship' Class '42' diesel-hydraulics between 1958 and 1961, 35 'Western' Class '52' diesel-hydraulics between 1961 and 1964, and 56 of the short-lived Type 1 Class '14' diesel-hydraulics between 1964 and 1965, as well as the Class '03' 0-6-0 diesel-mechanical shunters and multiple units – including some of the InterCity, Cross-Country and Trans-Pennine units. Locomotive construction ceased in 1965, with diesel locomotive repairs and carriage and wagon work continuing until March 1986 when the works was finally closed. Today the Swindon Steam Railway Museum occupies part of the former works.

Wolverton Works

Wolverton Works was first established by the London & Birmingham Railway in 1838, at the mid-point between the two major cities, and in 1865 the LNWR designated it as their carriage works. By 1901 it had become the largest in the country. After Nationalisation, Wolverton continued its construction work, manufacturing large numbers of the BR Mark 1 carriages. The works was downgraded to a repair facility in the wake of the 1955 Modernisation Plan, with the last new Mark 1 vehicle rolling off the production line in 1963. In 1977 the works completed an order for 24 new Royal Mail vehicles as well as 21 DMUs for Northern Ireland Railways. British Rail Engineering Ltd continued to repair loco-hauled and electric multiple units at Wolverton as well as maintaining and housing the royal train's fleet of carriages. Since 1986 the works has been gradually scaled back, with only a small portion remaining, under private ownership, and now being used for the maintenance of carriages and the royal train.

York Works

The Holgate Road carriage works in York opened in 1881, after which all carriage manufacturing was carried out there for the North Eastern Railway. Following the 1923 Grouping, the LNER had a construction capacity there of around 200 coaches per annum. Upon Nationalisation, BR's fleet of first-generation DMUs were maintained on the site, and the works went on to build electric multiple units, such as the Class '304' for the London Midland Region at Manchester. From the 1970s to 1989, under British Rail Engineering Ltd, the works manufactured much of BR's electric multiple unit passenger stock for the London Midland, Eastern and Southern Regions. The works continued building DMUs for BR after BREL was privatised, including Class '150' 'Sprinters'

Inside Swindon Works on 31 October 1983 with several diesel shunters, including Class '08' 0-6-0 No 08577 receiving attention. The Class '08' was built at Crewe Works as D3744 in 1959 and served at various sheds in South Wales, surviving into privatisation under ownership of EWS.

and Classes '165' and '166' 'Turbos'. In 1995 the then owner ABB announced the closure of the works due to lack of orders. American wagon manufacturer Thrall then reopened the plant as a wagon works in 1997 and produced over 2,500 wagons for English Welsh & Scottish Railway. Network Rail occupies the site today for maintaining its fleet of railhead treatment vehicles.

WALES

Oswestry Works

The Cambrian Railway's Works at Oswestry was opened around 1865. Although many carriages and wagons were built there only two locomotives were constructed, but many were extensively rebuilt there. Following the 1923 Grouping, the GWR maintained the works as its regional carriage and wagon works, as well as a locomotive repair shop. Oswestry Works enjoyed a full century of service before it was finally closed by BR in 1966, at the time of its closure being the last former GWR works to overhaul steam locomotives. The Grade II-listed buildings have survived for a variety of private uses.

SCOTLAND

Cowlairs Works

Located in Springburn, Glasgow, Cowlairs Works was built in 1841 for the Edinburgh & Glasgow Railway, before going on to become the main locomotive and carriage and wagon works for the North British Railway. Under Chief Mechanical Engineers such as Dugald Drummond, Matthew Holmes and William Reid, Cowlairs Works turned out some classic steam locomotives culminating in Reid's famous 'Glen' Class (LNER Class 'D34') 4-4-0s. Locomotive construction ended following the 'Big Four Grouping' of 1923, although locomotive, carriage and wagon repair work continued through the LNER era until 1948. Following Nationalisation most of the work was transferred to Horwich Works, and Cowlairs Works closed in 1968, with the remaining work being transferred to the other nearby BREL works at St Rollox.

St Rollox Works

Also located in Springburn, Glasgow, St Rollox Works was opened by the Caledonian Railway in 1856 as their

Various ex-LMS steam locomotives being overhauled at St Rollox Works in Glasgow on 10 June 1962.

locomotive and carriage and wagon works. It built many classic steam locomotives, designed by Dugald Drummond, John McIntosh and William Pickersgill. In 1948 St Rollox became the chief locomotive works for British Railways in Scotland, overhauling steam locomotives until 1966, but, despite modernisation in the 1960s, the works had been slimmed down by the early 1980s under BREL. Since then, a much-reduced St Rollox Works has been occupied by a succession of private owners.

Inverurie Works

Located about 17 miles north of Aberdeen, Inverurie Locomotive Works was opened in 1903 by the Great North of Scotland Railway. Designed by William Pickersgill, eight of the Class 'V' and two of their Class 'F' 4-4-0s (both later classified by the LNER as Class 'D34') were built at Inverurie. Despite only building ten new locomotives in its lifetime, the works continued to repair locomotives through the BR era, including the Classes '21' and '29' North British diesel-electric locomotives, as well as rolling stock, until it closed in 1969.

Lochgorm Works

Located in the triangle of lines outside Inverness station, Lochgorm Railway Works was built by the Inverness & Nairn Railway in 1855 and became the main locomotive works for its eventual successor, the Highland Railway. Lochgorm became part of the LMS in 1923 and continued to repair locomotives and rolling stock up until the early BR era. The works buildings were used as a diesel maintenance and running shed following closure of Inverness steam shed in 1961.

Kilmarnock Works

The Glasgow & South Western Railway's locomotive works was moved from Glasgow to Kilmarnock in 1854. When locomotive construction ceased in 1921 a total of 392 steam locomotives had been built at the works, however it continued to undertake locomotive repair work during the LMS era and, after Nationalisation, until 1952. Rolling stock repair ceased in 1959, since when the works has carried out repairs on rail-mounted cranes and BR Scottish Region's fleet of civil engineers' rail plant vehicles.

The remains of ex-LMS Class '2P' 4-4-0 No 40647 await their fate at Inverurie Works on 21 April 1962. Built at Crewe Works in 1931 this locomotive was withdrawn from Hurlford shed (67B) in October 1961.

What a glorious sight!! Inside Swindon Works on 3 May 1959. In the foreground is BR Standard Class '4MT' 4-6-0 No 75003, while behind are various ex-GWR locos including 'County' Class 4-6-0 No 1029 County of Worcester, 'King' Class 4-6-0 No 6029 King Edward VIII and in the distance BR Standard Class '7MT' 4-6-2 No 70027 Rising Star.

British Railways standard steam locomotives

Upon the creation of the Railway Executive in 1947 as a precursor to Nationalisation, Robert Riddles was appointed as British Railways' first Chief Mechanical & Electrical Engineer. With two principal assistants he went on to design and build twelve varied classes of steam locomotive which some argue should never have been built.

Born in 1892, Robert Riddles completed a premium apprenticeship with the LNWR at Crewe Works in 1913. As a visionary, he went on to further study electrical engineering, believing that there would be a future for electric traction. Rising through the ranks within the LNWR and later the LMS, Riddles developed a close relationship with Stanier and was responsible for much of the design work of the 'Princess Coronation' Pacifics. He also served with the Royal Engineers during the Second World War and, as the Deputy Director General, Royal Engineers Equipment, was involved in the design and construction of the cost-effective War Department 2-8-0 and 2-10-0 'Austerity' heavy freight locomotives. Several hundred of these were quickly produced and, post-war, went on to be widely used on BR, especially in the north of England and Scotland.

Riddles oversaw the 'Locomotive Exchanges' of 1948 (see pages 58–61), at a time when the LMS was first experimenting with mainline diesel traction, and he believed that Britain would, in the long term, introduce electric traction. He also believed that these experimental diesel-electric locomotives could not equal the tractive effort of a Class '8' Pacific, the design of which he had been involved with while at the LMS. In his new post he had the remit to continue with steam locomotive construction and believed that it was not worth changing to mainline diesel traction when the ultimate aim would be large-scale electrification. Riddles and his team then set about designing and building a range of efficient and cost-effective steam locomotives, incorporating the best practices of the 'Big Four' companies, as established during the interchange trials of 1948. These locomotives ranged from small, mixed traffic 2-6-2 tanks through to powerful, ten-coupled freight locomotives. Not unlike his wartime 'Austerity' locomotives, the BR Standard classes were designed for simplicity, ease of maintenance and the ability to burn poor-quality coal. Benefitting from the interchangeability of standardised parts across the range of classes, the emphasis was almost exclusively on two-cylinder designs, apart from the unique Class '8P' Pacific design, No 71000 *Duke of Gloucester*.

In 1951 the Standard Class locomotives began to roll off the production lines at BR's main workshops up and down the country, and by 1954 representatives from all of the twelve classes had been introduced. Construction of new steam locomotives continued until March 1960, when the 999th and final Standard steam locomotive emerged from Swindon Works, Class '9F' 2-10-0 No 92220 *Evening Star*. Although the BR Standards were generally considered to be a success, Riddles' policy attracted much criticism. Many of the Standard locomotive classes should not have been considered and Riddles failed to acknowledge the groundbreaking advances made in diesel and electric traction that had already been pursued by his peers, Fairburn, Ivatt and Bulleid. Riddles believed that diesels were too expensive in comparison to the mechanically simple steam locomotives, which were considered relatively easy to maintain and repair, not requiring high skills in technology and expensive equipment to keep them in traffic. And arguably his position was well-founded given the ill-conceived and costly decisions made later by the BTC with BR's pilot diesel locomotive scheme of 1955.

BR Standard Class '7MT' 'Britannia' 4-6-2 Nos 70000–70054 (▸) Designed by Robert Riddles, the BR Standard 'Britannia' Class '7MT' 4-6-2 locomotives were intended for mixed traffic work. Fifty-five were constructed at Crewe Works between 1951 and 1954 to a design intended to exploit the best from the locomotives of the four pre-nationalisation railways, incorporating various labour- and weight-saving measures, thereby reducing operating and maintenance costs. They proved to be popular with crews although difficulties in keeping to schedules were experienced on some routes. They were given names of notable Britons, former 'Star' Class locomotives,

The unique and very decrepit BR Standard Class '8P' 4-6-2 No 71000 Duke of Gloucester at Holyhead in 1961. Built at Crewe Works in 1954 this locomotive was withdrawn from Crewe North shed (5A) in November 1962 and has since been preserved.

BR Standard Class '7MT' 4-6-2 No 70013 without its precious nameplate Oliver Cromwell at Carlisle Kingmoor in June 1967. Behind it is a BR Standard Class '9F' 2-10-0. No 70013 was built at Crewe Works in 1951 and withdrawn from Carnforth Shed (10A) on 17 August 1968. It has since been preserved.

and the Scottish firths, one remaining unnamed. Two survived into preservation: No 70000 *Britannia* and No 70013 *Oliver Cromwell*.

BR Standard Class '8P' 4-6-2 No 71000 *Duke of Gloucester* (▸) Designed by Riddles, this unique three-cylinder Standard Class '8P' loco was built at Crewe in 1954. With its design based on the 'Britannia' Class '7MT' Pacifics, No 71000 *Duke of Gloucester* differed in having modern Caprotti valve gear but suffered in service due to high fuel consumption and poor steaming resulting from draughting problems. It was withdrawn in 1962 after only eight years' service and languished at Dai Woodham's scrapyard at Barry until 1975 when it was bought for preservation. Since then, it has been completely rebuilt with modifications that have resulted in a highly efficient and powerful steam locomotive.

BR Standard Class '6MT' 'Clan' 4-6-2 Nos 72000–72009 (▾) The Standard Class '6MT' 'Clan' 4-6-2 was designed by Riddles as a mixed traffic locomotive. It was based upon the 'Britannia' design but with an increased route availability more suited to its intended west of Scotland sphere of operation. Just ten were built at Crewe Works between 1951 and 1952, the intended order of 25 not being completed due to a shortage of steel. The class received a mixed reception from the crews, being less capable than the visually similar Class '7MT' 'Britannia' Pacific. The five locos allocated to Glasgow's Polmadie shed (66A) were withdrawn en masse in December 1962, and the Carlisle Kingmoor shed (12A) examples were all withdrawn by May 1966.

Preserved BR Standard Class '8P' 4-6-2 No 71000 Duke of Gloucester at work on the Severn Valley Railway on 8 March 2009.

From left to right at Crewe are ex-WD Class 2-8-0 No 90425, BR Standard Class '7MT' 4-6-2 No 70006 Robert Burns and BR Standard Class '6MT' 4-6-2 No 72002 Clan Campbell. The two BR Standard locos were built at Crewe Works in 1951 and 1952 respectively and withdrawn in May 1967 and December 1962 respectively.

BR Standard Class '5MT' 4-6-0 No 73002 at Sheffield Millhouse shed (41C) in September 1960. Built at Derby Works in 1951 this locomotive was withdrawn from Weymouth Radipole shed (70G) in March 1967.

BR Standard Class '5MT' 4-6-0 Nos 73000-73171 (▲)
The BR Standard Class '5MT' 4-6-0 designed by Riddles was based on the design principle of the highly successful LMS Stanier 'Black Five' and was arguably one of the most successful mixed traffic steam locomotives. Constructed between 1951 and 1957, Derby Works built 130 and Doncaster Works built 42. The class's standardisation, simplicity and high route availability, with an axle load of little over 19 tons, invariably found favour with locomotive crew and shed staff alike, who appreciated their rocking grates and self-emptying ashpans. Their versatility found them widely allocated around all BR regions, some working into the final year of BR steam traction.

BR Standard Class '4MT' 4-6-0 Nos 75000-75079 (▼) Of the two BR Standard 4-6-0 designs that were introduced in 1951, this was the smaller of the two. Built at Swindon Works, it was designed for mixed traffic use on secondary routes where the LMS Stanier and BR Standard Class '5's would be too heavy. As with many other BR Standard types, they were based on previous LMS designs, and in this instance the boiler had similarities to that on the Class '4MT' 2-6-4Ts, making them essentially a tender version of that locomotive. Having quite similar operating characteristics to the GWR 'Manor' Class, they went on to replace them on the Cambrian Coast and other Mid-Wales lines.

BR Standard Class '4MT' 2-6-0 Nos 76000-76114 (▼)
Designed by Riddles, the BR Standard Class '4MT' 2-6-0 s were built between 1952 and 1957 at Horwich and Doncaster Works. They were essentially a standardised version of the LMS Ivatt Class '4MT', primarily intended for freight use, with 115 locomotives of the class being built. They possessed considerable power despite an axle loading of less than 17 tons, giving them a high route availability and thereby making them virtually unrestricted on the BR network. They were allocated principally to the Southern, Midland, North Eastern and Scottish Regions. The four engines surviving in preservation were purchased from Dai Woodham's Barry scrapyard.

BR Standard Class '3MT' 2-6-0 Nos 77000-77019 (▼)
The Class '3MT' 2-6-0 locomotives were one of the smallest BR Standard classes and were essentially a tender version of the Class '3MT' 2-6-2T, both types being constructed at Swindon Works with boilers based on the GWR '5101' and '5600' Class locomotives. Sharing several parts and with a chassis closely based on the LMS Ivatt Class '4MT' 2-6-0, the locomotives were suitable for both mainline and secondary line duties throughout Britain, although

BR Standard Class '4MT' 4-6-0 No 75000 at its birthplace of Swindon in April 1956. Built at Swindon Works in 1951 this locomotive was withdrawn from Worcester shed (85A) at the end of 1965.

in practice the twenty locomotives built were equally divided between the North Eastern and Scottish Regions, the proposed order for the construction of further class members being cancelled.

BR Standard Class '2MT' 2-6-0 Nos 78000-78064

These were the smallest tender locomotives in the BR Standard series designed by Riddles. They were built at Darlington Works between 1953 and 1956. Their boilers were virtually identical to the LMS Ivatt '2MT' 2-6-0, but the locomotives were fitted with a cab of reduced dimensions to be compliant with the universal loading gauge. The class proved to be reliable and, apart from the Southern Region, they were widely distributed around the UK when withdrawal of the first locomotives commenced in 1963. The last remaining class members were taken out of service from Lostock Hall (10D) depot in May 1967, their final duties acting as station pilot at Preston.

BR Standard Class '4MT' 2-6-4T Nos 80000-80154

One of the earliest BR types built was this well-proportioned mixed traffic locomotive based on the LMS Stanier/Fairburn 2-6-4Ts, with the same boilers as the Standard Class '4MT' 4-6-0 but with sloping side tanks to conform with minimum loading gauge routes. Built at Derby (15), Doncaster (10) and Brighton (130) works between 1951 and 1956 for suburban and local passenger duties, many had a short working life due to impending dieselisation. They had been widely used on the

BR Standard Class '3MT' 2-6-0 No 77014 at Guildford shed (70C) in 1967. Built at Swindon Works in 1954 this locomotive was withdrawn in July 1967.

Southern Region and on suburban services from London's Fenchurch Street, St Pancras and Marylebone stations. Large numbers also worked in Scotland based at the Glasgow and Edinburgh area depots. All class members had been withdrawn by July 1967.

BR Standard Class '3MT' 2-6-2T Nos 82000-82044

Built at Swindon Works from 1952 to 1955 for light passenger duties, the '3MT' 2-6-2T was the fifth of the BR Standard locomotive designs and was

Very near the end of its life and the centre of attention is this decrepit BR Standard Class '4MT' 2-6-0 No 76031 at Guildford in 1967. Built at Doncaster Works in 1953 this locomotive was withdrawn from Guildford shed (70C) in July 1967.

influenced by the LMS Ivatt Class '2MT', though utilising the standard GWR No 2 type boiler, but with reduced length, used on the '5600' Class tank and large Prairie locomotives. It was envisaged that over 60 of the class would be built but the onset of dieselisation and branch line closures under the Beeching 'Axe' forced the order to be reduced to 45, and as such they had a short working life ranging between just nine and fifteen years.

BR Standard Class '2MT' 2-6-2T Nos 84000–84029 (▸)
Based on the LMS Ivatt '2MT', the BR Standard '2MT' 2-6-2T was the tank engine version of the Standard Class '2MT' 2-6-0, designed to fit within the universal loading gauge for light passenger duties. Twenty, numbered from No 84000, were built at Crewe Works from 1953 and were all push-pull fitted for use in the London Midland Region. A further ten were built at Darlington Works in 1957 for the Southern Region and were based at Ashford depot, but following electrification were transferred to the North Eastern Region in 1961. Plans to employ ten in the Isle of Wight, replacing the life-expired London & South Western Railway (LSWR) Adams Class 'O2' 0-4-4Ts, were abandoned.

BR Standard Class '9F' 2-10-0 Nos 92000–92250 (▾)
Riddles' final Standard design for BR was the Class '9F' Class 2-10-0 heavy freight locomotive, and these were to be the final BR steam locomotives built. Crewe Works

BR Standard Class '2MT' 2-6-2T No 84020 at Ashford station on 5 March 1960. Built at Darlington Works in 1957 this locomotive was withdrawn from Llandudno Junction shed (6G) after a very short working life in October 1964.

built 198 and Swindon Works 53. First appearing in 1954, construction continued until March 1960, when BR's last steam locomotive, No 92220, emerged from Swindon Works. Finished in GWR livery and with a copper-capped chimney, it was to be named *Evening Star*. Many of the class saw very few years of service due to the 1955 BR Modernisation Plan, and scrapping of the first members of the class commenced just four years after No 92220 had entered service. Appropriately, *Evening Star* hauled the final 'Pines Express' between Bath Green Park and Bournemouth over the Somerset & Dorset line on 8 September 1962.

This historic photograph shows the last steam locomotive built by British Railways, Evening Star, hauling the final 'Pines Express' via the Somerset & Dorset Joint Railway on 8 September 1962. BR Standard Class '9F' 2-10-0 No 92220 Evening Star was built at Swindon Works in 1960, withdrawn from Cardiff East Dock shed (88A) in April 1965 and has since been preserved.

BR Standard Class '7MT' 4-6-2 No 70027, minus its nameplates Rising Star, and Ivatt Class '4MT' 2-6-0 No 43044 at Bradford Manningham depot in February 1967. No 70027 was built at Crewe Works in 1952 and withdrawn from Carlisle Kingmoor (12A) in July 1967. No 43044 was built at Horwich Works in 1949 and withdrawn from Leeds Holbeck shed (55A) in September 1967.

Motive power depots

A necessary requirement for the smooth operation of the railways was the locomotive depot or engine shed, latterly termed a motive power depot (MPD), or during the diesel and electric era, the traction maintenance depot (TMD). Such facilities were essential for the routine care of the locomotives, including watering and coaling for steam and refuelling for diesel locomotives. In all but some minor facilities a turntable was provided for turning steam locomotives. Architecturally, the style of engine shed, particularly in the early days of the railway, could be quite different between the various companies. They were often built in a decorative style considered to be in keeping with the railway station, which was usually within close proximity. The depots could also act as the railway company's showcase for their latest locomotives.

As the railway system grew and conveyance of freight as well as passengers and mail further expanded, such facilities became more functional and tended to be built away from main residential areas. They were essentially based on three different design configurations. The straight shed covered one, two or a multiple of roads, either dead-ended or through-running, sometimes influenced by its topographical location. In order to accommodate larger engines a square building with multi-pitched roofs and a central turntable within, based on North American practice, proved to be suitable and especially found favour with the North Eastern and Midland Railways in the 19th century. Today's listed and publicly accessible Barrow Hill Roundhouse at Staveley in Derbyshire is a classic Midland Railway example of this type of building, as is the original and smaller London & Birmingham Railway's 1871-built Camden shed, long having passed into non-railway commercial use as an arts centre. Some sheds, or depots as they were later referred to, could be a combination of both designs. The semi-roundhouse, although popular with railways around the world, was not widely used in Britain. It was a semi-circular building with tracks radiating from a turntable. St Blazey in Cornwall is a survivor of this design.

The ramshackle engine shed at Meldon Quarry, near Okehampton, with departmental locomotive DS3152 inside. This loco was a former London & South Western Railway Class 'G6' 0-6-0T (previously BR No 30272) built at Nine Elms Works at the end of the 19th century and withdrawn in 1960.

York engine shed roundhouse (50A) on 6 July 1963. From left to right are 'A1' Class 4-6-2 No 60155 Borderer, 'B1' Class 4-6-0 No 61259, '9F' 2-10-0 No 92101 and 'A1' Class 4-6-2 No 60124 Kenilworth.

Middlesbrough engine shed roundhouse (51D) on 8 July 1956. Left to right are Class 'A8' 4-6-2T No 69892, Class 'Q6' 0-8-0 No 63375 and Class 'J25' 0-6-0 No 65720.

A scene soon to disappear forever, former GWR and BR Standard Class '9Fs' inside Ebbw Junction shed roundhouse (86A) in Newport in September 1963.

BR Class '9F' 2-10-0 No 92110 (left) and BR Standard Class '4MT' 4-6-0 No 75030 (right) at rest at Tebay engine shed (12E) on 9 December 1967.

Locomotives generally returned to their allocated home depot, where they would be prepared for their next duties. The engine sheds also housed locomotives awaiting or undergoing general repairs, cleaning or boiler examination. All depots had offices, stores and messroom facilities. The lack of natural light in some running sheds was not only an inconvenience, it also made the working conditions both primitive and dangerous for those employed there. Some of the principle MPDs were expansive and could have an allocation of several hundred locomotives. For example, Stratford in East London in the early 1950s had an allocation of nearly four hundred steam locomotives. So despite being filthy and dangerous, for the young rail fan engine sheds were places of pilgrimage, and they attracted many such visitors, both officially and illicitly! In order for the trainspotter to spot some illusive locomotives, perhaps in some far-reaching corners of the country, shed visits were an essential part of life. This activity was termed 'shed bashing' in trainspotters' parlance.

Each shed was allocated a code. For instance, Carlisle (Upperby) was variously coded 12A or 12B from Nationalisation until its closure. Steam locomotives assigned to that shed carried the code on a cast-iron oval plate affixed to the lower part of the smokebox door, and on diesel locomotives usually on the cab side. Minor 'sub-sheds' were not given separate codes as the locomotives using these came under the control of the local 'mother' shed. For example, Penrith was a sub-shed of Carlisle (Upperby). Although many locomotives were reallocated between various depots during their working lives, some celebrity locomotives were assigned to a specific 'home' shed. They would generally be returned there after their spell of duty, and would be cleaned and maintained, quite often becoming a source of local pride. For instance, 'Princess Coronation' Class 4-6-2 No 46238 *City of Carlisle* was based at Carlisle (Upperby) shed until its eventual withdrawal from service in 1964. Following the eradication of steam traction in 1968 such a practice was perpetuated at some diesel TMDs, such as at Stratford, where many

A bird's eye view of the former GWR engine shed at Worcester (85A) in the late 1950s. Former GWR locomotives of many classes feature in this wonderful photograph.

Inside the roundhouse at Leeds Holbeck engine shed (55A) in the summer of 1964. From left to right are Fowler Class '4F' 0-6-0 No 44240, Fowler Class '4MT' 2-6-4T No 42394, BR Standard Class '3MT' 2-6-0 No 77014 and Stanier Class '8F' 2-8-0 No 48029.

of their Brush Type 4 (Class '47') locomotives were not only immaculately presented but also had their roofs painted in a cream colour.

During the 1950s British Railways replaced some dilapidated or war-damaged MPDs with a standard concrete wall and flat-roof design, and some of these went on to accommodate both steam and diesel traction as a short-term measure. Although far from ideal, in the early 1960s thousands of steam locomotives were still employed around the country. By this time state-of-the-art diesel and electric TMDs for both locomotives and multiple units were being constructed to a similar modular design, though ranging in scale. Early examples of these, which replaced the steam MPDs, were in Bristol (Bath Road), Haymarket (Edinburgh) and Canton (Cardiff). For mainly freight locomotives these TMDs were located where traffic flows would start or end, such as in the vicinity of the marshalling yards at Tinsley (Sheffield), Kingmoor (Carlisle) and Basford Hall (Crewe). Many of these TMDs are now but a memory, today's diesel and electric locomotives being rotated around the network and stabled in freight yards and sidings, only returning to a handful of locations for their periodic examinations.

Inside the roundhouse at Leeds Holbeck engine shed (55A) in June 1966. From left to right are Stanier Class '5MT' 4-6-0 No 45204, Ivatt Class '4MT' 2-6-0 No 43130 and Fairburn Class '4MT' 2-6-4Ts Nos 42052 and 42271.

Locomotive exchanges

The first two instances of Britain's railway companies both evaluating their locomotives and comparing the speed and efficiency of their frontline engines and services took place in 1870 and 1888. In 1870 two LSWR locomotives were loaned to the South Eastern Railway (SER) for a two-month trial to evaluate and get the best out of burning poor-quality coal. In the 1888 'Race to the North', as named by the press, passenger trains of competing companies raced each other on the two principal East and West Coast routes between London and Edinburgh. Similar 'races' took place in 1895 between London and Aberdeen. More specific locomotive exchanges between rival railway companies took place both before and after Nationalisation. Arguably the most famous of these was in 1925 between a GWR 'Castle' Class 4-6-0 and a larger LNER 'A3' Class 4-6-2. While the GWR 'Castle', No 4079 *Pendennis Castle*, performed faultlessly on the East Coast Main Line, the LNER 'A3' No 2545 *Victor Wild* lost time on several of its journeys on the western route to Plymouth. During this and subsequent trials, the GWR proudly and rightfully claimed that its locomotive design was far superior to that of its rival!

In May 1948, Robert Riddles, the Railway Executive's official responsible for all matters concerning mechanical and electrical engineering, presided over a major programme of locomotive exchanges, so termed 'The 1948 Locomotive Exchanges'. He oversaw the use of specific locomotives of the four constituent 'Big Four' companies, seeking scientific evidence on the performance of the classes of locomotives exchanged. Data assessed was related to not just the performance but also the maintenance, reliability, operating costs and interchangeability. The process of evaluation ran over ten weeks across four regions, involving ten individual locomotives from five classes, all burning Yorkshire coal. To record the locomotive performance, one of three dynamometer cars were included in each train formation directly behind the locomotive, and they were tasked with hauling comparable trailing loads along predetermined designated routes. Riddles was assisted by Ernest Cox and Roland Bond, both of whom he had worked alongside on the LMS, and this team went on to oversee the design and introduction into service of the new BR Standard locomotives. It is understood that the testing possessed limited scientific precision, and railway political influence suggested that LMS practice was largely followed by the new standard designs regardless! The trials were, however, deemed by BR to provide valuable publicity showing the unity of the new British Railways.

The BR express passenger locomotive trials

The routes used for the BR trials were as follows:

London Euston to Carlisle
London King's Cross to Leeds
London Paddington to Plymouth
London Waterloo to Exeter

For the express passenger classification, the following types of 'Big Four' locomotives were chosen, each example being required to haul an identical load along each of the designated routes, burning the same grade of Yorkshire coal:

GWR – Collett 'King' Class 4-6-0
LMS – Stanier 'Coronation' Class 4-6-2
LNER – Gresley Class 'A4' 4-6-2
SR – Bulleid 'Merchant Navy' Class 4-6-2

A fifth locomotive class, the LMS Stanier 'Royal Scot' Class 4-6-0, was in the event added to the line up just before the trials commenced.

Whilst these pre-Nationalisation top link locomotives had been specifically designed to haul expresses on their own lines, some of them were not entirely well suited to the demanding and sometimes enduring gradients that confronted them during these trials. Furthermore, LMS locomotives assigned to the Southern Region, where there were no water troughs, were paired with four-axle ex-War Department tenders with larger water tanks. Similarly, ex-Southern classes used elsewhere were paired with ex-LMS tenders equipped with water scoops. As to be expected, the trials showed a diversity of results. Surprisingly, the smaller and less powerful 'Royal Scot' Class locomotive showed the best overall performance, as exemplified on a

With a dynamometer car next to the locomotive, ex-LNER Class 'A4' 4-6-2 No 60033 Seagull enters Paddington station with a test train from the West Country in the locomotive exchanges of 1948.

With a dynamometer car next to the locomotive, ex-LMS 'Coronation' Class 4-6-2 No 46236 City of Bradford leaves Paddington station with a test train during the 1948 locomotive exchanges.

run between Taunton and Paddington, where it arrived over 16 minutes ahead of schedule of the 'King' Class locomotive routinely used on the route. However, this illustrates the fact that the trials were not entirely conducted on a 'level playing field', since the 'King' probably suffered on account of having to burn Yorkshire coal instead of the higher calorific content of the South Wales steam coal that it had been designed to use. Similarly, apart from just one astonishing performance achieved on the Salisbury to Waterloo route, overall, the 'Coronation' delivered just satisfactory results. The 'Merchant Navy' performed well over the challenging section between Tebay and Carlisle on the climb to Shap summit, but the cost of this was a very high oil and coal consumption. Of the four larger locos, the ex-LNER 'A4' delivered the best overall performance, putting in a sensational run on the former GWR main line despite suffering from some mechanical issues.

It may have been an inexact science, but these passenger locomotive trials provided much useful data, subsequently, for the design of the BR Standard '7MT' 'Britannia' Class 4-6-2s, their introduction following three years later.

Ex-LMS 'Royal Scot' Class 4-6-0 No 46154 The Hussar with self-weighing tender leads a dynamometer car on the South Western Main Line at Farnborough during the 1948 locomotive exchanges on 15 June.

The BR mixed traffic locomotive exchanges

The routes used for these trials were as follows:

Exeter to Bristol
London Marylebone to Manchester
London St Pancras to Manchester
Perth to Inverness

For the mixed traffic classes the following types of 'Big Four' locomotive were used and, as before, each engine was required to haul the same type of train and trailing load along each of the designated routes, burning the same Yorkshire coal:

GWR – Collett 'Hall' Class 4-6-0
LMS – Stanier Class '5' 4-6-0
LNER – Thompson Class 'B1' 4-6-0
SR – Bulleid 'West Country' Class 4-6-2

Unlike the disparate results experienced during the express locomotive trials there was one clear winner from this phase. Without any doubt, the 'West Country' excelled on all routes, delivering remarkably impressive performances on even the most demanding of sections. Both the 'Hall' and 'B1' Classes performed well, but surprisingly the Stanier Class '5' showed extremely poor timings. Even though the 'West Country' was the undoubted winner, its heavy consumption of fuel let it down, so it was decided that the already proven Stanier Class '5' was to be used as the blueprint for the new Standard Class '5' 4-6-0 design subsequently introduced by BR in 1951. And rightly so – despite the misgivings during the trial, these new Standard locomotives gave excellent service for BR right up until the end of steam in 1968.

Sporting a Stanier tender, ex-SR 'West Country' Class 4-6-2 No 34006 Bude leads a dynamometer car on the Great Central Main Line on the northern outskirts of London during the 1948 locomotive exchanges.

Early diesel, gas turbine and electric locomotives

Gas turbine as a propulsion solution for Britain's locomotives had in theory been possible following Sir Frank Whittle's work of the 1940s. Early unsuccessful attempts had been based on using coal as a fuel, driving steam turbines. Even in the US in the 1930s, problems with coal supplies influenced by industrial unrest had prompted an early decision to actively pursue diesel-electric as a replacement for steam traction. Apart from a few tentative proposals during the 1930s, Britain procrastinated on this issue, and the first diesel locomotives were not actually introduced until well after the Second World War. The GWR experimented with gas turbine technology in the 1940s but it did not achieve the envisaged success, and eventually these projects were abandoned in the 1950s. Conversely, the LMS and SR had by then already had their sights set on diesel-electric traction, and their early prototypes, introduced around the time of Nationalisation, sowed the seeds for BR's fleet of first-generation diesel locomotives which were to be put into service from the late 1950s.

Gas turbine locomotives

Always forward thinking, the GWR's early belief regarding diesel-electric traction was that such engines would be unable to produce sufficient power to equal

Brown, Boveri gas turbine locomotive No 18000, nicknamed Kerosene Castle *for its heavy use of fuel, at Bristol Temple Meads with a train for Paddington in the mid-1950s.*

the frontline and largest locomotives in its fleet, the 'King' Class 4-6-0s introduced in the late 1920s, and that two diesel locomotives working in tandem would be needed to match its tractive effort. Delayed by the Second World War, the GWR's prototype gas turbine A1A-A1A locomotive was built in Switzerland jointly by the Swiss Locomotive Works and engineering company Brown, Boveri & Cie. It was ordered in 1946 and eventually delivered in 1950 to what was by then British Railways Western Region. An additional and slightly more powerful 3,000-hp locomotive – with Co-Co wheel arrangement – was ordered from the Manchester works of Metropolitan-Vickers Electrical Co. This was delivered just a few months later and was numbered 18100. Both locomotives were immediately put to work on services out of London Paddington but soon proved to be unpopular. Noisy, unreliable and not liked by the locomotive crews, they also were uneconomical on fuel.

It was recorded that No 18100's fuel consumption was roughly equivalent to three times that of a corresponding diesel-electric engine. The Brown, Boveri locomotive, with a power output of 2,500 hp, soon became nicknamed by the crews as the 'Kerosene Castle'. It was taken out of BR service in 1960 and subsequently returned to Switzerland where it was used as a testbed (minus its gas turbine equipment) by the International Union of Railways and, latterly, as a static exhibit in Vienna. It was returned to the UK in 1995 for preservation and is currently on display at the Great Western Society's Didcot Railway Centre. No 18100 was withdrawn in late 1957 and converted at GEC Stockton Works to run as a 25kV AC test bed electric locomotive for the West Coast Main Line electrification programme. In its new guise it ran as No E1000 (later renumbered E2001). It was withdrawn from service in 1968 and scrapped in the early 1970s.

Diesel-electric locomotives

Due to the shortage of good-quality coal in the period immediately following the Second World War, long-term plans were promulgated for mainline motive power. In addition to the conversion of steam locomotives to oil firing, the idea of diesel-electric traction found favour with the railway boards, with the LMS being the first to introduce mainline diesel-electric locomotives. Designed by their CME, H. G. Ivatt, two Co-Co locos, Nos 10000 and 10001, were built at Derby Works. The first of these was delivered towards the end of 1947, only two months prior to Nationalisation, and No 10001 followed later in 1948. With English Electric power units, both locomotives had a power output of just 1,600 hp. Due to this low power output compared to the LMS 'Coronation' Pacifics, it was necessary for them to work in multiple when diagrammed on heavy passenger trains. After working on the Midland and West Coast Main Lines, in 1953 the pair were transferred to the Southern Region, where their performance could be compared with the three more powerful new Bulleid diesel-electric locos, Nos 10201–10203. In 1955, the five locos were permanently transferred to the LMR and were allocated to Camden depot. After modification, Nos 10000 and 10001 regularly worked in multiple on the WCML expresses such as the 'Royal Scot'. No 10000 was withdrawn in 1963 with parts cannibalised to keep No 10001 operational until it was finally withdrawn from Willesden depot in 1966. The Ivatt Diesel Recreation Society is rebuilding a replica of No 10000.

Three SR slab-fronted diesel-electric locomotives, Nos 10201–10203, were designed by Oliver Bulleid and delivered after Nationalisation. The first two, built at Ashford Works in 1950 and with 1,750-hp English Electric power units, were initially evaluated on passenger services on the St Pancras and Derby route of the Midland Main Line, later working out of Waterloo, and were joined in 1953 by the two LMS diesels Nos 10000 and 10001 for a performance comparison. The third Bulleid-designed locomotive, No 10203, emerged from Brighton Works in 1954, but with a power output of 2,000 hp. Upon completion of the trials on the Southern Region, all five diesels were permanently reallocated to the London Midland Region's Camden depot from where they were diagrammed on WCML passenger services. The three SR locos were placed into store at Derby Works during 1962–63 and were eventually scrapped in 1968.

Electric locomotives

The SR's extensive pre-war third-rail passenger network radiated out of London to the south and southwest and was operated entirely by electric multiple units. However, its freight traffic was exclusively steam hauled, something which the SR was keen to address in order to make cost savings on fuel, maintenance and human

Built at Derby Works and delivered in 1948 is the London Midland Region's 1,600 hp Co-Co diesel-electric No 10001. Seen here at speed with a freight train, this pioneering locomotive was withdrawn from Willesden shed (1A) in 1966.

Designed by Oliver Bulleid and built at Brighton Works in 1954, 1Co-Co1 2,000 hp diesel-electric No 10203 ended its working life at Willesden shed (1A) before being withdrawn at the end of 1963.

resources. Oliver Bulleid had a hand in designing three 1,470-hp Co-Co electric locomotives. Nos 20001 and 20002 emerged from Ashford Works in 1941 and 1945 respectively. The third, No 20003, was eventually placed into traffic in 1948 under the auspices of British Railways. All three proved to be highly successful, but in 1968 they were classed as 'non-standard' locomotives by BR and were withdrawn from traffic.

The Second World War had interrupted LNER's project to electrify the steeply graded route across the Pennines via Woodhead Tunnel. A prototype electric locomotive, No E26000, had been designed by Gresley and had already emerged from Doncaster Works as early as 1941. The route between Sheffield and Manchester, however, was not completed until 1954. Between 1950 and 1953 BR's Gorton Works turned out for this route 57 1.5kV DC Class 'EM1' Bo-Bo mixed traffic locomotives to join the Doncaster-built prototype. Seven more powerful Class 'EM2' Co-Co express passenger locomotives, Nos E27000–E27006, were also built by Gorton Works and continued to ply the route until the short-sighted decision was taken to withdraw its passenger services in 1970. The 'EM2's were sold on to the Dutch National Railway, but the 'EM1's continued to be entrusted to freight services, mainly transporting coal from the Yorkshire pits, until the closure of the route in 1981, when all remaining locomotives in traffic were taken out of service. One 'EM2' locomotive, E27001, is now on display in the Science and Industry Museum in Manchester and 'EM1' No 26020 is with the National Railway Museum.

At the head of this this line up of redundant EM1 Class '76' Bo-Bo electric locomotives is No 26045. Delivered from Gorton Works in July 1952, this locomotive was withdrawn in November 1971.

Another view of London Midland Region's 1,600 hp Co-Co diesel-electric No 10001. It is seen here at Bletchley with a local train on 1 September 1958.

Diesel shunters

Many years before Nationalisation, several of the 'Big Four' companies had introduced diesel shunters to replace the thousands of steam locomotive shunters that could be found working their humble duties in all parts of the country, manoeuvring carriages and wagons around stations, works and dockyards. First off the block with this was the LMS, which pioneered the use of these diesel locomotives, commissioning Hudswell, Clarke & Co in 1930 to build an 0-4-0 diesel-mechanical shunting locomotive for their Crewe Works' 18-in gauge internal railway. It survived until 1957, latterly at Horwich Works. There then followed an experimental diesel shunter, rebuilt from a steam locomotive, which was introduced in 1932. Nine further diesels followed in 1934 and ten, built by Armstrong Whitworth, in 1936. Finally, a further twelve 0-6-0 diesel shunters were built between 1934 and 1952, firstly by English Electric and, from 1948, by British Railways at both Derby and Darlington Works. These locomotives were later designated as Class '11' by BR.

Not to be outdone, the GWR first used a John Fowler-built diesel-mechanical shunter at Swindon Works in 1933. There followed a Hawthorn Leslie-built 0-6-0 diesel-electric shunter in 1935, numbered 15100, followed by six further diesel-electrics which were built at Swindon Works in 1948. Upon Nationalisation, they were given the numbers 15101–15106. These were all withdrawn in 1967, preceded by 15100 in 1965.

The SR introduced three Class 'D3/12' 350-hp 0-6-0 diesel-electric shunters in 1937, designed by Richard Maunsell and built at Ashford Works for shunting Norwood Junction yard. These were numbered 15201–15203 after Nationalisation, and all were withdrawn at the end of 1964.

Finally, the LNER built four 0-6-0 diesel-electric 350-hp shunters at Doncaster Works in 1944 and 1945, which were numbered 15000–15003 after Nationalisation. They all initially worked at March marshalling yard, and ended up at Crewe before their withdrawal in 1967.

British Railways soon embarked on ordering and building hundreds of 0-4-0 and 0-6-0 diesel shunters of several different classes, designed to replace even more ancient steam locomotives. Twelve classes survived to be classified under the TOPS classification (a computer-based system adopted by BR in 1971). By far the most numerous and successful design was the humble 0-6-0 diesel-electric shunter (later classified as Class '08') which was introduced in 1952. Nearly one thousand of these locomotives had been built by 1962 and the survivors are still a familiar sight across the length and breadth of the network.

Class '02' 0-4-0 diesel shunter D2869 at Newton Heath on 10 April 1971. Built by the Yorkshire Engine Company in 1961 this diminutive locomotive had been withdrawn in December 1969.

BR Class '01' 0-4-0DM Nos 11503–11506 (later D2953–D2956 and 01001–01002) (▼) Built by Andrew Barclay Sons & Co, these short-wheelbase 153-hp diesel-mechanical shunters were designed to operate in docks where there were tight curves and limited clearances. A very reliable class, the shunters were initially based at Stratford depot in East London. D2954 and D2955 (later 01001 and 01002) ended up working on the Holyhead Breakwater Railway until this line closed in 1980. D2953 and D2956 were sold into industrial use in 1966 and both were later preserved, the former on Peak Rail and the latter on the East Lancashire Railway.

BR Class '02' 0-4-0DH Nos D2850–D2869 (later 02001–02004) Built between 1960 and 1961 by Yorkshire Engine Company and widely used in industry as well as by BR, these 170-hp diesel-hydraulic shunters were also designed for operating in docks where there were tight curves and a restricted loading gauge. The door to the cab was at the rear, where there was, unusually, a railed veranda. The majority were allocated to depots in Liverpool and Manchester. They were withdrawn between 1969 and 1975, and eleven were sold to private industry. Seven locomotives have been preserved including D2860 at the National Railway Museum.

BR Class '03' 0-6-0DM Nos D2000–D2199, D2370–D2399 One of BR's most successful short-wheelbase diesel-mechanical 0-6-0 shunters, the Class '03' was built at both Doncaster and Swindon Works between 1957 and 1961 for light duties, especially for shunting at locomotive and carriage depots and as station pilots. With a power output of 204 hp, they could be found at docks in Kings Lynn, Ipswich, Boston, Birkenhead and Poplar, or doing freight trips along the height-restricted Gwendraeth Valley branch line. One worked on the Isle of Wight while others worked on the Channel Islands boat trains through the streets of Weymouth. Fifty-six members of this class have been preserved.

BR Class '04' 0-6-0DM Nos D2200–D2341 The 204-hp Class '04' diesel-mechanical shunters formed the basis for the later Class '03' shunters that were built by British Railways. Built by the Drewry Car Company between 1952 and 1962, the first four of these locomotives were fitted with side skirting and cowcatchers for working on the Wisbech & Upwell Tramway and in Yarmouth Docks, and a later two for serving the Ipswich Docks tramway. Nineteen examples are preserved on heritage lines across England.

BR Class '05' 0-6-0DM Nos D2550–D2618 The 204-hp Class '05' diesel-mechanical shunters were built by Hunslet Engine Company for duties on the Eastern and Scottish Regions. Most were withdrawn after a short working life and replaced by classes '03' and '04', apart from D2554 which was shipped to the Isle of Wight in 1966 to assist with the electrification of the Island Line and remained in BR service until 1983,

0-4-0 departmental diesel shunter No 81 at Doncaster in July 1967. Built by Andrew Barclay in 1956, this locomotive was withdrawn in November 1967. Upon purchase by BR, it immediately entered departmental service, numbered as Departmental No. 81, and it was not until July 1967 before it was taken into BR capital stock, then renumbered D2956, just 4 months before its withdrawal at Doncaster (36A).

Diesel shunter No 2164 at Stratford depot on 7 June 1970. This Class '03' 0-6-0 locomotive was built at Swindon Works in 1960 and withdrawn as No 03164 in January 1976. It was exported for industrial use in Italy and finally cut up in May 1997.

Built at Doncaster Works in 1959, Class '03' 0-6-0 diesel shunter No 03063 providing station pilot duties at Newcastle Central station on 24 May 1985. This locomotive was withdrawn in November 1987. It is now preserved at the Mid-Norfolk Railway.

latterly as departmental 97803. Four members of this class have been preserved, including D2554 which has been given the name *Nuclear Fred* at the Isle of Wight Steam Railway.

BR Class '06' 0-4-0DM Nos D2410–D2444 The entire 204-hp diesel-mechanical class was built by Andrew Barclay for shunting duties on the Scottish Region. Mass withdrawals started in 1968, with the last member, 06003 (D2420), being withdrawn in 1984, by then in BR departmental service at Reading as 97804. This locomotive is the only member preserved and can be seen at the Heritage Shunters Trust at Peak Rail in Rowsley, Derbyshire.

BR Class '07' 0-6-0DE Nos D2985–D2998 Built by Ruston & Hornsby in 1962 with an off-centre cab, this short-wheelbase class of diesel-electric shunters were mainly used at Southampton Docks and Eastleigh Works. Their 'Achilles heel' came in the form of overheating axleboxes, which meant that they had to be transported by road when visiting locomotive works for overhaul. On withdrawal between 1973 and 1977, the vast majority were sold into industrial use, and consequently six have found their way into preservation. D2991 (07007) is still in use at the now privately owned Eastleigh Works.

BR Class '08' 0-6-0DE Nos D3000–D3116, D3127–D3136, D3167– D3438, D3454–D3472, D3503–D3611, D3652–D3664, D3672–D3718, D3722–D4048, D4095–D4098, D4115–D4192 Introduced in 1952, the 350/400-hp Class '08' 0-6-0 diesel-electric shunter was the most successful and numerous of BR diesel locomotive classes, and many of its members can still be seen at work across the length and breadth of the railway network. Nearly 1,000 members had been built by 1962 and over 100 are still in service. In the 1980s, five examples were reduced in height for working on the coal-carrying Gwendraeth Valley Railway in southwest Wales. Examples have been exported to Australia, Liberia and France. In 1965 six of the locomotives were converted to three Class '13' shunters (see page 73). Sixty-eight members are preserved on heritage railways.

BR Class '09' 0-6-0DE Nos D3665–D3671, D3719–D3721, D4099–D4114 Built at both Darlington and Horwich Works, this 350/400-hp class is virtually identical to the Class '08' diesel-electric shunter but it has a much higher top speed with a lower tractive effort, allowing it to operate on longer trip workings. These shunters were occasionally used on short-distance passenger trains such as the Clapham Junction to Kensington Olympia service. Ten members are still in service while a further twelve are preserved.

Built by Andrew Barclay in 1960, Class '06' 0-4-0 diesel shunter D2436 is seen at Ayr in August 1967. This short-wheelbase locomotive was withdrawn in November 1971.

Class '08' 0-6-0 diesel shunter No 3309 at Stratford depot on 7 June 1970. Built at Darlington Works in 1956, this versatile locomotive was withdrawn in July 1984. Purchased from BR for parts recovery by Harry Needle Railroad Company, it was eventually cut up at EMR Kingsbury in 2005.

Class '09' 0-6-0 diesel shunter No 09005 at Clapham Junction on 14 June 1985. Built at Darlington works in 1959, this powerful locomotive was withdrawn in 2009 and cut up by C.F. Booth, Rotherham, in 2011.

BR Class '10' 0-6-0DE Nos D3137–D3151, D3439–D3453, D3473–D3502, D3612–D3651, D4049–D4094 With the same general outline, 0-6-0 wheel arrangement and outside frames as the Class '11' (see below), and a variant of the Class '08' diesel-electric shunter, the 350-hp Class '10' shunters were fitted with Lister six-cylinder, four-stroke, ER6T engines and two GEC nose-suspended electric motors. Built at both Darlington and Horwich Works in 1959 and from 1961 to 1962, the class was distributed to the North Eastern and Eastern regions of BR. As it was non-standard, the class had a short working life, with 77 being withdrawn in one year alone (1968). Three examples later found use at English China Clays' Fowey Harbour and four examples are now preserved.

BR Class '11' 0-6-0DE Nos 12033–12138 Based on similar shunters built by the LMS before Nationalisation, the 350-hp Class '11' 0-6-0 diesel-electric shunters were built at both Derby and Darlington Works between 1945 and 1952. The War Department also purchased fourteen, including one that saw action on the Continent at the end of the Second World War. Other members were purchased by the Danish and Dutch state railways and the National Coal Board (NCB). Withdrawal took place between 1967 and 1972, and eight have been preserved.

BR Class '12' 0-6-0DE Nos 15211–15236 A development of Maunsell's experimental batch built for the Southern Railway in 1937, the 350-hp Class '12' diesel-electric shunters were built at Ashford Works between 1949 and 1952. They were fitted with English Electric six-cylinder engines and main generators, and distributed between the South London marshalling yards at Norwood Junction and Hither Green. They were later used for the Bournemouth line electrification, at Dover for shunting continental ferry vans, and as works shunters at Ashford, Brighton and Eastleigh. Only one example survived scrapping: No 15224 once worked in the Kent coalfield after having been bought by the NCB and is now based on the Spa Valley Railway.

BR Class '13' 0-6-0+0-6-0DE Nos D4500–D4502 (later 13001–13003) (▼) In 1965 British Rail converted six Class '08' diesel-electric shunters to three pairs of more powerful Class '13' 0-6-0+0-6-0 'master and slave' locomotives for working at the Tinsley marshalling yard in Sheffield. With a power output of 700 hp, the three pairs were made up of D4190 with D4189, D4187 with D3697, and D4188 with D3698. They had a short working life as hump shunting soon became obsolete at Tinsley, and all three had been withdrawn by early 1985.

Class '13' 'master and slave' 0-6-0+0-6-0 No 13003 (previously D4500) diesel shunter at Doncaster Works on 12 May 1985. Originally Class '08' locos D3698 and D4188, this strange combination used at Tinsley marshalling yard was withdrawn in early 1985 and scrapped at Doncaster Works in 1986.

The 1955 'Modernisation Plan'

British Railways recorded its first operating loss in 1955 and, albeit by then having been nationalised for seven years, the tired and outdated railway network was in dire need of countrywide modernisation. On 24 January 1955 the British Transport Commission (BTC) published its 35-page *Modernisation and Re-Equipment of British Railways* plan, which it launched at three separate press conferences, all chaired by the BTC's chairman Sir Brian Robertson. The plan recommended a programme of modernisation and re-equipment over a 15-year period, with an investment of £1.24 billion (about £40 billion in today's money). This included £345 million for the replacement of steam locomotives by several thousand diesel and electric locomotives, although it was acknowledged that widespread electrification would have been an enormous commercial proposition

MODERNISATION
AND
RE-EQUIPMENT
OF
BRITISH
RAILWAYS

NOT FOR PUBLICATION, BROADCAST OR USE ON CLUB TAPES BEFORE 00.30 HOURS G.M.T. TUESDAY, JANUARY 25TH, 1955. ANY MESSAGES SENT IN ADVANCE TO ADDRESSES OVERSEAS SHOULD BE PREFACED WITH THIS EMBARGO.

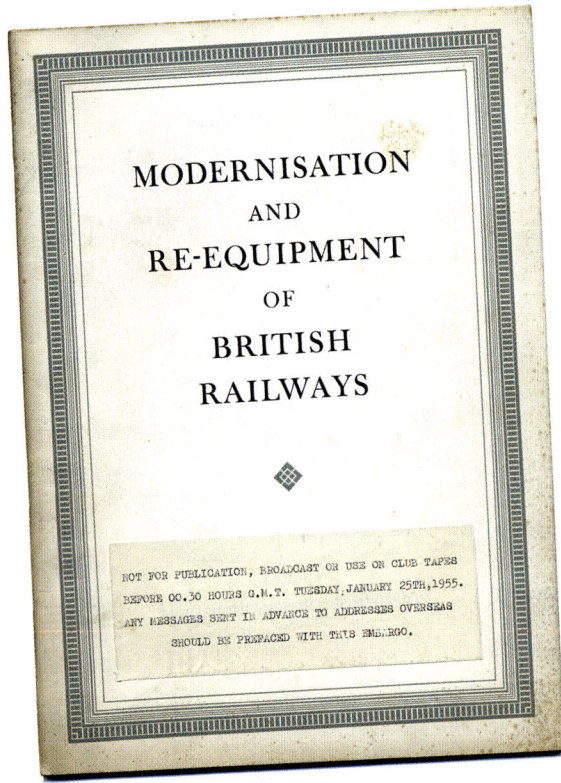

ABOVE: *British Railways' 'Modernisation Plan' was published on 24 January 1955.*

BELOW: *Brand new Type 4 1Co-Co1 diesel-electric locomotive D200 (later Class '40') is shown off at Liverpool Street station in London before departing for Norwich. Built by English Electric at the Vulcan foundry in 1958 this locomotive was condemned as No 40122 in August 1981. After extensive repairs being sanctioned, BR reinstated it in July 1983, it ultimately being withdrawn in April 1988. It is now preserved at the National Railway Museum in Shildon.)*

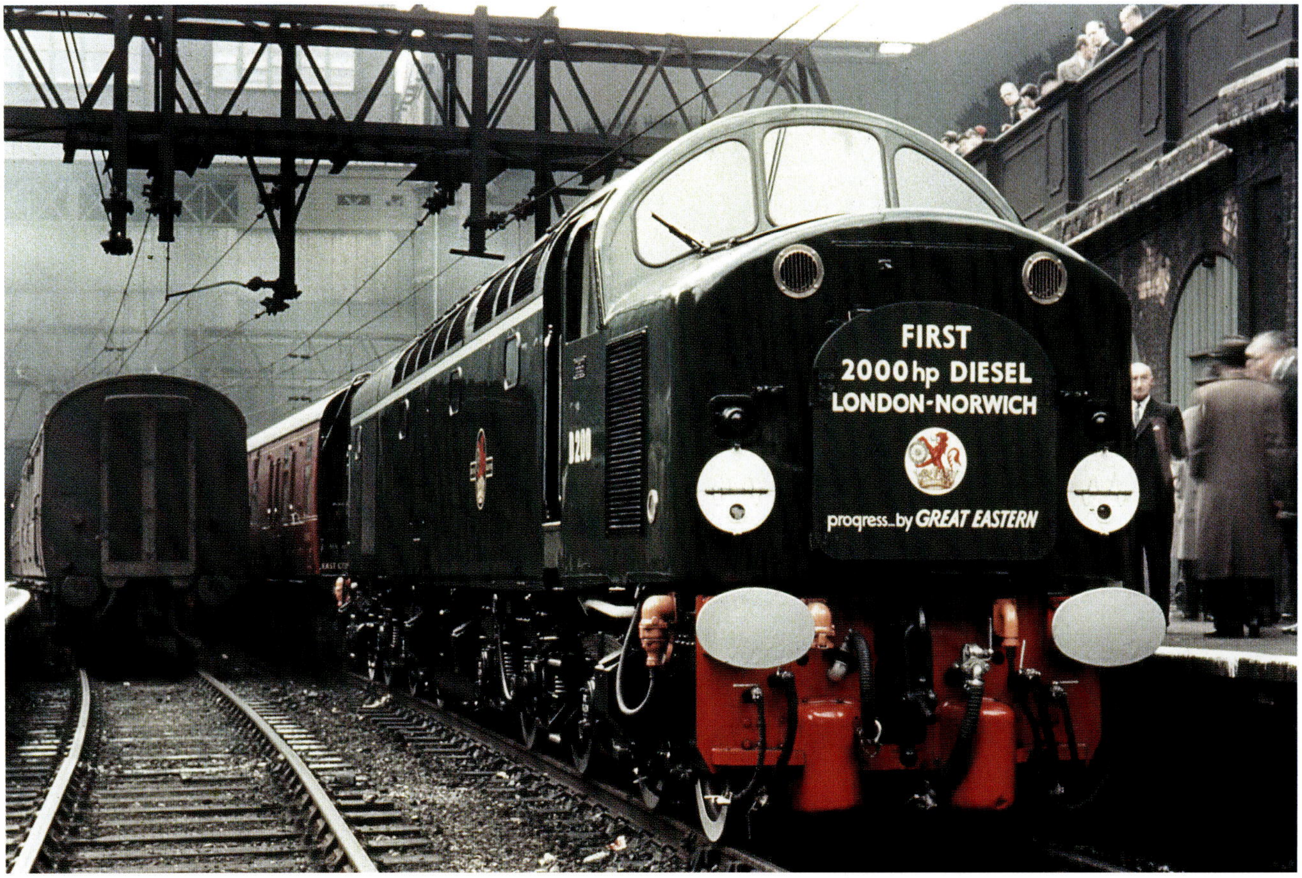

BR Standard Class '9F' 2-10-0 No 92220 Evening Star was the last steam locomotive built by British Railways. Built at Swindon Works in 1960, it was withdrawn in March 1965 and has since been preserved.

to undertake and that only principal routes would be so upgraded. Also acknowledged was that there were some 19,000 steam locomotives remaining in service, a large proportion of which were of a modern design and had a remaining service life of up to 40 years, and that further capital expenditure would be necessary to upgrade some steam motive power depots for their upkeep. A further £285 million would be needed for the modernisation of passenger stations and the replacement of much outdated steam-heated passenger rolling stock, inherited from the 'Big Four' companies, with redesigned modern passenger coaches for the mainline locomotive-hauled services, and electric and diesel multiple units for suburban and rural services, although in the latter's case it was accepted that many loss-making branch lines would have to be closed.

On the freight side, a sum of £365 million was proposed for the entire remodelling of BR's freight wagon fleet, with the design and introduction of larger mineral wagons, continuous brakes fitted to all freight wagons and a substantial expansion of containerised intermodal transport. The number of freight depots and marshalling yards would be reduced, and a small number of modern marshalling yards built. Those remaining would be either upgraded or re-sited, and freight modal transfer equipment would be modernised. To allow for higher line speeds on the main trunk routes, the sum of £210 million would be channelled into the improvement of track and signalling, with increased use of colour aspect signals, power-operated signal boxes and centralised traffic control. A further sum of £35 million would be invested to make improvements at the ferry ports, for the streamlining of office procedures and for research and development work.

While vast amounts of taxpayers' money were to be expended on these proposals, those responsible for drawing up the Modernisation Plan had failed to consider the expertise required for building and maintaining modern diesel and electric locomotives and, critically, had overlooked the overall autocratic management within the various BR regions, not a lot having changed during the seven years since Nationalisation. The Modernisation Plan's intention was to bring Britain's railway system into the 20th century and a government white paper lodged in 1956 affirmed that modernisation would help eliminate British Railway's financial deficit by 1962. The then Conservative Government appeared to endorse the 1955 programme, including the eventual elimination of steam traction, but accepted that not all

Type 2 Bo-Bo diesel-electric D8002 (later Class '20') heads a local passenger train over Bushey troughs soon after being delivered. Built by English Electric at Vulcan Foundry in 1957, this locomotive was withdrawn as 20002 in February 1988.

modernisation projects would be effective at reducing costs. This endorsement was of course made from a political perspective. The figures quoted in both the white paper and the initial plan had a political bias and were in no way based on a detailed analysis (and by 1960 the Government would be having second thoughts). The aim was to improve reliability and safety as well as to increase speed, and in turn the line capacity, thereby making rail services more attractive to passengers and freight operators alike, and thus recovering traffic that had already been lost to road transport.

For the dieselisation programme, contracts had been awarded primarily to British companies that possessed limited experience in diesel locomotive manufacture, with pressured commissioning based on the assumption that rapid electrification would be taking place. This resulted in several non-standard locomotive designs being developed. Despite the lessons learnt from the standardising of steam locomotive design in the 1950s, standardisation was never part of the master plan for dieselisation and, within a few years, perfectly good and in many cases nearly new steam locomotives were being sent to the scrapyards to make way for a motley fleet of first-generation diesel-hydraulic and diesel-electric locos. By far the biggest offender was the autonomous Western Region, which had decided to opt for lightweight diesel-hydraulic transmission based on a successful German design. But here the similarity ended, as the early British examples (Type 4 'Warships' and Type 2 'Baby Warships'), built by the North British Locomotive Company in Glasgow and by BR at Swindon, were unreliable, expensive to maintain and of a non-standard design. Introduced in 1961, Beyer, Peacock & Co's Type 3 'Hymeks' were a vast improvement but even they, and the more powerful 'Westerns', had a short working life, with the last being withdrawn in 1977. Opting for heavier diesel-electric transmission, other regions had more success than the Western Region, with the London Midland Region's Sulzer-engined Type 4 'Peaks' and the Eastern Region's English Electric Type 4s and Brush Type 2s being reasonably successful, especially the latter when re-engined. Introduced in 1961, the Type 5 'Deltics' were impressive machines but even this small class of 22 had a working life of only 20 years, plying up and down the East Coast Main Line. Probably the most successful design was not a mainline locomotive at all, but the humble diesel shunter (now classified '08') which BR introduced in 1953 (see page 71). It is still to be seen on the privatised railway of today, but ironically it was based on a pre-Nationalisation LMS design.

Built by Metropolitan-Cammell, Class '111/1' diesel multiple unit headed by motor composite E50278 stands at Huddersfield station with a train for Wakefield in the late 1950s.

The electrification programme was much slower in its development, despite the obvious benefits that could be delivered with energy efficiency, absence of pollution, unlimited range and rapid acceleration. Unfortunately, the government of the day was unprepared to invest in the high initial cost of widespread electrification of BR and because of this only a limited, but nevertheless successful, programme was embarked upon, with new 25kV schemes for the London–Birmingham/Liverpool/Manchester route and suburban lines out of London Liverpool Street being some of the earliest projects to be successfully delivered. The work having initially commenced in 1959, electrification of the entire WCML was not achieved until 1974, while full electrification of the former Great Eastern Main Line from London Liverpool Street to Norwich was not completed until 1987. Elsewhere in the country, the Glasgow electric suburban 'Blue Trains' were 'switched on' in 1960 and the extension of the Southern Region third-rail system to Bournemouth in 1967. Electrification of the East Coast Main Line was completed in 1990, but only a few short 'infill' schemes have been undertaken since then, other than in Scotland, where re-opened lines for passenger traffic from Glasgow to Larkhall and from Airdrie to Bathgate have been electrified.

The delivery of new BR passenger stock has been a success story, but indeed this building programme had already commenced in earnest in 1951, well before the publication of the Modernisation Plan. Thousands of the so-called BR Mark 1 coach – including compartment stock, open saloons, kitchen and sleeping cars, and brake composites – were built at BR workshops between 1951 and 1974, including adaptations for electrified suburban lines around the country. The design proved to be so successful that many of these coaches remained in passenger traffic until 2001.

On the other hand, the building programme for new marshalling yards and freight vehicles had proved to be a total failure, a broad assumption being made at the outset that wagon-load freight traffic would continue to be a viable operational solution in the face of increasingly cost-effective road competition. No effective forward planning and comprehension of future freight transport requirements, solutions and logistics had been considered. The Modernisation Plan had not been entirely implemented when, in 1963, Dr Beeching's report *The Reshaping of British Railways* was published (see page 168–171), heralding sweeping changes for Britain's railways.

First-generation diesel-electric locomotives

It took until the publication of the 1955 Modernisation Plan before British Railways started to invest in diesel locomotives, although five examples had already been built by the LMS and Southern Railway immediately after the war. In the mid-1950s there were around 19,000 operational steam locomotives on BR's books, and it was estimated that it could take approximately 30 years to replace them with a somewhat reduced fleet of both diesel and electric locos. The first contracts for new diesels went not only to BR's own locomotive workshops, but also to the private sector – including Brush Traction, Clayton Equipment Company, The English Electric Company, Metropolitan-Vickers Electrical Co, and the North British Locomotive Company – where the experience needed to build such complex and powerful machines was limited.

Categorised by their engine power, five types of mainline diesel locomotive were introduced under the Modernisation Plan: Type 1 (800–1,000 hp), Type 2 (1,001–1,499 hp), Type 3 (1,500–1,999 hp), Type 4 (2,000–2,999 hp), and Type 5 (over 3,000 hp). There was a mixed bag of designs within each of these categories, with some being disposed of by BR even before the end of steam in 1968. With hindsight the whole exercise was flawed, with enormous amounts of taxpayers' money literally going up in smoke at the breakers' yards.

While the Western Region was the biggest culprit when it came to scrapping recently developed non-standard diesel locomotives, other regions also possessed in their fleets their own astonishingly inadequate locomotives. Notable among these were the Scottish Region's Type 2s (some with a life of barely 8 years) – whose chronic unreliability brought about the collapse of their builders, the world-renowned North British Locomotive Company – as well as the same region's Clayton Type 1s (6 years), the LMR's Metro-Vick Type 2s (10 years), and the ER's English Electric Type 2 'Baby Deltics' (11 years).

Fortunately, BR made good decisions with a few of their first-generation diesels, such as the English Electric Type 1 (or Class '20' in later parlance) and Type 3 (Class '37'), and Brush Type 4 (Class '47'), some of which are still in service after over sixty years. By the late 1980s the writing was on the wall for British diesel-electric locomotive manufacturing and now, sadly, new mainline locomotives are mainly procured from overseas, including from the US, Canada and Spain.

Type 1

English Electric Bo-Bo Type 1 BR Class '20' Nos D8000–D8199, D8300–D8327 (▶) Introduced in 1957, the 1,000-hp English Electric Type 1 was the first British mainline diesel locomotive built on a large scale. Intended for lighter freight duties, it was fitted, unusually, with just a single cab, comparable to the steam locomotives that it was replacing. It proved to be the most successful of the early Type 1 diesel locomotives, and by 1962 128 had been built by The English Electric Company and Robert Stephenson & Hawthorns. Reliability issues with other Type 1s resulted in a further BR order of 100 from the Vulcan Foundry, these being delivered between 1965 and 1968. Crew visibility issues led to the locomotives predominantly being paired together at the nose end, providing a useful 2,000 hp that was increasingly used on heavier freights. They were also diagrammed on some summer-dated passenger workings. A handful of privately owned locos still see occasional mainline use in addition to preserved examples.

Diesel-electrics at Stratford depot on 7 June 1970. From left to right Type 1 Bo-Bo D8056 (later Class '20') and Type 4 Co-Cos (later Class '47') D1524 and D1563.

The British Thomson-Houston Company Bo-Bo Type 1 BR Class '15' Nos D8200–D8243 The first ten British Thomson-Houston (BTH) 800-hp Type 1s (Class '15') built under the Pilot Scheme were intended for local freight and empty coaching stock duties in East Anglia. Although the contract was placed with British Thomson-Houston, the construction work was subcontracted to the Yorkshire Engine Company. These were delivered between 1957 and 1958. A further 34 were subcontracted to the Clayton Equipment Company, delivered between 1959 and 1961. Withdrawal of steam traction from the London area saw them allocated to East London depots for use on the Great Eastern and London, Tilbury & Southend lines. Proving unsuccessful compared to the English Electric Type 1 Class, no further class members were built. General decline in freight duties saw withdrawals between 1968 and 1971. All were scrapped apart from four that were retained in departmental service for carriage heating duties.

North British Locomotive Company Bo-Bo Type 1 BR Class '16' Nos D8400–D8409 Another Pilot Scheme order of 1955 – based on an earlier LMS prototype, No 10800, built just before Nationalisation – was for just ten 800-hp Class '16' locomotives for the Eastern Region to be built by the North British Locomotive Company in 1958. They were initially allocated to Devons Road (Bow) depot in London for evaluation purposes but were soon transferred to Stratford depot, where they remained for their short BR career. They proved to be utterly unreliable, suffering with oil contamination in the coolant and overheating, resulting in engine seizures. Their non-standard red star (electro-mechanical) control equipment prevented them from working in multiple with other more common types of locomotive having blue star (electro-pneumatic) equipment. Having such poor attributes and being a small non-standard class they were all withdrawn from service during 1968.

Clayton Bo-Bo Type 1 BR Class '17' Nos D8500–D8616 (▼) The Clayton Class '17' was intended to be the BR standard Type 1 locomotive, replacing the early Pilot Scheme Type 1s by offering the crew unhindered vision from its centre-cab with its low bonnet design but, arguably, it proved to be the least successful diesel locomotive ever employed on BR. Built between 1962 and 1965, it was principally assigned to freight traffic in Scotland and northern England, although the Beyer Peacock-built examples were initially allocated to Thornaby, Gateshead and Tinsley depots. Their twin Paxman engines were prone to cylinder head and camshaft problems resulting in just around 60% availability of the class despite modifications. Relatively low-powered and unreliable, they were usually used in pairs. Withdrawals took place between 1968 and 1971, some class members experiencing fewer than 5 years in traffic. All were scrapped except for one, which was sold for further private industrial use and eventually passed into preservation.

BELOW: *Clayton Type 1 Bo-Bo diesel-electric locomotive D8590 hauls a goods train through Pelaw in 1966. Built by Beyer, Peacock in 1962, this short-lived Class '17' locomotive was withdrawn in March 1971.*

Type 2

BR-built Sulzer Bo-Bo Type 2 BR Class '24' Nos D5000–D5150 (▼) The first twenty of the 1,160-hp Sulzer Type 2 locomotives (Class '24') were built between 1958 and 1961 as part of BR's 1955 Modernisation Plan, and a further 131 were built at BR Derby, Crewe and Darlington Works, with initial allocations covering freight and parcels traffic in the Crewe and Derby areas. To replace steam duties prior to completion of the Kent Coast electrification scheme, fifteen were initially allocated to the Southern Region before moving on to Crewe depot. Further deliveries saw them more widely allocated on the London Midland, Eastern, and Scottish Regions, some also seeing use in Wales. After evaluation, they formed the basis for the Type 2 variant (later BR Class '25'), a follow-on build upon completion of this order. The first Class '24's were withdrawn in 1969, and the rest progressively between 1973 and 1980.

BR-built Sulzer Bo-Bo Type 2 BR Class '25' Nos D5151–D5299, D7500–D7677 (▼) Built directly following the Sulzer Type 2 (Class '24') order, the 1,250-hp Class '25' variant was built by British Railways (Derby, Crewe, Darlington) and Beyer, Peacock & Co in large numbers during the mid to late 1970s, also benefitting from modifications that increased its top speed and power

In ex-works condition, Type 2 (later Class '24') Bo-Bo diesel-electric D5096 stands at York in June 1966. Built at Darlington Works in 1960, this locomotive was withdrawn as 24096 in August 1975.

Built by the Birmingham Railway Carriage & Wagon Company in 1961, Type 2 Bo-Bo diesel-electric D5350 (later Class '27') at Eastfield depot (65A) in August 1966. It was withdrawn as 27004 in May 1986. Behind it is Stanier Class '5MT' 4-6-0 No 45467.

output. Although designed primarily for freight work, a large number were fitted with boilers for heating passenger trains, for example on some services between Crewe–Cardiff and in Scotland. The changing trend of freight traffic from the 1980s found them gradually replaced by more powerful second-generation locos, and also ousted by DMUs on their remaining passenger diagrams. All but one 'celebrity', 25322, had been taken out of operational service by March 1987.

Brand new Type 2 Bo-Bo diesel-electric locomotive D7599 (later Class '25/3') and nearly new D7632 (later Class '25/3') at Wath in March 1966. Built at Derby Works D7599 was withdrawn as 25249 in January 1987. D7632 was built by Beyer, Peacock in October 1965 and withdrawn as 25282 in March 1986.

Birmingham RC&W Company Bo-Bo Type 2 BR Class '26' Nos D5300–D5346 The first twenty of the Birmingham Railway Carriage & Wagon Company (BRCW) 1,160-hp Type 2s (Class '26') built in 1958 were part of BR's Modernisation Plan for Type 2 locos, powered by the same Sulzer engine as fitted to the Class '24's. Their early success saw a further 27 ordered, with deliveries made during 1959. They were initially allocated to the Eastern Region in the London area, notably working commuter services based on London King's Cross, before being transferred to Scotland, where from the early 1960s they saw widespread mixed traffic use including passenger services over the Waverley route and on the Highland Main Line. Their gradual withdrawal took place between 1975 and 1994. Their success and popularity are reflected in the thirteen examples preserved from the original 47 built.

Birmingham RC&W Company Bo-Bo Type 2 BR Class '27' Nos D5347–D5415 (▲) Essentially a more powerful version of the Class '26' and delivered between 1961 and 1962, the BRCW 1,250-hp Type 2s (Class '27') were initially allocated to London Midland, North Eastern and Scottish depots. Those at Cricklewood depot worked Tilbury boat trains, cross-London freights and empty stock workings based on London St Pancras station. From 1969 the entire class was concentrated at Scottish depots, enabling the ailing Clayton Class '17's to be finally taken out of service. They were used on mixed traffic diagrams, and some were converted to work the 90-mph push-pull services between Glasgow and Edinburgh. The final class members were taken out of service during 1987, outlived by the older Class '2' locos.

Brush A1A-A1A Type 2 and 3 BR Classes '30' & '31' Nos D5500–D5699, D5800–D5862 (▶) The first twenty Pilot Scheme 1,250-hp Brush Type 2s were delivered from late 1957, allocated to the Eastern Region, and immediately followed from the Brush Falcon Works by a further 243. The Mirrlees engines fitted proved unsuccessful and between 1965 and 1969 all were replaced with English Electric 1,470-hp engines. The Pilot Scheme (Class '30') and the first of the production (Class '31') locos had disc headcodes and no roof-mounted headcode box. At first allocated to the Eastern Region, some later migrated to the London Midland and Western Regions. They were used on secondary and relief passenger duties as well as on freight and parcels traffic. Some were fitted with Electric Train Heating (ETH) during the 1970s and reclassified as '31/4's. A successful design, most of the class survived into the 1990s.

Brush Type 2 A1A-A1A diesel-electric D5528 (later Class '31/1') at Liverpool Street station in the summer of 1959. Built at Brush Traction, Loughborough, a few months before, this locomotive was withdrawn as 31110 in May 2006. In the background is BR Standard Class '7MT' 4-6-2 No 70036 Boadicea on an express for Norwich.

Metropolitan-Vickers Co-Bo Type 2 BR Class '28' Nos D5700–D5719 The Pilot Scheme Metro-Vick 1,200-hp Type 2 (BR Class '28'), often referred to as Co-Bos due to their unusual wheel arrangement, emerged in July 1958. Allocated to the Midland Division, they were immediately put to work in tandem on the overnight London–Glasgow 'Condor' express freight services. Although having a very high tractive effort, their Crossley two-stroke diesel engines proved troublesome. After refurbishment by the manufacturer, the entire twenty class members were concentrated in Cumberland, based at Barrow-in-Furness and finally Carlisle Upperby depots. Problematic and considered by BR to be non-standard, withdrawals commenced before the end of BR steam. One that was latterly used as a carriage heating unit at Bristol Bath Road depot survived in preservation.

English Electric Bo-Bo Type 2 BR Class '23' Nos D5900–D5909 Ten Pilot Scheme English Electric Bo-Bo 1,100-hp Type 2s (Class '23') entered service in 1959, being used on outer suburban duties from London King's Cross and on the 'widened lines' peak services based on Moorgate. The single diesel-electric engine, a half-sized version of those used in the Class '55' 'Deltic', and their overall but shorter appearance, led to their nickname 'Baby Deltic'. Initially unreliable and overweight, subsequent modifications led to them becoming a reliable workhorse when based at Finsbury Park depot, although still beset with some operational issues. BR's so-called National Traction Plan in the late 1960s saw them targeted for early withdrawal, which duly took place between 1968 and 1971. None have survived, although the project for a new-build 'Baby Deltic' is making good progress.

North British Locomotive Company Bo-Bo Type 2 BR Classes '21' & '29' Nos D6100–D6157 From 1958 the North British Locomotive Co built 58 Type 2 1,000-hp diesel-electric Bo-Bo locos (Class '21'), which were arguably the most maligned of BR's Pilot Scheme diesel classes. Two thirds were initially allocated to the Eastern Region, with the remainder based in Scotland. Suffering with mechanical and electrical problems, by spring 1960 the entire class was concentrated in the Scottish Region to facilitate the manufacturer's input and their consequent rectification. In the mid-1960s, twenty locos were re-engined to 1,350 hp and designated Class '29'. Both classes saw widespread use in Scotland on freight and passenger duties, but all Class '21s' were withdrawn by 1969. Despite the costly Class '29' rebuilding programme, all had been taken out of traffic by 1971.

English Electric Type 2 Bo-Bo ('Baby Deltic') diesel-electric D5901 (later Class '23') emerges from Hadley Wood Tunnel with a long freight train in the summer of 1959. Built at Vulcan Foundry a few months before, this short-lived locomotive was withdrawn in December 1969 but was used in departmental service until 1975.

Type 3

Birmingham RC&W Company Bo-Bo Type 3 BR Class '33' Nos D6500–D6597 (▼) The BRCW 1,550-hp Type 3 (Class '33') 'Crompton' was essentially a more powerful development of the earlier Class '26'. The most powerful and flexible Bo-Bo diesel locomotive within BR, it was able to handle heavy loads at low to moderate speeds. Occasionally used in multiple, such as on heavy inter-regional cement trains, it offered the power of a Type 5 locomotive. It was originally intended to replace Southern Region steam traction but later saw use on the Western and Midland Regions. Twelve were built with narrow 'Hastings Line Gauge' bodies (Class '33/2') for use through narrow tunnels in Kent and Sussex, and in 1967 a total of 19 were converted for push-pull operation (Class '33/1'). A reliable locomotive popular with crews and maintenance staff alike, 28 have survived, the majority in preservation.

Type 3 (Class '33') Bo-Bo diesel-electric No 33052 Ashford stands at Hereford station with a train for Cardiff on 30 March 1984. Built as D6570 by the Birmingham Railway Carriage & Wagon Works in 1961, this locomotive was withdrawn in February 1997.

English Electric Co-Co Type 3 BR Class '37' Nos D6700–D6999, D6600–D6608 (▶) First introduced for mixed traffic duties in 1960, the 1,750-hp English Electric Type 3 (Class '37') is arguably considered to be the most versatile and successful of the Modernisation Plan diesel-electrics and it very soon ousted several of the Type 2 classes, seeing widespread use throughout England, Wales and Scotland. Its design bears a strong resemblance to other English Electric designs. Due to its low axle loading, low power-to-size ratio it found good use on secondary passenger duties especially in East Anglia and Scotland. It was selected by BR as its standard Type 3, which heralded the early withdrawal of other Type 2 and 3 locomotives. In the 1980s large numbers of the fleet enjoyed heavy overhauls to prolong their life, with many of the class still in use today.

RIGHT: Type 3 (later Class '37') Co-Co diesel-electric locomotives D6959 and D6811 at Wath in March 1966. Both locos were built by English Electric at Vulcan Foundry, D6959 in 1965 and D6811 in 1963. 37326 (formerly D6811) was renumbered back to 37111 in July 1989 and was withdrawn as such in September 1998. 37380 (formerly D6959) was renumbered back to 37259 in September 2002 and is still in service.

Type 4

BR-built 1Co-Co1 Sulzer Type 4 'Peak' BR Class '44' Nos D1–D10 Intended for express passenger service, the ten Pilot Scheme 2,300-hp Sulzer Type 4 locos (Class '44') were built at Derby Works and introduced from 1959. They were named after British mountains and so became known as 'Peaks'. Drawing from the experience gained with the LMS prototypes 10000 and 10001 and the Southern Railway 10201–10203, they were the first large locos commissioned for the BR Modernisation Plan, precursors to a further 183 built by both Derby and Crewe Works between 1960 and 1963 (Classes '45' and '46'). After initial use on London St Pancras–Manchester Central passenger services and overcoming some teething problems, they settled down from the early 1960s into a mundane life based at Toton depot working freight services around the East Midlands. Withdrawals took place between 1976 and 1980.

BR-built 1Co-Co1 Sulzer Type 4 'Peak' BR Class '45' Nos D11–D137 From 1960, these 2,500-hp Sulzer Type 4s (Class '45') followed the initial pilot batch of ten 'Peaks' that had entered traffic in 1959. The class was built at Derby and Crewe Works between 1960 and 1962. With some named after British Army regiments and the Royal Marines, they proved to be both reliable and versatile workhorses, equally at home on express passenger or freight duties. From 1962 until the early 1980s they were the prime motive power on the Midland Main Line between London St Pancras, Nottingham, Derby and Sheffield. The majority were taken out of service between 1981 and 1986 after being ousted by InterCity 125s on major routes, with the last class member being withdrawn in 1989.

Midland Line diesels at Leeds Holbeck shed on 21 May 1967. Third from the left is Type 4 (later Class '45') 1Co-Co1 diesel-electric D109 which was built at Crewe Works in 1961 and withdrawn as 45139 in April 1987.

BR-built 1Co-Co1 Sulzer Type 4 'Peak' BR Class '46' Nos D138–D193 These 2,500-hp Sulzer Type 4s (Class '46') were built at Derby Works between 1961 and 1963. The 56 locos were structurally like the preceding Class '44's/'45's, also having Sulzer engines, but differed in the fitment of a Brush generator and traction motors in place of the Crompton Parkinson equipment installed in their predecessors. Used on both longer-distance freight and passenger duties, they regularly handled North East–South West, Trans-Pennine and secondary North East–London King's Cross services. By the 1980s remaining class members were based at Gateshead depot and final withdrawal of the last five came by the end of 1984. Just one was officially named, D163 (later 46023), *Leicestershire & Derbyshire Yeomanry*.

English Electric 1Co-Co1 Type 4 BR Class '40'
Nos D200–D399 Drawing from experience gained from the LMS prototypes 10000 and 10001 and notably the Southern Region's 10203, whose bogie design was used, an initial order for ten 2,000-hp English Electric Type 4s (Class '40') was placed, these evaluation prototypes entering service on the Eastern Region during 1958. Immediately deemed a success, a further 190 were constructed by English Electric and Robert Stephenson & Hawthorns, the class seeing widespread use on all regions except the Western and Southern. By the end of their production line their top link passenger turns were already being taken over by more powerful locos, and by the mid-1970s they were confined chiefly to the north of England on secondary passenger services and freight. They were progressively withdrawn between the mid-1970s and the end of 1985. Locos in the range D210–D235, which in the 1960s were regularly diagrammed on London Euston–Liverpool services, were named after Liverpool-based shipping companies.

Brush/BR-built Co-Co Type 4 BR Class '47'
Nos D1500–D1999, D1100–D1111 (▼) Drawing on the operational experience gained from the Brush 1961-built prototype D0280 *Falcon* (see page 89), and the success of the initial twenty Brush Type 4 2,750-hp diesel-electric locos (Class '47') delivered from Brush's Falcon Works at Loughborough, Brush Traction and Crewe Works fulfilled the large order between 1962 and 1968 that eventually accounted for a class of 512. The class was the most numerous and successful of British mainline diesel locomotives. As mixed traffic locomotives, they soon replaced many steam traction classes throughout the national network, particularly on important express passenger services and mail trains. Apart from those previously withdrawn due to accident damage, inroads commenced from 1986 as a result of a decline in passenger work and the introduction of new more powerful locomotives and InterCity 125s. Nevertheless around seventy remain, either in private ownership or based on heritage railways.

English Electric Co-Co Type 4 BR Class '50'
Nos D400–D449 (▶) Built at the English Electric Vulcan Foundry in Newton-le-Willows, Lancashire, the 2,700-hp Type 4s (Class '50') were the final first-generation diesel locomotives ordered by BR, commissioned due to a delay in government funding forthcoming for further electrification of the WCML north of Crewe. Delivered between 1967 and 1968, they initially worked in tandem on express passenger services on the unelectrified northern section. After completion of WCML electrification by 1974 they were redeployed to London Paddington and South

Type 4 Co-Co diesel-electric D1718 (later Class '47') at Leeds Holbeck Shed in June 1966, Built by Brush Traction in 1964, this locomotive was withdrawn as No 47539 in September 1996.

West England services, coinciding with the ending of days of the final Western Region diesel-hydraulics. Nicknamed 'Hoovers', they were named after Royal Navy ships from 1978. As principal West of England services from London Paddington moved over to InterCity 125s, they took over Waterloo–Exeter and Paddington–Hereford and Worcester services, but all too soon were steadily retired in the late 1980s and early 1990s.

RIGHT: *Class '50' No 50001 speeds through Great Bedwyn on 21 April 1975. Built as Type 4 D401 by English Electric at Vulcan Foundry in 1967, this locomotive was later named* Dreadnought *and was withdrawn in April 1991.*

Type 5

English Electric Co-Co Type 5 'Deltic' BR Class '55' Nos D9000–D9021 (▼) Gaining their name from the English Electric 1955-built prototype *Deltic* (see page 88), 22 English Electric Type 5 (Class '55') 'Deltics' were built at the Vulcan Foundry between 1961 and 1962. Named after British Army regiments and thoroughbred racehorses, few engines have captured the imagination of enthusiasts as much as these powerful 3,300-hp locomotives. They dominated principal ECML services throughout the 1960s and 1970s before their displacement by InterCity 125s. The most powerful single unit diesel locomotives in the world, they were officially capable of 100 mph but speeds of up to 125 mph were occasionally recorded. After ending their days on semi-fast passenger services, their sad demise was greatly mourned after 55019 *Royal Highland Fusilier* brought the final 'Deltic'-hauled service into York at just before midnight on 31 December 1981, the 1630 service from Aberdeen.

Type 5 Co-Co 'Deltic' diesel-electric (later Class '55') D9019 Royal Highland Fusilier *speeds through Haringay with the 11.00 Kings Cross to Edinburgh on 25 July 1973. Built by English Electric at Vulcan Foundry in 1961, this powerful locomotive was withdrawn as No 55019 at the end of 1981. It is now preserved by the Deltic Preservation Society at Staveley Barrow Hill.*

Diesel and gas turbine locomotive prototypes

The 1955 Modernisation Plan included the gradual and progressive replacement of steam by diesel traction, but in its haste, BR ordered far too many locomotives of unproven designs and many of these early classes proved to be unreliable. In the course of BR's initial evaluation process, several leading British locomotive manufacturers developed experimental designs for BR's appraisal. Some of these prototypes enjoyed a very limited service life, one even disappearing under a cloud, exported to the Soviet Union, but there were also some noteworthy success stories.

The English Electric Company led the way with experimental locomotive designs, the most well known of these being DP1 (Development Prototype 1) *Deltic* which emerged from their Dick Kerr Works at Preston in 1955. Their externally similar DP2 design of 1962, built on the same production line as the BR Class '55' 'Deltic' fleet, was the test bed and forerunner of what was to be the most successful BR Class '50'. Both of these prototypes were developed in a bid to promote fast and powerful diesel locomotive designs that would prove an attractive alternative to expensive railway electrification.

English Electric's 1961-built gas turbine experimental prototype *GT3*, externally resembling an 'air-smoothed' steam locomotive and tender, was built to investigate the application of gas turbine traction for railway use, as had previously been attempted by the GWR with the experimental locomotives 18000 and 18100 around the time of Nationalisation. Despite *GT3* performing well during trials, BR opted to remain with the conventional diesel-electric locomotive design.

Closely following English Electric with experimental locomotives in the 1960s was the Brush Traction company at Loughborough, with their *Falcon* and *Kestrel* prototypes. The 1961-built *Falcon*, along with the lesser-known Birmingham Railway Carriage & Wagon Co's 1962-built *Lion*, was built to evaluate lightweight diesel-electric Type 4 designs to meet BR's requirements for a second-generation mixed traffic Type 4 diesel-locomotive. However, these prototypes were soon superseded by Brush's own successful Type 4 (later Class '47') design. HS4000 *Kestrel* was Brush's prototype high-powered Type 5 diesel-electric locomotive, powered by a Sulzer 4,000-hp engine. It was trialled, working from Shirebrook depot, on heavy 2,000-ton coal trains in Nottinghamshire and on ECML expresses between London King's Cross and Newcastle. Despite its apparent success, BR did not proceed further with the proposal and, after a refit at Brush, *Kestrel* 'flew' off to the Soviet Union where, undoubtedly, valuable knowledge was gained from this advanced British locomotive design.

DELTIC DP1 (▸)

Built at Dick Kerr Works by English Electric, the *Deltic* prototype, producing a combined power output of 3,300 hp from its twin Napier Deltic marine engines, was a familiar sight in the mid-1950s working London–Liverpool freights. Following modifications and subsequent tests on the Settle–Carlisle Line, it was then employed on passenger services on both the WCML and ECML. Also known as DP1, it was finished in a striking powder-blue livery with cream side stripes and speed whiskers. Remaining in service until 24 November 1960 when a severe engine oil leak was found, no further repairs were authorised, and it was withdrawn in March 1961. It has been preserved as part of the National Collection, noteworthy as the forerunner of the successful Class '55' 'Deltic' Class.

The 3,300-hp prototype Deltic DP1 was built by English Electric in 1955, remained in service until 1960 and is now preserved at the National Railway Museum in Shildon.

FALCON D0280 (▸)

Emerging from Brush's Falcon Works in September 1961 as a second-generation lightweight diesel-electric locomotive, the one-off experimental D0280 *Falcon* was fitted with twin Maybach 1,350-hp diesel engines. It was one of the three prototypes – DP2, *Lion* and *Falcon* – which eventually led to the production of Class '47' and '50' locomotives. Finished in a striking lime green and brown livery, *Falcon* saw trials on the Eastern and London Midland Regions, as well as on the Lickey Incline south of Birmingham. It was also allocated for a time to Bristol Bath Road diesel depot (82A) and operated mainline services to London Paddington in its new two-tone green livery. When its use as a prototype locomotive was no longer required it was sold to BR in 1970 for its scrap value and was subsequently rebuilt at Swindon as No 1200 and classified under TOPS as Class '53'. Due to its non-standard design, it was withdrawn in 1975 and subsequently scrapped.

GT3 (▾)

This unusual-looking 2,750-hp 4-6-0 gas turbine locomotive was built by English Electric between 1958 and 1961 and commenced trials with BR. Resembling a slab-sided steam locomotive, *GT3* required turning at the end of each journey, with its tender carrying the kerosene fuel. Finished in a beech leaf brown livery, it earned the

Type 4 (later Class '53') prototype D0280 Falcon, seen here at Reading on 21 October 1966, was built by Brush Traction in 1961 and withdrawn in 1975.

nickname 'The Chocolate Zephyr'. It was tested on the Great Central Main Line and on the WCML over Shap summit between Crewe and Carlisle before returning to its manufacturer in December 1962 and placed into store. It was finally scrapped in 1966, having ironically been towed to Thomas Ward's Salford scrapyard by a BR Standard Class steam locomotive!

LION D0260

Prototype 2,750-hp mainline diesel D0260 *Lion* was built in 1962 as a private venture at Birmingham Railway Carriage & Wagon Co's Smethwick Works by a consortium

Gas-turbine prototype 4-6-0 GT3 ascending to Shap Summit at Scout Green in 1961. It was scrapped in February 1966.

The new prototype diesel-electric D0260 Lion on display at Marylebone station in 1962.

comprising BRCW, Associated Electrical Industries, and Sulzer. Its aim was to meet BR's requirement for a powerful Type 4 Co-Co locomotive superseding earlier 1Co-Co1 locomotives such as the 'Peak' Class '44's, but with a more reliable bogie design and offering a lighter weight. Tested on both London Paddington–Wolverhampton and ECML expresses, the resplendent gleaming white *Lion*, probably not coincidentally resembling a Brush Type 4, was withdrawn at the end of 1963 when BR decided to order a fleet of Type 4 (later Class '47') diesels from competitor Brush Traction.

DP2 (▸)

Similar in outline to the 'Deltic' Class '55' diesels, but internally very different, equipped with a single engine and generator, English Electric's successful 2,700-hp prototype DP2 formed the test bed for their Type 4 diesels (later Class '50') introduced in 1967. Built at the Vulcan Foundry, DP2 entered service in February 1962, initially seeing service on the WCML and then on the Eastern Region. Following a major overhaul in 1965 it was briefly used on the 'Sheffield Pullman' followed in 1966 by a regular balanced diagram between London King's Cross and Edinburgh. Suffering a serious accident at Thirsk in July 1967, and damaged beyond repair, it was withdrawn from BR service in September 1967 and was subsequently dismantled at the Vulcan Foundry.

The prototype English Electric DP2, a basis for the eventual Class '50' fleet production, was withdrawn following a serious accident at Thirsk in July 1967.

KESTREL HS4000 (▸)

Prototype Co-Co 4,000-hp diesel HS4000 *Kestrel* was built by Brush Traction and Hawker Siddeley and entered service in January 1968. It was finished in a two-tone yellow ochre and dark brown livery separated by a thin white bodyside line. The Type 5 locomotive's design principal considered that a locomotive with a powerful single engine required less maintenance than one with a twin engine, with its high power obviating the need for double-heading heavy freight trains. Apparently drawing no further interest from BR, *Kestrel* was sold to the Soviet Union in 1971 for the equivalent sum of £1.8 million today.

Prototype DP2 passes through Barlby near Selby with an East Coast Main Line express in 1966.

The prototype Brush Traction 1968-built HS4000 Kestrel on display at Staveley Barrow Hill in 1969.

Railway unions and labour disputes

RAILWAY UNIONS

The life of a railway worker in Britain was fraught with danger before the formation of the trade unions in the 1870s. Every year hundreds of workers were killed in accidents, the chances of these increased by the very long working hours that were expected of the workforce. And as a result, passengers were also being placed in danger. Today's concept of 'Health and Safety at Work' quite simply did not exist back then. Although some railway employees had previously attempted to form workers' associations, these were invariably overturned in their infancy by the management of the all-powerful railway companies. The first recognised railway union was the Amalgamated Society of Railway Servants of England, Ireland, Scotland & Wales (ASRS) which was founded in 1871 with the support of the Liberal MP Michael Thomas Bass. Membership of the union was small and its initial growth faltered as drivers and firemen migrated to their own union, the Associated Society of Locomotive Engineers and Firemen (ASLEF), which was formed in 1880. By the turn of the century the by then powerful ASRS helped to found the Labour Party but was subsequently reprimanded for the misappropriation of union funds in a bid to support its parliamentary representation.

The National Union of Railwaymen (NUR)

In 1913 two railway unions, the United Pointsmen and Signalmen's Society which had also been founded in 1880, and the General Railway Workers' Union founded in 1889, merged with the ASRS to form the largest workers' union in Britain, the National Union of Railwaymen. With a membership of around 267,000, the NUR became influential in the national trade union movement, and during the strikes of the 1920s proved to be an unquestionable force to be reckoned with. Leading up to the nationalisation of the railways in 1948, membership peaked at 462,000 but from thereon numbers declined, falling to 369,400 by 1956. Ten years later, following the large number of railway closures and consequent workforce redundancies, membership stood at just 227,800. The NUR's last General Secretary, Jimmy Knapp, was a brusque former railway signalman from Ayrshire who played a pivotal role in the merger of the NUR with the National Union of Seamen in 1990. The combined unions emerged as the National Union of Rail, Maritime and Transport Workers (RMT for short), which is today a growing force of over 83,000 members from almost every sector of the transport industry.

Early 20th century banner for the Hornsey branch of the National Union of Railwaymen.

Associated Society of Locomotive Engineers and Firemen (ASLEF)

The members of ASLEF have always been considered among the elite of railway employees, although they are comparatively small in numbers. The trade union was founded after the GWR's decision in October 1879 to extend the working hours and cut the wages of their longest-serving footplatemen prompted a bitter dispute. Having received no support from the recently formed ASRS union, a total of 56 drivers and firemen united to form ASLEF in February 1880, successfully negotiating a cut in the working hours for the footplatemen. ASLEF membership had surpassed the 1,000 mark by 1884, reaching 12,000 members some two decades later. The union has always taken a proud independent stance, despite often expressing solidarity with other unions, and today has a membership of over 21,000.

A public notice warning passengers about an ASLEF rail strike in July 1982.

THE 1955 NATIONAL RAIL STRIKE

In 1955, the year coinciding with the £1.24-billion Modernisation Plan, British Railways recorded its first operating loss. Losses continued to mount in the face of outmoded working practices and technology and infrastructure dating to the Victorian era, exacerbated by overmanning and labour disputes. Especially problematic were labour relations, and a pay dispute led to ASLEF calling a national rail strike that lasted from 29 May to 14 June 1955. The action did irreparable damage to the railways, especially for rail freight revenue where the already dwindling traffic was increasingly being lost to competitive and more flexible road transport. The Government reacted by declaring a state of emergency on 31 May as Britain ground to a halt. There were no passenger trains, no coal deliveries, no milk, no newspapers and no food – the country had found itself at the mercy of the ASLEF union. Anthony Eden's new Conservative government eventually conceded and British Railways had to foot the bill. Full railway services could not be resumed quickly and many people for several days continued to use alternative means of transport. Coal had been stockpiled at the mines, enabling supplies to be quickly turned around and the effects of the strike on steelworks and other industries was marginal. The main outcome of the strike was that BR's losses kept on rising exponentially, and by 1960 the figure had reached £67.7 million per year, nearly £1.6 billion in today's money.

The national rail strike in 1955 did irreparable damage to Britain's railways. This chalked reminder was written on ex-LBSCR 0-6-2T 'E4' Class locomotive No 32502 at Guildford on 29 May 1955.

Diesel multiple units

Born of the need to revolutionise and quickly streamline passenger train operations on the national railway system, the development of diesel multiple units (DMUs) by British Railways preceded the 1955 Modernisation Plan by several years. Between 1952 and 1955 Derby Works constructed 100 single-car and two/three/four-car DMUs. With diesel engines fitted below carriages, rather than as a separate unit, their lightweight bodies were constructed entirely of alloy, chosen not only in terms of its ability to lessen vehicle tare weight, but also addressing concerns over steel supply shortage. With fast acceleration, reduced operating costs, and their cleanliness compared to steam-hauled coaching stock, the concept heralded a new era of travel when first launched in West Yorkshire in June 1954, where they proved to be an immediate success with both BR and the travelling public alike.

In 1958 BR contracted four manufacturers – Bristol/Eastern Coach Works, D. Wickham & Co, Park Royal Vehicles and AC Cars – to build seventeen four-wheel railbuses, while a further five were supplied by Waggon & Maschinenbau of West Germany. Additionally, a unique two-car battery electric unit, nicknamed 'The Sputnik' and used on the Dee Valley line west of Aberdeen, was built by BR jointly at Derby and Cowlairs Works. The BR service life of these vehicles was short-lived due to the ongoing closure of the branch lines upon which their use had been envisaged.

Following the success of the 'Derby Lightweight' DMUs, the 1955 Modernisation Plan (see pages 74–79) ambitiously proposed the building of around a further 4,500 mostly diesel-mechanical multiple units and single-unit railcars and parcels vans. While some of these were built by BR at both Swindon and Derby Works, many were sub-contracted to private sector companies such as the Birmingham Railway Carriage & Wagon Co, the Gloucester Railway Carriage & Wagon Co, Metropolitan-Cammell Carriage & Wagon Co, Park Royal Vehicles, D. Wickham & Co, Pressed Steel Company, and Cravens Railway Carriage & Wagon Co. These first-generation DMUs were all later classified

A two-car Class Derby Lightweight diesel multiple unit at Verney Junction station on 30 March 1965.

Three-car Class '207' 'East Sussex' diesel-electric multiple unit (nicknamed 'Thumpers') No 207001 approaches Uckfield station on 26 August 1988.

Class '108' two-car diesel multiple unit comprising Nos 53964 and 54247 in the bay platform at Huddersfield station on 28 May 1991.

A Metropolitan-Cammell 1954-built 'yellow diamond' 4-car diesel multiple unit departs from Wroxham station in the early 1960s.

A rural railway scene that was soon to disappear – Class '121' 'Bubble Car' at Halwill Junction on 19 March 1966.

under TOPS as Classes '100' to '188' (both motor cars and trailers). Eastleigh Works also built a series of diesel-electric multiple units for the Southern Region, some with narrow 'Hastings Gauge' bodies. These were later classified under TOPS as classes '201' to '207'.

The publication of the Beeching Report in 1963 and the subsequent closure of around 4,500 route miles of railway put an end to further first-generation DMU construction. By the late 1970s many of these units were life-expired. Some had been refurbished to prolong their lives, but many had been condemned due to their hazardous blue asbestos content. A cost-effective DMU solution was needed, and during the concept stage two different applications were considered: one for local services involving a modular bus body, thereby reducing procurement and ongoing operational costs, and the second for a more conventional solution offering passenger comfort on longer-distance services, delivering a superior performance.

In 1981 the cost-effective DMU solution came in the form of the prototype two-car Class '140' 'Pacer' unit, essentially two British Leyland bus bodies, each mounted on a four-wheel chassis. British Rail Engineering Ltd (BREL) went on to build the production Class '141'–'144' two- and three-car DMUs, totalling 165 sets. Despite their somewhat basic design, lack of passenger comfort and poor ride, the later-build Class '142'–'144' units saw widespread use across northern England for almost four decades, their longevity demonstrating an informed decision made by BR in the early 1980s.

With the gradual demise of loco-hauled trains, BR's solution for regional services across Britain was seen in the form of two- and three-car diesel-hydraulic 'Sprinters' (Classes '150' and '153'), 'Super Sprinters' (Classes '155', '156' and '158'), and 'Turbo' (Class '159') units. After the evaluation of the BREL Class '150', Metro-Cammell Class '151' and BREL Class '154' prototypes, the production 'Sprinter', 'Super Sprinter' and 'Turbo' units went on to be constructed between 1987 and 1992 by BREL York Carriage Works (Class '150' – 130 units), Hunslet-Barclay (Class '153' – 70 units), British Leyland (Class '155' – 42 units), Metro-Cammell (Class '156' – 114 units) and BREL Derby (Class '158' – 180 units; Class '159' – 22 units).

The final second-generation DMUs built under Nationalisation were in the early 1990s: 76 Class '165' 'Network Turbo' and 21 Class '166' 'Network Express Turbo' units constructed by BREL York Works and introduced by Network Southeast on the Thames Valley and the Chiltern routes out of London's Paddington and Marylebone stations between 1990 and 1993.

With a passenger body based on a Leyland National bus, prototype Class '140' 'Pacer' diesel multiple unit railbus No 140001 stands at Colne station on 1 October 1981. This historic unit is now preserved on the Keith & Dufftown Railway in Moray.

A young boy waits in anticipation as Cravens Class '113' diesel multiple unit approaches Burnley Manchester Road station on 4 November 1961.

Blue Pullmans

In 1954 the British Transport Commission took over ownership of the British Pullman Car Company, a private business offering prestigious travel in luxury coaches on the nationalised railway. BR's Modernisation Programme was published the following year and one of its main objectives was the eradication of steam locomotives, to be rapidly replaced by clean, modern diesel and electric traction. A committee was initiated to examine the prospect of introducing diesel-hauled express passenger trains. Soon thereafter, in 1957, it was announced that the Birmingham-based Metropolitan-Cammell Carriage & Wagon Company would be contracted to build five high-speed diesel multiple units and that these would be introduced during the following year on the London Midland Region between London St Pancras and Manchester Central, and on the Western Region between London Paddington and Bristol/Birmingham.

The blueprint for these luxurious trains was ground-breaking for its time, with the classic and highly acclaimed brown and cream Pullman livery being replaced by a striking 'Nanking' blue accented with a broad white band extending the length and width of the windowed section on the side of each passenger car. The passenger cars also benefitted from air conditioning, double glazing and lavish seating. A power car was placed at either end of the train, each displaying the Pullman Car Company's crest and equipped with a 1,000-hp NBL/MAN diesel engine driving electric transmission, delivering a top speed of 90 mph. The two LMR sets were in a six-car formation (this included the two non-accommodating power cars) providing 132 first-class seats, and the three WR

The six-car 'Midland Pullman' entered service between London St Pancras and Manchester Central on 4 July 1960.

sets were in an eight-car formation providing 108 first-class and 120 second-class seats.

Delays arose due to extended trials and the subsequent requirement for modifications, as a result of which the first Blue Pullmans did not enter revenue-earning service on the LMR until 4 July 1960, on their initial London St Pancras to Manchester Central route. The service was essentially targeted at catering for business executives, and passengers enjoyed at-table service from catering staff wearing a coordinating blue uniform. The up service left Manchester Central during weekdays at 8.50 a.m. and, after a Cheadle Heath station stop, completed the 189-mile journey to St Pancras in 193 minutes. Departing from St Pancras at 6.10 p.m., the return journey was timetabled to take 191 minutes. A shorter fill-in diagram between St Pancras and Nottingham proved to be short-lived. Following the completion of electrification between Euston and Manchester Piccadilly, the 'Manchester Pullman' was launched on 18 April 1966. The new integrally constructed Pullman cars, although based on the BR standard Mark 2 carriage, were presented in individual livery, each named after a famous British statesman. Following the introduction of these services the two LMR Blue Pullman sets were transferred to the WR.

The WR's Blue Pullman services had commenced on 12 September 1960. The drivers were initially attired in a predominantly white jacket with Pullman insignia but were derided for resembling 'ice cream salesmen'! The service operated between London Paddington and Bristol, and Paddington and Wolverhampton Low Level, with an additional service between Paddington and Swansea introduced in summer 1961. A steam-hauled set of traditional brown and cream Pullman cars was maintained at Old Oak Common on standby. Following the transfer of the two six-car sets from the LMR, an additional service to Bristol and a new service to Oxford were introduced in March 1967. The introduction of High Speed Trains (InterCity125s) on the WR heralded the demise of Blue Pullman services, with the last train, an enthusiasts' farewell special, running on 5 May 1973. None have been preserved.

The Western Region's eight-car 'Blue Pullman', seen here at Chippenham on 14 March 1962, entered service between London Paddington and Bristol Temple Meads on 12 September 1960. A second route was also operated between Paddington, Birmingham Snow Hill and Wolverhampton Low Level.

Diesel-hydraulic locomotives

With the 1955 Modernisation Plan sounding the death knell for steam locomotive haulage in Britain, the British Transport Commission hurriedly ordered nearly 3,000 mainline diesel locomotives to be built, even before the results of prototype testing were fully available. The orders were placed with British Railways themselves, along with an assortment of other manufacturers around the country, and a variety of non-standard locomotive types were built.

Most of the new locomotives used diesel-electric power, whereby a diesel engine drives a generator, which in turn produces electric power that is then used to power the driving axles/wheels via electric motors. Taking the lead from the US, all BR regions, with the exception of the Western Region, decided on this type of engine. The Western Region, still maintaining a degree of autonomy that lingered from the days before and after the 'Big Four Grouping', followed the German example and opted for a diesel-hydraulic locomotive instead. In these, a torque converter is used to transmit hydraulic power from the diesel engine to the driving axles/wheels. Lightweight diesel-hydraulic locomotives had been operating on the Deutsche Bundesbahn since 1953, with an impressive show of performance and reliability, and so, in 1956, the Western Region placed an order for a British version of the German 'V200' locomotive to be made under licence.

Three Class '52' 'Western' diesel-hydraulics and a solitary Class '42' 'Warship' diesel-hydraulic wait for their next turns of duty in the murky surroundings of Old Oak Common depot (81A) in the early 1960s.

North British Locomotive Company A1A-A1A Type 4 'Warship' BR Class '41' Nos D600–D604 (▼) Built by the North British Locomotive Co between 1957 and 1959, these five prototype 2,000-hp A1A-A1A 'Warship' locomotives, ordered by the British Transport Commission as a comparison with the diesel-electric Class '40', were at odds with the Western Region's policy for a Swindon Works fleet of 'Warship' Class locomotives, which were being built at around the same time. After some early successes on the London Paddington to West Country mainline expresses, they were based for most of their short lives at Plymouth Laira depot. All five locomotives were withdrawn in December 1967 and subsequently scrapped.

The first of five North British Locomotive Company 'Warship' (Class '41') diesel-hydraulics, D600 Active, at Swindon on 28 February 1959. Delivered new in January 1958, this locomotive was withdrawn at the end of 1967.

BR Swindon Works B-B Type 4 'Warship' Class BR Class '42' Nos D800–D832, D866–D870 These formed the first batch of the Swindon Works-built 'Warship' Class locomotives, later known as Class '42' and numbered D800–D832 and D866–D870. Their power output was increased from 2,070 hp to 2,400 hp. They entered service between August 1958 and October 1961 and were initially employed on London Paddington–Penzance expresses, eliminating steam traction on the severely graded route west of Newton Abbot. All except D800 and D812 were named after Royal Navy vessels. The first withdrawals of Class '42' locomotives began just ten years after the first had entered service, in August 1968, with the final withdrawals taking place in December 1972.

North British Locomotive Company B-B Type 4 'Warship' BR Class '43' Nos D833–D865 (▼) The second batch of 2,200-hp 'Warship' Class locomotives, later known as Class '43' and numbered D833–D865, were built by the North British Locomotive Co. Deliveries were made between July 1960 and June 1962. They differed mechanically from the Class '42' 'Warships', being equipped with MAN engines and Voith transmissions, and proved to be less operationally reliable than their Swindon Works-built counterparts which had Maybach engines and Mekydro transmissions. The first Class '43' was withdrawn in March 1969 and, although still being

'Warship' Class diesel-hydraulics (Class '42') under construction at Swindon Works on 3 May 1959.

'Warship' Class diesel-hydraulic D842 Royal Oak (Class '43') at Plymouth North Road station on 26 September 1964. Built by the North British Locomotive Company at the end of 1960, this locomotive was withdrawn in October 1971.

entrusted with London Paddington to West Country services into summer 1971, the entire class withdrawal was concluded by October 1971, influenced by BR's decision to standardise its fleet with diesel-electric traction.

BR Swindon Works C-C Type 4 'Western' BR Class '52' Nos D1000–D1073 The first thirty 2,700-hp 'Western' (later Class '52') was outshopped from Swindon Works in December 1961. Forty-four were also built at Crewe Works. They were necessary for hauling the top link expresses, since the 'Hymeks' and 'Warships' proved to be underpowered. Fitted with two Maybach 1,350-hp diesel engines, the 'Westerns' suffered from inherent design, transmission and train heating faults and, more importantly, were, as with the other types of WR diesel-hydraulics, of a non-standard design compared to the majority of BR's diesel-electric locomotive fleet on other regions. Due for replacement by the InterCity 125 sets, the first members of the class were taken out of service in May 1973, with the final withdrawals taking place in February 1977.

North British Locomotive Company B-B Type 2 BR Class '22' Nos D6300–D6357 (▼) Very similar in appearance to the Class '21' diesel-electric, a BR Pilot Scheme order was initially placed with the North British Locomotive Co for six 1,000-hp Type 2 diesel-hydraulics, duly delivered to the Western Region in 1959. A further 52 were ordered without the benefit of any meaningful operational feedback. Most of the class worked in the West Country and Bristol areas on mixed traffic duties, although a handful worked empty stock duties between Old Oak Common and London Paddington. In a similar fashion to the Class '21's, engine and transmission faults were commonplace, but rectification eventually proved them to be reliable. Their withdrawals took place between 1967 and 1972.

Built by the North British Locomotive Company in 1959, B-B diesel-hydraulic D6300 (later Class '22') is seen here at Swindon Works in the 1960s. Behind it is a Class '41' diesel-hydraulic made by the same manufacturer. D6300 was withdrawn in May 1968.

The first of its class, brand new C-C diesel-hydraulic D1000 Western Enterprise, stands outside its birthplace, Swindon Works, at the end of 1961, uniquely finished in a desert sand colour. This Class '52' locomotive was withdrawn in February 1974.

B-B diesel-hydraulic D6318 (later Class '22') is the centre of attention at Barnstaple Junction on 8 June 1967. Built by the North British Locomotive Company in 1960, this locomotive was withdrawn in May 1971.

BRITISH RAILWAYS | 105

**Beyer Peacock Type 3 B-B 'Hymek' BR Class '35'
Nos D7000–D7100** (▶) This popular mixed traffic class was built by Beyer, Peacock & Co between May 1961 and February 1964. After initially suffering from coolant and transmission problems it went on to become the most reliable diesel-hydraulic locomotive type used by the Western Region. Very soon into its all-too-short career it was entrusted to express passenger services between London Paddington and Swansea, displacing 'King' Class steam locomotives. Facing early withdrawal due to its non-standard hydraulic transmission, this began in earnest during 1971, with the final six members lasting into early 1975.

**BR Swindon Works Type 1 0-6-0 BR Class '14'
Nos D9500–D9555** (▼) The Swindon Works-built Type 1 650-hp 0-6-0 (later Class '14') entered service between July 1964 and October 1965 and was chiefly allocated to depots in South Wales, but a small number were based at Old Oak Common and Bristol Bath Road depots. Its short career with BR was in this case not down to poor reliability of the locomotive but indirectly due to the Beeching 'Axe'. Having experienced such limited use on the mainline, most were to be keenly snapped up for a second lease of life in industry, and three were regauged and exported to Spain.

B-B 'Hymek' D7014 (later Class '35') pauses at Dawlish station in the late 1960s. Built by Beyer, Peacock in 1961 this locomotive was withdrawn at the beginning of 1972.

0-6-0 diesel-hydraulic D9505 (later Class '14') outside its birthplace of Swindon Works in the late 1960s. Built in 1964, this short-lived locomotive was withdrawn in April 1968.

Diesel engine sheds

During the transition period from diesel to steam power, the new diesel locomotives were forced to rub shoulders with their old and dirty counterparts at grimy and mainly outmoded steam motive power depots. This was far from being an ideal situation, so by the early 1960s modern diesel traction maintenance depots (TMDs), or at least smaller servicing points, were being erected alongside or in the vicinity of the steam depots. These were each assigned a unique alpha-numeric shed code and included, for example, Crewe South (5B), Longsight (9A), Toton (18A), Haymarket (64B), Bristol Bath Road (82A) and Cardiff Canton (86A), to name but a few.

At this time there were still thousands of steam locomotives at work on Britain's railways, in spite of the sudden influx of diesels, and in the summer of 1961 there remained around 300 steam-age depots, with only a small number of dedicated TMDs dotted around the country. But as the balance shifted from steam to diesel locomotion, and mass withdrawals – or, in the case of East Anglia and the West Country by the mid-1960s, elimination across the entire geographical region – of steam engines took place, it became imperative to redevelop or replace the dilapidated facilities that had supported them with state-of-the-art diesel TMDs.

Diesel maintenance sheds, in some cases just a single road, were installed at a few key locations in the vicinity of steam sheds to provide routine maintenance and refuelling facilities for the new diesel locomotives, for instance at Ayr, Bescot, Carlisle (New Yard), Feltham, Holbeck (Leeds) and Heaton Mersey (Stockport). Some of these smaller depots experienced a very short lifespan as rail freight or wagonload services contracted, resulting in some of the freight yards or railway routes which supported the depots closing very soon after their installation.

Principal TMDs built following the 1955 Modernisation Plan were generally of a very similar modular construction, offering clean ergonomic facilities, good illumination, and raised inspection

The new and the old in Willesden shed (1A) roundhouse in 1964. From left to right are Type 2 diesel-electrics D5026 and D5077 (both later Class '24') and Stanier Class '5MT' 4-6-0 no 45280.

Brush Type 4 (Class '47') diesel-electrics Nos 1777 and 1774 at Ripple Lane diesel depot on 7 June 1970.

platforms, in addition to inspection pits, fume extraction and end doors that could be closed during inclement weather. In most cases these TMDs were located at the traditional key railway hubs around the country, and usually in the immediate vicinity of the steam sheds which they were replacing, such as Cardiff (Canton), Carlisle (Kingmoor), Crewe South, Cricklewood, Derby, Eastleigh, Haymarket, Lincoln, Longsight (Manchester), Newport (Ebbw Junction), Old Oak Common, Plymouth (Laira), Saltley, Stratford, Toton and Willesden. On the other hand, the TMD at Tinsley (Sheffield), which was opened in 1965, was part of the plan to rationalise all aspects of rail freight handling and distribution in the entire Sheffield area and was located on a greenfield site adjacent to the new Tinsley hump and marshalling yard. In a few cases some steam motive power depot buildings that had been erected during the early BR era were converted into TMDs and continued to provide many more years of service, such as at Doncaster, Eastfield (Glasgow), Gateshead, Norwich, and Perth. At some, such as Gloucester (Horton Road), only the workshop building was retained for further diesel traction use and the remaining structure demolished.

The gasometer looms large over Horton Road depot, Gloucester, on 16 May 1980. From left to right are Class '45' No 45022 Lytham St Annes, Class '47' No 47101, Class '46' No 46027 and Class '37' No 37181.

Class '47' diesel-electrics abound inside Tinsley diesel depot on 7 July 1996.

Post-war electrification

Although a government committee chose 1,500V DC as the national standard for the electrification of railways in Britain as far back as 1921, in essence little implementation followed and many different systems coexisted. The only major electrification scheme that took place on Britain's railways before the Second World War was the expansion of the Southern Railway's third-rail network between London and the south coast, where it reached as far as Brighton and Portsmouth. The company drew up a plan in 1946 to electrify all lines east of Portsmouth to third rail, aiming to complete the work by 1955, but this was overtaken by the Transport Act 1947 bringing about the creation of British Railways and its regions. Under BR's 1955 Modernisation Plan, the Southern Region's first major project was the Kent Coast electrification scheme of 1956. This scheme extended third-rail electrification beyond Gillingham and Orpington to Dover, Folkestone, Ramsgate and Margate. Electrification of these routes was completed by 1961 and, concurrently, the voltage across the entire Southern Region third-rail network was increased from 660V DC to 750V DC.

Completion of the Southern Region's final major third-rail electrification programme, on the South Western Main Line between London Waterloo, Southampton and Bournemouth, did not take place until 1967. To reduce overall costs the Southern Region adopted an ingenious form of push-pull working to accommodate the unelectrified section beyond Bournemouth to Poole and Weymouth, using four-car

Class 'AL5' (later Class '85') 25kV AC electric locomotive E3074 at Manchester Piccadilly with a train from Crewe in September 1963. Built at Doncaster Works in 1962, this locomotive was withdrawn as 85019 in December 1989.

Mark 1 trailer units (designated 4TC) and a push-pull converted Class '33/1' diesel locomotive. The 4TC units were compatible with the four-car Mark 1 electric multiple units (designated 4-REP), which provided the electric traction for the services between London Waterloo and Bournemouth.

On the Isle of Wight most of the lines had been closed between the early 1950s and the 1960s, leaving just one main route remaining, between Ryde Pierhead and Shanklin. This was electrified to standard third rail from 1966, trains being formed of renovated London Transport tube stock dating to 1923.

In the north of England, the electrification of the LNER's 41½-mile Woodhead Line between Manchester and Sheffield was suspended during the Second World War, but work was soon resumed following the ending of hostilities. Problems were encountered with the existing tunnel at Woodhead, the bore having insufficient headroom to accommodate the overhead cables, which made it necessary to bore a new tunnel.

Britain's first overhead-electrified railway, using new locomotives constructed at Gorton Works, was not to be fully opened until 1954. Whilst its overhead wires, energised at 1,500V DC, used technology that was tried and tested in Britain, the comparatively low voltage meant that many substations and much heavy cabling were required. The Woodhead Line later became the only main line in the country so equipped, when 25kV AC became the new network standard in Britain.

The 1955 Modernisation Plan laid out plans for the completion of major electrification schemes on Britain's railways, but progress proved to be extremely slow due to the challenging economic climate, which limited the funding available for the costly programme. As an interim measure, it was therefore necessary to precede the electrification schemes with a period of dieselisation.

The first major mainline electrification programme was undertaken on the West Coast Main Line between London Euston, Liverpool and Manchester. The

Dating from 1923, former London Underground Class '485' third-rail electric multiple unit at Ryde St John's Road station on the Isle of Wight, 25 September 1970.

section between Crewe and Manchester was first to be opened, on 12 September 1960, followed by Crewe to Liverpool on 1 January 1962. Electrification was then extended south from Crewe, with the first electric locomotive-hauled trains from London departing on 12 November 1965. It was not until April 1966 before a full, direct, public electric service was operating between London, Manchester and Liverpool. Electrification to Birmingham and Wolverhampton, and on the route to Manchester via Stoke-on-Trent, was completed on 6 March 1967.

In Glasgow, electrification of the suburban lines commenced in 1960 with the introduction of the new 'Blue Train' electric multiple units (later Class '303') on the North Clyde Line. These units were state of the art at the time, featuring pneumatically operated sliding passenger doors and passenger-operated door buttons.

The suburban lines out of London's Liverpool Street and Fenchurch Street stations were also electrified in the 1960s, but due to bridge clearances these lines were at first electrified at 6.25kV AC instead of the Modernisation Plan standardised 25kV AC voltage, although they were later converted. The section between Liverpool Street and Southend Victoria was completed in November 1960, and from Fenchurch Street to Tilbury and Southend in 1962.

4 CEP (later Class '411') third-rail electric multiple unit led by No 7151 arrives at Birchington-on-Sea station on 11 July 1965.

BRITISH RAILWAYS | 113

BRITAIN'S FIRST ALL

January 1955 saw the completion of electrification of the Manchester-Sheffield-Wath lines of British Railways to afford the first example, in this country, of a main line over which all passenger and freight train operation is carried out by electric traction.

The Manchester, Glossop and Hadfield suburban service is provided by multiple-unit electric trains, but elsewhere all haulage is performed by mixed traffic electric locomotives of the two types depicted in the above view of the line between Hadfield and Woodhead.

With artwork by V. Welch, this poster was produced by British Railways to promote the first mainline service in Britain to operate all freight and passenger services by electric traction. 1955 saw the completion of electrification of the Manchester–Sheffield–Wath lines.

ELECTRIC MAIN LINE

In the centre is a Manchester (London Road)—London (Marylebone) express headed by 2,760 h.p. Co–Co (12 wheeled double bogie) locomotive No. 27000, of which seven are now at work. On the left is a westbound coal train hauled by No. 26051, one of a fleet of fifty-eight 1,868 h.p. Bo+Bo (8 wheeled double bogie) locomotives in service.

Over the Manchester-Sheffield main line there are operated about 100 trains each way every 24 hours, nine out of ten of which consist of loaded coal wagons or empties.

Electric locomotives and multiple units

Prior to Nationalisation, the development of electric locomotives in Britain involved two third-rail locomotives built by Southern Railway for use on its electrified lines between London and Kent, and LNER's prototype E26000, which was built at Doncaster Works for the proposed Woodhead Line electrification. Electrification of the Woodhead Line was delayed by the Second World War, but work resumed afterwards and the EM1 and EM2 locomotives were built for it at Gorton Works. The 1955 Modernisation Plan envisaged that all future mainline electrification and busy suburban routes would be 25kv AC overhead, leaving the Southern Region, London District, Wirral, Merseyside and Tyneside lines with their existing third-rail electrification. Following this, locomotive development gathered pace as the electrification programme was rolled out across the country.

British Railways electric locomotives

BR Class '70' Co-Co No 20003 Oliver Bulleid designed the two Southern Railway Co-Co 1,470-hp third-rail electric locomotives built at Ashford Works before Nationalisation. They were numbered CC1 and CC2, then, after Nationalisation, Nos 20001 and 20002. A third was built at Eastleigh Works in 1948. A pantograph was added to the three locomotives to allow them to work in marshalling yards such as Hither Green. All three were withdrawn between 1968 and 1969 without receiving TOPS numbers.

BR Class '71' Bo-Bo Nos E5000–E5023 (▶) Twenty-four of these mixed traffic 650-750V DC third-rail 2,552-hp locomotives were built for the Southern Region at Doncaster Works between 1958 and 1960. They were designed to work on the newly electrified Kent Coast main lines, where they hauled freight and passenger trains, including both the 'Golden Arrow' and the heavy 'Night Ferry' boat trains. Ten members of the class were converted in 1967-68 to electro-diesels at Crewe Works and renumbered E6101–E6110, later classified as Class '74'. The remaining fourteen locomotives were later renumbered 71001–71014. Withdrawals of these came in November 1977. The rebuilt Class '74' locos were withdrawn during 1977. E5001 is preserved at the National Railway Museum (NRM).

BR Class '73' Bo-Bo electro-diesel Nos E6001–E6049 (▶) Six of these versatile mixed traffic locomotives were built to the 'Hastings Line Gauge' at Eastleigh Works during 1961-62. Their power output was 1,600 hp on 650-750V DC third-rail electric and 600 hp with an English Electric diesel engine. These six locos were later reclassified as Class '73/0' and numbered E6001–E6006. A further

The first of its class, third-rail Bo-Bo electric locomotive E5000 (later renumbered E5024 and subsequently rebuilt as an elctro-diesel Class '74') pauses at Broadstairs station in the summer of 1961. This locomotive was withdrawn as 74004 in December 1977.

43 locomotives were built by English Electric at Vulcan Foundry between 1965 and 1967, numbered E6007–E6049 and later classified as Class '73/1'. Class '73' was designed to work in multiple with electric multiple units as well as with normal carriages and freight wagons. In 1984, twelve were modified to work on the Gatwick Express, becoming Class '73/2'. Following privatisation, five GB Railfreight

Class '73' third-rail Bo-Bo electro-diesel No 73006 at London Bridge station on 12 August 1985. Built at Eastleigh Works in 1962 this locomotive is still in service as No 73967.

Class '73's were re-engined by Brush Traction in 2013 and classified as Class '73/9'. Fitted with 1,600-hp diesel engines they are used on 'Caledonian Sleeper' services in Scotland, from Edinburgh to Aberdeen, Inverness and Fort William. Although ten Class '73's have been scrapped, many are either still in service or have been preserved.

BR Class '74' Bo-Bo Nos E6101–E6110 See Class '71' on page 116.

BR Class '76' (EM1) Bo-Bo Nos 26000–26055 Prototype locomotive No E26000 was built by the LNER in 1941 at Doncaster Works for the planned 1,500V DC overhead electrification of the Manchester to Sheffield via Woodhead Tunnel route. The latter was delayed by the Second World War but was finally completed in 1954. To work this route a further 57 1,300-hp locomotives were built at Gorton Works between 1950 and 1953 and classified as EM1. Fitted with twin diamond-shaped pantographs these locomotives worked both freight and passenger trains across the Pennines. Fourteen received classical Greek names between 1959 and 1961. Although the Woodhead Line closed to passengers early in 1970 it remained open for freight trains, in particular 'merry-go-round' coal trains, which kept the reliable Class '76's (often working in multiple) busy until the line closed in 1981. The entire class was then scrapped apart from No 26020, which has been preserved at the NRM.

BR Class '77' (EM2) Co-Co Nos 27000–27006 (▼) Also designed to work on the overhead 1,500V DC Woodhead Line, seven of these more powerful 2,490-hp locomotives were built at Gorton Works between 1953 and 1954. Originally, 27 locomotives had been planned but when BR chose to pursue the 25kV AC overhead system, the Woodhead Line's system became obsolete, so the order was reduced. Between 1959 and 1960 the locomotives were

The first of its class, 1,500V DC Class 'EM2' No 27000 Electra at Sheffield Victoria station with a Manchester train in the 1950s. Built at Gorton Works in 1953, this locomotive was withdrawn as a Class '77' and sold to Dutch national railway operator Nederlandse Spoorwegen in 1970 where it survived until 1985. As NS '155' Class No 1506, this locomotive is now preserved at Manchester Museum of Science and Industry.

named after characters from ancient Greek mythology. In service they were mainly employed on express passenger trains between Manchester Piccadilly and Sheffield Victoria. The entire class was withdrawn in 1968 and later sold to the Dutch national railway. No 27000 *Electra* is now preserved at the Midland Railway – Butterley heritage railway and museum, No 27001 *Ariadne* is at the Science and Industry Museum in Manchester and No 27003 *Diana* is preserved at the Railway Museum in Utrecht, Netherlands.

BR Class '80' A1A-A1A No E1000 (later E2001) Originally built as a prototype Co-Co gas turbine locomotive (No 18100) for the Western Region by Metropolitan-Vickers in 1951 (see page 62), it was rebuilt in 1958 to operate on the 25kV AC overhead system, preparing the ground for electrification of the West Coast Main Line. Once the Class '81' and onwards locomotives (see below) were in service, E2001 was no longer needed and it was withdrawn in 1968.

Class '81' 25KV AC electric locomotive No 81011 at Carlisle with a Euston to Glasgow Central train on 24 May 1985. Built as E3013 by the Birmingham Railway Carriage & Wagon Works in 1960, this loco was withdrawn as No 81011 in April 1989.

BR Class '81' (AL1) Bo-Bo Nos E3001–E3023, E3096, E3097 (▼) Built between 1959 and 1964 by Associated Electrical Industries at Birmingham Railway Carriage & Wagon Works, the 25 members of Class AL1 (later Class '81') Bo-Bo 25kV AC overhead 3,300-hp locomotives were the first such locomotives ordered by BR for use on the fledgling electrified WCML, then chiefly restricted to the Crewe to Liverpool and Manchester routes. Under the TOPS system the remaining 22 locomotives were numbered 81001–81022. Nos 81001 and 81016 were withdrawn in 1983 and 1982 respectively while the remainder was withdrawn between 1983 and 1991. No 81002 has been preserved at Barrow Hill Engine Shed.

BR Class '82' (AL2) Bo-Bo Nos E3046–E3055 Ten members of this 25kV AC overhead 3,300-hp class were built by Metropolitan-Vickers and Beyer Peacock between 1960 and 1962. Designed to haul express trains on the fledgling WCML, all locomotives were allocated to Longsight depot in Manchester. Under the TOPS scheme they were renumbered 82001–82008 (two had previously been destroyed by fire). The entire fleet was withdrawn in 1983, with the exception of two examples that survived until 1987. No 82008 is preserved at Barrow Hill Engine Shed.

BR Class '83' (AL3) Bo-Bo Nos E3024–E3035, E3098–E3100 (▼) The fifteen members of this 25kV AC overhead 2,950-hp class were built by English Electric at Vulcan Foundry between 1960 and 1962. Designed to haul expresses between London Euston (from 1965), Birmingham, Crewe, Liverpool and Manchester, the class was placed in storage from 1967 to 1971 due to problems with their rectifiers. After rectification they were reinstated to work on the extension of electrification to Glasgow in the early 1970s. Two were

25kV AC electric locomotive E3100 (later Class '83') at Manchester Piccadilly in the early 1960s. Built by English Electric at Vulcan Foundry in 1962, this loco was withdrawn as 83015 in February 1988.

Class '86' 25kV AC electric locomotive No 86246 with a parcels train at Crewe on 31 March 1984. Built by English Electric at Vulcan Foundry in 1966, this loco was renumbered to 86505, but reverted to 86246 when used on Anglia services between Liverpool Street and Norwich and withdrawn as such in 2004.

withdrawn after accidents in 1975 and 1977, ten were withdrawn in 1983 and the final three in 1989. E3035 (83012) is preserved at Barrow Hill Engine Shed.

BR Class '84' (AL4) Bo-Bo Nos E3036–E3045 Built in 1960–61 by the North British Locomotive Company, the ten 25kV AC overhead 3,560-hp locomotives of this class were plagued by technical issues. Taken out of service in 1963, the entire class was returned to GEC, the manufacturer of the electrical equipment, who carried out remedial work. The problems persisted and the class was put into storage in 1967. Then in 1972 the locomotives were rebuilt and classified under TOPS as Class '84', Nos 84001–84010. The class was withdrawn between 1979 and 1980. 84001 is preserved at the Museum of Scottish Railways in Bo'ness.

BR Class '85' (AL5) Bo-Bo Nos E3056–E3095 (▼) Built by BR at Doncaster Works from 1961 to 1964, the 40 members of this 25kV AC overhead 3,200-hp class were designed to haul expresses on the WCML between Euston (from 1965), Birmingham, Crewe, Liverpool and Manchester. Under the TOPS scheme they were renumbered 85001–85040 in 1968. They were withdrawn between 1985 and 1991. E3061 (85006) is preserved at Barrow Hill Engine Shed.

BR Class '86' (AL6) Bo-Bo Nos E3101–E3200 (▲) One hundred of this long-lived 25kV AC overhead 3,600/4,000-hp class were built at Doncaster Works (E3101–E3140) and English Electric (E3141–E3200) between 1965–66. Under the TOPS scheme they were renumbered 86001–86048, 86201–86252. Designed to haul passenger and freight trains on the WCML, in the 1980s members of the class were also employed on the newly electrified Great Eastern Main Line between London Liverpool Street and Norwich. Following privatisation, members of the class were operated by Anglia Railways, Colas Rail, Caledonian Sleeper, English Welsh & Scottish Railway, FM Rail, Freightliner, Hull Trains, Vintage Trains, Virgin Rail Group and Network Rail. Thirty-one examples have more recently been exported to Bulgaria and Hungary, three operational examples have been preserved (E3137, E3191 and E3199) and the remainder scrapped.

BR Class '87' Bo-Bo Nos 87001–87035, 87101 (▼) Built by BREL at Crewe Works between 1973 and 1975, the 36 members of the 25kV AC 5,000-hp class were designed to haul passenger and freight trains on the WCML. They had a maximum speed of 110 mph. 87101 had major equipment differences making it very suitable for hauling freight trains, but was the first to be withdrawn in 1999. As flagships of the Anglo-Scottish fleet, many members of the

Celebrating the 'Golden Jubilee' of the 'Royal Scot' express, Class '87' 25kV AC electric locomotive No 87003 Patriot pauses at Preston station on 2 May 1977. Built at Crewe Works in 1973, this locomotive was exported to Bulgaria in December 2008.

class were later named. Following privatisation, the class was operated by Virgin Trains, English Welsh & Scottish Railway, Cotswold Rail, Direct Rail Services and GB Railfreight. More recently, 21 members have been exported to Bulgaria, two have been preserved (87001 and 87002) and thirteen have been scrapped.

BR Class '89' Co-Co No 89001 Designed potentially to haul freight trains through the Channel Tunnel, this prototype 25kV 50Hz AC overhead 6,000-hp electric locomotive 89001 was built by BREL at Crewe Works in 1986. After test runs on the WCML and ECML it was withdrawn in 1992, reinstated in 1996 and withdrawn again in 2000 before being saved for preservation at Barrow Hill Engine Shed. Following an overhaul there is a plan to return it to operational status.

BR Class '90' Bo-Bo Nos 90001-90050 Fifty members of this 25kV AC overhead 5,000-hp class were built by BREL at Crewe Works between 1987 and 1990. These mixed traffic locomotives had a top speed of 110 mph and, after privatisation, were employed by Greater Anglia, Virgin Trains and Great North Eastern Railway, as well as DB Cargo UK and Freightliner. Twenty-five are still in service, nineteen are stored and six have been scrapped.

BR Class '91' Bo-Bo Nos 91001-91031 (from 2003, 91101-91122, 91124-91132) See page 199.

BR Class '92' Co-Co Nos 92001-92046 Built jointly by ABB Transportation of Switzerland and Brush Traction between 1993 and 1996, the 46 members of this dual-voltage class were specifically designed to operate freight trains through the Channel Tunnel. They can operate on 25kV AC overhead or 750V DC third rail, with a power output of 6,760 hp and 5,360 hp respectively. Current operators include DB Cargo UK, GB Railfreight, DB Cargo Bulgaria, DB Cargo Romania and Transagent Rail Cargo (Croatia). Seven locomotives have been repainted in 'Midnight Teal' for hauling the 'Caledonian Sleeper' services in the UK.

British Railways operated a wide variety of electric multiple units (EMUs) around its network following Nationalisation, a mix of 25kV AC overhead (which eventually replaced 1,500V DC systems, such as on the Manchester–Altrincham and the Woodhead lines), and third-rail 650–850V DC, used on the Southern Region, the London District Euston to Watford and Broad Street services, and on the Wirral, Merseyside and Tyneside suburban services. Clearances for overhead wires on the Great Eastern Main Line, North Clyde Line and London, Tilbury & Southend Railway routes were low, and these lines demanded a lower voltage of 6.25kV AC. First-generation EMU stock numbered thirteen classes (Classes '300' to '312') built at British Railways workshops between 1949 and 1978. Second-generation units (Classes '313' to '322') numbered ten classes, all built between 1976 and 1991 at British Rail Engineering Ltd, York. A final batch of non-passenger Royal Mail Class '325' units were built by ABB at Derby in 1995–96. Just two third-generation EMU classes were built before privatisation, the Class '323' for Regional Railways built by Hunslet Transportation Projects, and the Class '365' 'Networker' units for Network SouthEast's Great Northern and South Eastern services.

Class '506' 1500V DC electric multiple unit M59404 at Manchester Piccadilly in 1965 with a train from Hadfield. These three-car units, built to an LNER design, were withdrawn in December 1984.

Class '506' 1500V DC electric multiple unit M59604M at Manchester Piccadilly with a train for Hadfield on 21 October 1984.

Two four-car third-rail Class '404' electric multiple units 3123 and 3081 depart from Guildford with a Portsmouth to Waterloo train on 18 July 1970. The last of these late 1930s-built Southern Railway units were taken out of service during 1972.

Marshalling yards and freight services

Until the 1960s, the usual means of moving large volumes of freight by rail was to transport it in a series of separate goods wagons which would be coupled together to form a train. Even before the 'Big Four Grouping' of 1923, several rail companies had built marshalling yards at strategic locations around their networks to handle and sort wagons into specific formations for onward transport. One of these, the Great Central Railway, opened a colossal hump yard at Wath in South Yorkshire in 1907 to manage the output from around 45 collieries located within a 10-mile radius. Two yards, each totalling 31 departure sidings amounting to 36 miles of track, could handle up to 5,000 wagons a day. In Feltham, southwest London, the London & South Western Railway's hump marshalling yard opened ten years later and used two gravity shunts, electrically operated points and 32 miles of track to handle over 3,000 wagons daily. The former Midland Railway's Nottinghamshire marshalling yard at Toton was dealing with over one million wagons a year by the 1950s and was the largest of its kind in Europe.

The 'hump method' used in Britain's marshalling yards involved the wagons from incoming trains being individually uncoupled, then shunted forwards over a hump before being propelled by gravity into their allotted marshalling siding. Each wagon in the completed rakes for onward haulage would display a card denoting its contents, weight and destination. It was a straightforward process but also laborious, and an extremely dangerous operation too since each wagon had to be slowed by manually pinning down the brakes, and directed into the correct siding by ground shunting staff who would run alongside them. Innumerable lives were saved by the introduction of hydraulic wagon retarders. These were first used in 1933 by the LNER at Whitemoor yard at March in Cambridgeshire, once the largest in Britain and the second largest in Europe, though it was not until the 1960s before all yards were so equipped.

Class '08' diesel shunter at the control centre of Toton marshalling yard.

Class '13' diesel shunter D4500 ('master and slave') at Sheffield Tinsley marshalling yard on 11 April 1971. Withdrawn in 1985.

By the time of Nationalisation there was often more than one traditional-style freight yard within the same local area. As part of the 1955 Modernisation Plan, an £80-million programme was put into place to rationalise and modernise the provision by building a total of 55 new hump yards, each equipped with wagon retarders and controlled from a central tower. This was in spite of the continuing loss of freight traffic to road transport. By the 1960s many of the new yards had been completed. Several opened in 1963 including Carlisle New Yard at Kingmoor, Millerhill at Edinburgh, Healey Mills near Wakefield, Tees Yard at Middlesbrough and Tyne Yard at Newcastle. Tinsley yard at Sheffield, opened by BRB chairman Dr Richard Beeching in 1965, contained 50 sorting sidings and used a new computerised system to control all wagon movements.

Within ten years these yards had become virtually obsolete, with the freight that they were built to handle having dwindled away. An effort to claw back rail traffic previously lost to road had already been made with the introduction of the 'Condor' express container train between London and Glasgow, with a second route between Birmingham and Glasgow added in 1963. At this time there were still about 850,000 individual wagons on BR. The traditional wooden-bodied type was being replaced by wagons made of steel, which had been introduced following a 1951 review by the Ideal Stocks Committee, whose task was to oversee the standardisation of freight rolling stock with the widespread use of steel.

In some respects, the 1963 Beeching Report proved to be a 'home goal' as it conflicted with the ambitions of the Modernisation Plan by closing around 4,500

Stanier Class '8F' 2-8-0 No 48084 passing Carlisle Kingmoor with a freight train, c.1965.

Ex-GWR '2800' Class 2-8-0 No 2874 thunders through Ludlow with a mixed freight on 15 May 1956.

route miles of railway and cutting off the freight traffic feeding into the main trunk freight routes.

The report did, however, correctly forecast that the primary rail freight role would comprise bulk-fitted freight such as coal and mineral traffic. These amounted to 146 million tons in 1961 and 54 million tons in 1963 respectively. The report recommended the introduction of 'merry-go-round' trains for power station coal deliveries from some of the main collieries, and there were 620 of these remaining in 1961. These coal trains got their nickname as they continued to move, albeit very slowly, at the loading bays at coal mines then at the delivery bay at the power station. The loading and unloading was done mechanically as the wagons moved very slowly at these two points.

Beeching also foresaw the transfer of long-haul freight from road to rail, albeit ultimately with government aid, and made the important proposal to introduce intermodal liner trains to convey road/rail ISO shipping containers. Superseding the pioneering 'Condor' services, the first Freightliner service was launched in 1965. Some six decades later, at least two of Dr Beeching's recommendations have proved to be highly successful, with an ever-increasing volume of Britain's long-distance freight traffic now being transported by rail.

The 1963 Beeching Report map showing liner train routes and terminals under consideration.

A new freightliner train hauled by a Class '47' diesel-electric locomotive, c.1965.

British Railways Mark 1 carriages

Faced with replacing thousands of ageing locomotive-hauled railway carriages on its network, including some with wooden bodies, each with its own unique design, the newly nationalised British Railways embarked on a massive building programme of new steel coaching stock incorporating the best safety features of the former 'Big Four' railway companies. From 1951 these Mark 1 carriages were built in their thousands at British Railways' carriage workshops in Derby, Doncaster, Eastleigh, Swindon, Wolverton and York. The design was not used exclusively for locomotive-hauled carriages, and large numbers of electric multiple unit stock variants were also built to the same design, especially for use on the Southern Region third-rail electrified lines.

Most of the Mark 1 carriages were built with an underframe of 63 ft 5 in but a smaller number had a shorter length of 56 ft 11 in, to be used on lines with a sharper track curvature. The first-class and second-class carriages incorporated corridors with individual seating compartments and low windows to give a clear view for passengers. The third-class carriages were open, with eight seating bays and a central gangway. Toilets were provided at one end of each carriage. Orders for prototypes incorporating the best designs were also placed in 1955 with Cravens and the Gloucester Railway Carriage & Wagon Company. The earlier carriages had interiors finished in timber veneer, with labels giving the type of wood and its country of origin.

The Mark 1s were finished in various liveries. From 1951 the corridor versions were painted in crimson lake and cream (nicknamed 'blood and custard') and non-corridor stock in crimson. However, in 1956 the

A BR Mark 1 buffet restaurant and kitchen car on the Southern Region in 1966.

A Western Region BR Mark 1 brake third coach at Salisbury on 22 May 1963.

Based on a BR Mark 1 coach, this Royal Mail Letters coach is seen at Crewe on 11 August 1987.

Western Region broke with tradition and reverted to chocolate and cream for their named express trains, the Southern Region reverted to green, and other regions opted for maroon. In 1962 the Southern Region introduced a yellow strip above first-class carriages and a red strip above dining cars, and by the late 1960s these visual devices were being used throughout BR. In 1962 the Western Region ceased using chocolate and cream and reverted to maroon.

Over the years there were many variants of the Mark 1 carriages, including those built for multiple units and non-passenger stock such as Travelling Post Office vehicles, and these continued to be built until 1974. In 1960 Metro-Cammell built 44 Pullmans as a more luxurious version. From 1961 until construction ended in 1963, new Mark 1 carriages were fitted with US-designed Commonwealth bogies.

British Railways and other contractors also built 380 sleeping cars between 1957 and 1964, and these remained in service until the 1980s. In 1962 Eastleigh Works built one fibreglass-bodied Mark 1 carriage, first used on the Hayling Island branch and latterly on the Clapham Junction to Kensington Olympia peak services, but this venture went no further. Towards the end of production an eight-car train of experimental carriages was unveiled by BR as the XP64 set. Derby Works built three Corridor Firsts, two Corridor Seconds and three Tourist Second Opens, all finished in a powder-blue livery and accompanied by Brush Type 4 diesel No D1733, finished in the same experimental blue livery.

The last Mark 1 locomotive-hauled coaching stock was withdrawn in the 1990s, to be replaced by more modern Mark 2 and Mark 3 versions (see pages 180–182), but Network Southeast and other sectors continued to use the multiple unit variants of Mark 1 for many more years. Currently, many Mark 1s are still used by many heritage railways, and for mainline charter trains with retrofitted central door locking.

A 'blood and custard' BR Mark 1 Third Class coach on an Aberdeen to Edinburgh train in the 1950s.

An Eastern Region BR Mark 1 sleeping car.

BRITISH RAILWAYS | 129

Named trains

During most of the 19th century passengers on Britain's railways had to endure slow and uncomfortable journeys in order to reach their destinations. The introduction of Pullman cars and interconnected corridor coaches, as well as dining and sleeping cars, on Britain's railways had transformed rail travel around the country by the beginning of the 20th century. This was especially so with the development of more powerful and faster steam locomotives. As early as 1904 the Great Western Railway, always leading the way with its innovations and marketing strategies, introduced the 'Cornish Riviera Limited'. This express service ran between London Paddington and Penzance, taking just seven hours and completing the first 245.6-mile leg between London and Plymouth at an average speed of 55 mph. Not wishing to be outdone, other railway companies soon introduced yet-to-be named expresses offering at-table dining in restaurant cars running between London, Wales, the north of England and Scotland. This heralded the start of the golden age of rail travel for the travelling public which lasted for almost a century, albeit interrupted by the two world wars.

In the early 1930s the challenge was on between competing British railway companies for the title of the 'World's Fastest Train'. Unsurprisingly, the Great Western Railway was leading the way, claiming the title in June 1932 with its record-breaking 'Cheltenham Flyer' hauled by 'Castle' Class No 5006 *Tregenna Castle*, which completed the 77.3-mile journey in under 57 minutes at an average speed of no less than 81.6 mph. Not to be beaten, the London & North Eastern Railway in 1935 introduced its non-stop 'Silver Jubilee' between London King's Cross and Newcastle. This streamlined train was entrusted to one of Nigel Gresley's new streamlined 'A4' Class locomotives, one of which, No 4468 *Mallard*, still holds the world speed record for a steam locomotive, of 126 mph, set in 1938.

Ex-GWR 'King' Class 4-6-0 No 6000 King George V *hauling the 'Cornish Riviera Limited' at Stoneycombe near Newton Abbot on 7 September 1956.*

These were heady days for such trains during the 1930s but the high-speed streamlined era of rail travel was very soon to be brought to an abrupt end upon the onset of the Second World War, in September 1939.

The period of austerity that followed the war and the subsequent nationalisation of Britain's railways at first witnessed a very slow return of these named express trains on Britain's rundown and woebegone railways. The publicity departments of the formative British Railways were, however, undaunted and were soon working hard at marketing and attracting customers to rail travel once again. They brought out a profusion of named trains, not only reintroducing many of the well-known names of the inter-war period but also presenting a host of newly named trains. Ornate headboards bearing the train's name graced the front of locomotives and roofboards on carriage sides also bore the name and route. Publicity material, restaurant car menus, luggage labels and fold-out route guides were all designed to lend an air of romanticism to rail travel on these esteemed trains that crisscrossed Britain throughout the 1950s and into the 1960s.

Late 1950s restaurant car tariff for the 'Cheltenham Spa Express'.

Type 5 'Deltic' diesel-electric D9018 Ballymoss approaches Great Ponton on the East Coast Mainline with the 'Flying Scotsman' on 7 July 1962.

Experimental London Midland Region diesel-electric No 10001 (with No 10000 behind) stand at Euston station after hauling the 'Royal Scot' express from Glasgow, early 1950s.

Sadly, this relatively short post-war period of golden-age rail travel would shortly come to an end with the demise of the steam locomotive. During their early years the new diesel locomotives – such as the English Electric Type 4s (later Class '40'), Brush Type 4s (later Class '47') and 'Deltics' (later Class '55') – still carried these all-important train headboards or, in the case of the 'Flying Scotsman' London to Edinburgh service, the winged thistle emblem, in an attempt to perpetuate the glamour, but these were soon quietly forgotten as the railways entered a new age of uniformity, followed by the unmitigated disaster of railway privatisation.

Pullman Trains

Providing a luxurious form of travel, Pullman cars had run on Britain's railways since 1874. The first all-Pullman train began service on the London, Brighton & South Coast Railway's London Victoria to Brighton route in 1881. Carriages for these services were built at the Pullman Car Company's works in Brighton, and later by Metropolitan Cammell and the Birmingham Railway Carriage & Wagon Company. In exchange for a supplementary charge, passengers enjoyed luxurious seating with stewards providing table-served refreshments and meals.

With their distinctive brown and cream livery, Pullman trains continued to run on British Railways and by the 1960s still operated from London to many destinations. In their later years the carriages were repainted in a bland grey livery with blue window surrounds. The last Pullman service, the 'Manchester Pullman', was withdrawn in 1993.

Ex-LNER Class 'A4' 4-6-2 No 60003 Andrew K. McCosh with the 'Tees-Tyne Pullman' express in the early 1950s.

WESTERN REGION
'The South Wales Pullman' Paddington to Newport, Cardiff and Swansea. Replaced by diesel 'Blue Pullman' (1960–73)
'Bristol Pullman' Diesel 'Blue Pullman' from London Paddington to Bath and Bristol (1960–73)
Other 'Blue Pullman' services
London Paddington to Birmingham and Wolverhampton Low Level (1960–67)
London Paddington to Oxford (1967–73)

SOUTHERN REGION
'Golden Arrow' London Victoria to Dover – for Calais and Paris (ended 1972)
'Brighton Belle' Electric multiple units, London Victoria to Brighton (ended 1972)
'Bournemouth Belle' London Waterloo to Southampton and Bournemouth (ended 1967)
'Devon Belle' London Waterloo to Plymouth/Ilfracombe (1947–52/1954)
'Thanet Belle' London Victoria to Ramsgate (1948–51). Renamed *Kentish Belle* (1951–58)
'Ocean Liner Expresses' London Waterloo to Southampton Docks (ended 1970s)

LONDON MIDLAND REGION
'The Midland Pullman' Diesel 'Blue Pullman' from London St Pancras to Manchester Central (1960–67)
'Manchester Pullman' London Euston to Manchester Piccadilly (1967–93)

EASTERN/NORTH EASTERN REGIONS
'The Master Cutler' London King's Cross to Sheffield (1958–68)
'The Queen of Scots' London King's Cross to Leeds, Edinburgh and Glasgow Queen St (ended 1964)
'Harrogate Sunday Pullman' London King's Cross to Bradford/Harrogate (ended 1967)
'The White Rose' London King's Cross to Leeds and Bradford (ended 1967)
'Yorkshire Pullman' London King's Cross to Harrogate/Bradford/Hull (Hull portion became separate train 1967. Ended 1978)
'Hull Pullman' London King's Cross to Hull (1967–78)
'Tees-Tyne Pullman' London King's Cross to Newcastle (1948–76)

British Railways ferries

On its formation on 1 January 1948 the newly nationalised British Railways inherited 27 seagoing ferries which had formerly been operated by the 'Big Four' railway companies. Until the formation of Sealink in 1970, the BR regions, overseen by District Marine Superintendents, were individually responsible for operating cross-Channel services to Holland, Belgium and the Channel Islands, as well as ferry services to the Isle of Wight, across the Irish Sea to the Isle of Man, and to the Western Isles. The shipping services, known collectively as British Transport Ships, were essentially an extension of the railways, enabling rail and sea passenger services as well as carrying mail and cargo traffic. Some of the ships dated to the First World War, but British Railways (from 1970 Sealink) commissioned over fifty new ferries that were launched between 1948 and 1983.

Fifteen of the ferries that were used for carrying combined road and rail vehicles were later accorded the 'celebrity' distinction of receiving the TOPS number as BR Class 99 – for instance, No 99006 *Twickenham Ferry*.

Ports handling the services to the Continent were Folkestone, Dover, Newhaven, Southampton and Harwich. Fishguard, Holyhead, Heysham and Stranraer handled services to Ireland and the Isle of Man. Weymouth and

The Sealink Antrim Princess *ferry to Larne at Stranraer Harbour station on 27 May 1983.*

134 | BRITISH RAILWAYS

Portsmouth served the Channel Islands; Portsmouth and Lymington served the Isle of Wight. Until privatisation in 1994 BR even operated the steamer passenger services on Lake Windermere in the Lake District.

On 1 January 1968 the BR regions lost control of the shipping upon the formation of the Shipping and International Services Division, the precursor to the formation of Sealink. This was responsible for all BR shipping services, the railway-owned ports, for the marketing of traffic, and liaising with the Irish and continental railway organisations. Formed in 1970, Sealink was the new brand name for all ferry services in the UK and Ireland that were previously operated by BR. As part of a consortium, Sealink also used ferries owned by French National Railways (SNCF), the Belgian Maritime Transport Authority and the Dutch Zeeland Steamship Company. In the 1960s British Rail started operating hovercraft services from Dover to Calais and Boulogne and across the Solent from Portsmouth to Ryde on the Isle of Wight – these services were marketed as Seaspeed and Solent Seaspeed respectively. The ferries even carried the famous double-arrow logo of British Rail as their Sealink house flag. This logo was reversed on one side so that the top arrow on the funnel always pointed towards the bow of the ship, and on flags towards the pole.

The end for Sealink as a wholly owned British Rail subsidiary came in 1984 when it was sold to Sea Containers at the extremely low price of £66 million, which earned it the nickname 'The Sale of the Century'. However, the Sealink brand name lived on in various forms until 1996, when the UK services were rebranded as Stena Line, which had acquired the British ferry services six years earlier.

The Sealink paddle steamer Tattershall Castle *approaches New Holland pier with a ferry service from Hull on 23 October 1971.*

Sleeping car trains

The North British Railway introduced the first sleeping car on 2 April 1873, running between London King's Cross and Glasgow Queen Street, and it was not long before other railway companies were offering similar facilities, using Pullman cars with convertible seating. Unlike double or single-berth cabins that are used on today's sleeper trains, all arrangements were communal until the GWR introduced double-berth cabins in 1890.

Sleeping car trains became very popular and by the turn of the century they were running between London and Scotland, the West Country, North Wales and northern England. By summer 1961, the LMR timetable included the following sleeping car services running from London: Barrow-in-Furness, Carlisle, Corkickle (Whitehaven), Edinburgh Waverley, Galashiels, Glasgow Central, Glasgow St Enoch, Holyhead, Inverness, Leeds City, Liverpool Lime Street, Manchester Piccadilly, Motherwell, Oban, Perth, Preston and Stranraer Harbour. Additionally, there were services between Birmingham and Glasgow, Newcastle and Bristol, Edinburgh Princes Street and Birmingham, Glasgow and Liverpool, Glasgow and Manchester, and Manchester and Plymouth.

The Eastern, North Eastern and Scottish Regions were, in their winter 1960/61 timetables, served by the following destinations from London: Aberdeen, Arbroath, Dundee, Edinburgh Waverley, Fort William, Montrose and Newcastle.

There were no sleeping car services offered on the Southern Region apart from 'The Night Ferry' cross-Channel services connecting London Victoria with Paris and Brussels. The Western Region operated services between London Paddington and Birkenhead Woodside, Carmarthen, Penzance and Plymouth, as well as between Plymouth and Manchester.

BR made major investments in its sleeping car fleet, initially between 1957 and 1964 when 380 Mark 1 sleeper

Class 55 'Deltic' diesel-electric No 55008 The Green Howards *with the Newcastle to Kings Cross sleeping car service at York on 26 November 1981.*

carriages were built to replace those mixed fleets that had been inherited from the 'Big Four'. A decision was made in 1969 to market sleeper trains as 'InterCity Sleepers', reinforcing the InterCity brand that had caught the public's imagination since its launch in 1966. BR's second major build of sleeping cars came about in the early 1980s when Derby Works turned out 208 air-conditioned Mark 3 vehicles to support what was still quite an extensive network of services.

Since the heady days of the 1960s, BR's network of sleeping car trains has shrunk substantially with the advent of cheaper domestic air travel and the growth of Britain's motorway network. Today, only two routes remain. These trains run six nights of the week and are notably among the last regular, timetabled locomotive-hauled trains in the UK. The 'Caledonian Sleeper' is effectively two trains that are run as a dedicated franchise using new sleeping cars built from 2018. The 'Lowland Caledonian Sleeper' carries two portions between London Euston and Glasgow/Edinburgh. The 'Highland Caledonian Sleeper' carries three portions between Euston and Aberdeen/Inverness/Fort William.

The 'Night Riviera' sleeper service operates between London Paddington and Penzance, where it connects with *Scillonian III* for sailings to the Isles of Scilly.

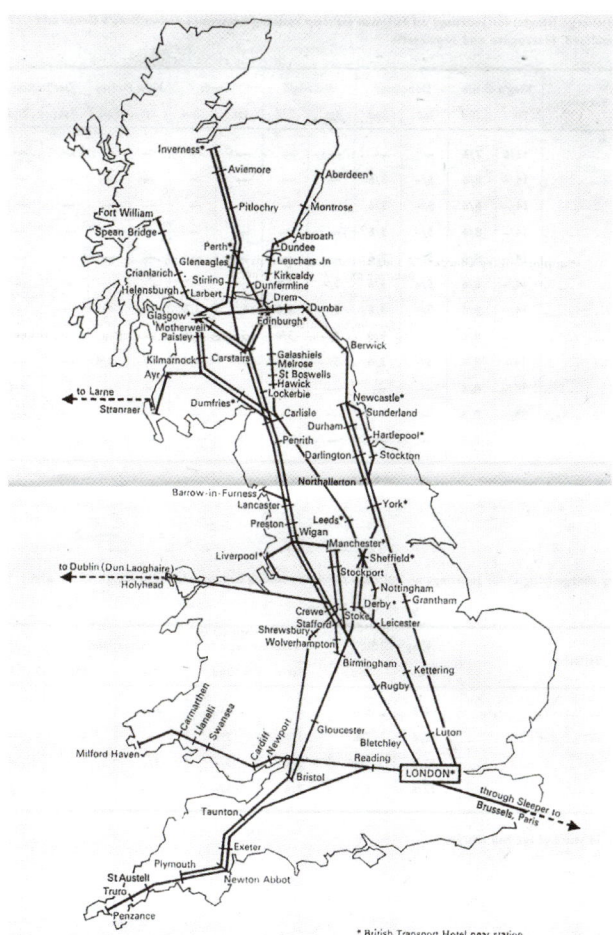

BR sleeping car services in 1968.

Class '47' diesel-electric No 47635 at Glasgow Queen Street station with a Scotrail BR Mark 3 sleeping car train on 20 September 1989.

Motorail

Privately owned horse-drawn carriages were regularly transported in Britain by train during the early days of the mainline railway, usually conveyed in a separate carriage truck attached to a scheduled passenger train. With the increasing ownership of motor cars from the early 20th century, the railway companies began using a similar method to transport cars and their passengers.

Transporting road vehicles across rivers and sea lochs created opportunities for the enterprising railway companies. After the opening of the Ballachulish branch of the Callander and Oban Railway in Scotland in 1903, cars were conveyed across the single-rail Connel Bridge between Connel Ferry station and North Connel using a specially adapted goods wagon. This service ran until 1914, when the bridge was resurfaced and upgraded to accommodate both road and rail traffic.

Then, in 1924 the GWR introduced a scheduled car-carrying service through the Severn Tunnel between Severn Tunnel Junction and Pilning High Level stations as an alternative to using the irregular Aust Ferry that crossed the River Severn. While passengers were conveyed in separate standard carriages, the vehicles travelled on open bogie wagons attached to the rear of the train. Upon reaching their destination,

The 1961 timetable for the 'Anglo-Scottish Daytime Car Carrier' service between London Holloway and Edinburgh.

The finest of British cars leave a Motorail service at Totnes station on 2 August 1973.

the cars were invariably filthy after being transported through the sooty and damp Severn Tunnel by a steam locomotive! This service lasted until 1966 when the Severn Bridge was opened.

British Rail commenced its long-distance car-carrying services in 1955 on the Eastern Region, where overnight services between London and Perth initially operated as the 'Car-Sleeper' service. Similarly, a London Holloway to Edinburgh daytime service was introduced in 1960. These and other early services, including the 'Continental Car Sleeper', proved there was a demand for car-carrying trains between some of Britain's major cities, ports and holiday destinations. The Motorail brand was accordingly launched in 1966 and within just a few years the network had expanded to include destinations radiating from a dedicated terminal at Kensington Olympia in London to destinations such as St Austell, Fishguard, Stirling and Inverness. Outside of London there were services between Manchester and Dover, Newcastle and Dover, Newcastle and Exeter, York and Inverness, and Sutton Coldfield and Inverness. Most of these were scheduled overnight services with sleeping cars attached to either flat car-transporter wagons on converted general utility vehicle (GUV) covered wagons, with cars being loaded on and off via an end-loading dock at a station. The loading point at the western end of Reading station could be seen for many years after it had fallen into disuse. London's Kensington Olympia was the only purpose-built Motorail terminal, opening in 1961 and remaining in use until 1981.

The peak of Motorail services was in the late 1970s when around thirty destinations were served and close to 100,000 passengers were using the service annually. The expansion of the country's motorway network, together with the increasing reliability of motor vehicles and the provision of faster InterCity rail services, gradually led to a decline in the number of Motorail routes offered. The impending privatisation of BR made the service difficult to market as an effective franchise, and although there was an interesting proposal put forward between Scotrail and Royal Mail to integrate some Motorail services onto existing overnight mail trains, this idea did not develop further. The downturn in passenger numbers to around 20,000 per annum finally led to Motorail's demise, with the last service running in May 1995. Following privatisation the franchised train operator First Great Western relaunched a Motorail-style service in 1999, with vans attached to the 'Night Riviera' London Paddington to Penzance sleeper train, but this facility was withdrawn in 2005.

A Motorail service on the West Coast Main Line in 1974.

Rural branch lines

When Britain's developing railway network reached rural areas in the 19th century, the benefits this brought to the people that lived there were immeasurable. Travel to urban centres suddenly became much easier and farmers could sell their fresh produce over a wider area, while livestock and locally made goods could reach more distant markets than ever before. As these new branch lines made transport from rural areas more possible, so they created opportunities for city-dwellers to access the countryside, opening up new markets in leisure and tourism and increasing employment. Milk was one commodity whose distribution was transformed by the arrival of the railways. Milk churns were collected at wayside stations for delivery to creameries, and by the 1930s specialised milk tanker trains were travelling overnight from the far corners of England and Wales to bottling plants in London.

On Nationalisation in 1948, British Railways inherited thousands of miles of rural branch lines serving scattered communities across the land (see map on pages 9–10). For most of them this was their only link with the wider world. However, BR prioritised economics and, years before Dr Beeching came onto the scene, around 3,300 miles of loss-making rural branch lines were either closed or converted to freight-only status by the newly formed Branch Lines Committee. The most significant loss during this period was borne by the former Midland & Great Northern Joint Railway in 1959.

Influenced by the societal changes of the 1950s and early 1960s, and with the consequent haemorrhaging of passenger and freight traffic from rail to road transport, worse was yet to come when Beeching published his report in 1963. Beeching's brief was to stem the loss of around £100 million per year, and over the following years another 4,500 miles of mainly rural lines were closed, including virtually every branch line in Scotland. Although not all of Beeching's recommended closures were implemented, the extent of the country's rail network was reduced by a third and around 2,300 stations were closed. It was the rural branch lines countrywide that most certainly took the brunt of those losses. By ignoring the social benefits of their retention, BR denied a railway link for so many rural communities.

Gone but not forgotten.

Ex-GWR '5101' Class 2-6-2T No 5167 at Much Wenlock station with a train for Wellington in August 1959.

Scottish Region railbus SC79970 at Craigellachie station with a Spey Valley service on 16 June 1962.

BR Standard Class '2MT' 2-6-2T No 82039 at Cheddar station with a Strawberry Line train in the early 1960s.

BRITISH RAILWAYS | 141

Ex-LMS Class '2P' 0-4-4T No 41900 at Upton-on-Severn station with a train for Ashchurch on 4 July 1959.

Seaside branch lines

Back in the 1950s and early 1960s the highlight of each year for me was without doubt the family seaside holiday. Fortunately my father did not own a car so we travelled to seaside resorts from our hometown of Gloucester to our holiday destination by train. I can well remember those exciting journeys to resorts in the southwest of England such as Swanage, Lyme Regis, Perranporth and Woolacombe – for most of the journey I would stand in the corridor with trainspotting notebook and pencil in hand accompanied by the rhythmic clickety-clack of the track and the whistling of the steam locomotive as it rushed through sleepy country stations. Adding to the anticipation, even some of the locos were named after seaside holiday destinations such as *Padstow*, *Westward Ho!* and *Seaton*. Towards the end of these journeys we would finally get our first exciting glimpse of the distant, sparkling sea.

A 1950s BR Western Region poster extolling the delights of Coney Beach at Porthcawl in South Wales. Artwork by Harry Riley.

Ex-GWR 'Hall' Class 4-6-0 No 4948 Northwick Hall *arrives at Kingswear station with a local train from Newton Abbot in the summer of 1958.*

144 | BRITISH RAILWAYS

At that time it was still possible to travel by train from virtually anywhere to virtually anywhere in Britain. My memories of these halcyon days have not been dimmed by the passage of time.

During the late 19th century the arrival of the railways to Britain's coastal towns and villages not only enabled fishermen to quickly transport their daily catches to distant cities but also led to a boom in homegrown tourism which the various railway company publicity departments were keen to promote, transforming previously sleepy harbour villages into thriving holiday destinations.

However, by the time of the Beeching Report's publication on 27 March 1963 (see page 168–171) British holidaymakers were changing their habits. The train journey to an annual holiday at the seaside was gradually becoming history, and with more disposable income the British were becoming a nation of car owners, in possession of convenient personal transport that was cheaper and quicker than rail travel. Low-cost package holidays to Mediterranean resorts were also taking off thanks to entrepreneurs such as Freddie Laker.

Although many rural and seaside branch lines closed in the 1960s and 1970s, there have been a few survivors which are fortunately still open for business. Notable among these are the former GWR branch lines in Cornwall that serve St Ives, Falmouth, Newquay and Looe.

The seaside branch lines that were closed to passengers from the time of Nationalisation in 1948 through to the Beeching closures, post-1963, are listed in chronological order by geographical region overleaf.

Beside the Camel estuary ex-LSWR 'T9' Class 4-4-0 No 30715 leaves Padstow with a train for Wadebridge on 1 August 1958.

Ex-LB&SCR Class 'A1X' 0-6-0T No 32650 crosses Hayling Bridge over Langstone Harbour with a Hayling Island to Havant train just before closure in 1963.

Ivatt Class '2MT' 2-6-2T No 41292 calls at remote Combpyne station with an Axminster to Lyme Regis train on 18 May 1963.

SOUTHWEST ENGLAND
Highbridge to Burnham-on-Sea – 29 October 1951
Upwey Junction to Abbotsbury – 1 November 1952
Chacewater to Newquay – 4 February 1963
Churston to Brixham – 13 May 1963
Brent to Kingsbridge – 16 September 1963
Axminster to Lyme Regis – 29 November 1965
Seaton Junction to Seaton – 7 March 1966 (now a heritage tramway)
Halwill Junction to Bude – 3 October 1966
Yatton to Clevedon – 3 October 1966
Wadebridge to Padstow – 30 January 1967
Sidmouth Junction to Sidmouth/Exmouth – 6 March 1967
Barnstaple Junction to Ilfracombe – 5 October 1970
Taunton to Minehead – 4 January 1971 (now a heritage railway from Norton Fitzwarren)
Wareham to Swanage – 3 January 1972 (now a heritage railway)
Maiden Newton to Bridport – 5 May 1975

SOUTHERN ENGLAND
Queenborough to Leysdown-on-Sea – 4 December 1950
Merstone to Ventnor West (Isle of Wight) – 15 September 1952
Fareham to Gosport – 8 June 1953
Brading to Bembridge (IoW) – 21 September 1953
Newport to Freshwater (IoW) – 21 September 1953
Hoo Junction to Allhallows-on-Sea – 4 December 1961
Havant to Hayling Island – 4 November 1963
Smallbrook Junction to Cowes (IoW) – 21 February 1966 (now a heritage railway to Wootton)
Shanklin to Ventnor (IoW) – 18 April 1966
Appledore to New Romney – 6 March 1967

EASTERN ENGLAND
Heacham to Wells-next-the-Sea – 2 June 1952
Cromer to Mundesley-on-Sea – 7 April 1953
Little Bytham to Yarmouth – 2 March 1959
Beccles to Yarmouth – 2 November 1959
Louth to Mablethorpe – 5 December 1960
Melton Constable to Sheringham – 6 April 1964 (now a heritage railway from Holt)
Wivenhoe to Brightlingsea – 15 June 1964
Dereham to Wells-next-the-Sea – 5 October 1964
North Walsham to Mundesley-on-Sea – 5 October 1964
Saxmundham to Aldeburgh – 12 September 1966
Kings Lynn to Hunstanton – 5 May 1969
Lowestoft Central to Yarmouth South Town via Gorleston-on-Sea – 4 May 1970
Willoughby to Mablethorpe – 5 October 1970

WALES
Lampeter to Aberayron – 7 May 1951
Denbigh to Rhyl – 19 September 1955
Pontypridd to Barry – 10 September 1962
Whitland to Cardigan – 10 September 1962
Pyle to Porthcawl – 9 September 1963
Bridgend to Barry – 15 June 1964
Lampeter to Aberystwyth – 14 December 1964
Penarth to Cadoxton via Lavernock – 6 May 1968

NORTHERN ENGLAND
Chathill to Seahouses – 29 October 1951
Aintree Central to Southport Lord Street – 7 January 1952
Loftus to Whitby West Cliff – 3 May 1958
Preston to Southport – 6 September 1964
Carlisle to Silloth – 7 September 1964
Hull to Hornsea – 19 October 1964
Hull to Withernsea – 19 October 1964
Monkseaton to Newbiggin-by-the-Sea – 2 November 1964
Scarborough to Whitby – 8 March 1965
Kirkham to Blackpool South – 2 November 1965
Lancaster (Green Ayre) to Morecambe – 3 January 1966

SCOTLAND
Stranraer Town to Portpatrick – 6 February 1950
Newton Stewart to Whithorn – 25 September 1950
Inveramsay to Macduff – 1 October 1951
Montrose to Inverbervie – 1 October 1951
The Mound to Dornoch – 13 June 1960
Burnmouth to Eyemouth – 5 February 1962
Elgin to Lossiemouth – 6 April 1964
Tillynaught Junction to Banff – 6 July 1964
Castle Douglas to Kirkcudbright – 3 May 1965
Fraserburgh to St Combs – 3 May 1965
Maud Junction to Peterhead – 3 May 1965
Leven to St Andrews – 6 September 1965
Dyce to Fraserburgh – 4 October 1965
Elgin to Cairnie Junction via Cullen – 6 May 1968
Ayr to Heads of Ayr – 16 September 1968
Leuchars Junction to St Andrews – 6 January 1969

Camping coaches

The increasing popularity of the great outdoors, particularly with those living in heavily populated urban areas, presented commercial opportunities for the railways in the 1930s. Camping and hiking in the countryside had become more viable for many as transport links and standards of living improved. And not only did the campers need to use the railways to travel to their holiday destination, they also needed somewhere to stay when they got there. The 'Big Four' railway companies were ready to capitalise on this demand with the provision of 'camping coaches' positioned in sidings at rural or coastal stations. In addition, the railway companies profited from the holidaymakers' use of local networks to explore the area while they were there.

The LNER became the first company to make camping coaches available when it converted ten disused Great Northern Railway carriages into holiday accommodation and sited them at a series of strategic locations around its network in 1933. During the following year the GWR and LMS jumped on the bandwagon, quickly followed by the Southern Region in 1935. Their camping coaches not only offered comfortable sleeping accommodation but also cooking and daytime living quarters, and as they became ever more popular, carriages of up to eight berths were made available, examples of which were to be found on the Norfolk Coast. By the late 1930s there were around a hundred such coaches dotted around the country.

During the Second World War the use of camping coaches was suspended but in 1947 they were reintroduced. British Railways rapidly expanded the number of available locations, with some key seaside destinations offering a long line of coaches, such as at Dawlish Warren in Devon. Catering for all tastes and pockets, BR also offered more upmarket

Nine ex-GWR camping coaches at Dawlish Warren station on 2 December 1967.

accommodation using converted Pullman cars which comprised six berths in three bedrooms, sited at some especially attractive locations. By 1957 there were over 120 sites where camping coaches were available, spanning from Glenfinnan in Scotland to St Erth in Cornwall. The Western Region alone had camping coaches in 44 locations, mainly in Wales and the West Country.

Camping coaches were also made available to BR staff and their families at privileged rates, three such coaches being available until 1970 at Blue Anchor station, located on the branch line between Taunton and Minehead in Somerset. Today, three of the coaches previously used at Dawlish Warren have been preserved and stand alongside the heritage West Somerset Railway at Blue Anchor.

Changing holiday habits with the convenience of travel by family motor car and the advent of the overseas package holiday, together with the decreasing appeal of the standard of accommodation on offer, led to the demise of camping coaches. BR rented out its last camping coach during 1971.

In more recent years, a few businesses, including some heritage railways, have identified a niche market in providing a holiday with a difference, and have resurrected the idea of turning redundant railway carriages into holiday accommodation. Refurbished and well-appointed coaches are available in a number of locations around the country including at St Germans and Hayle stations in Cornwall, alongside the Ravenglass & Eskdale Railway at Ravenglass station in Cumbria, at Goathland and Levisham stations on the North Yorkshire Moors Railway, Cloughton station also in North Yorkshire, Heacham on the closed line to Hunstanton in Norfolk, Loch Awe station and also Cromdale station on the closed Spey Valley line in Scotland.

Happy campers relax outside their ex-GWR camping coach at Cheddar station in 1951.

Travelling Post Office

In 1830, mail coaches travelling by road between the two commercial cities of Liverpool and Manchester were proving to be no match for the speed and frequency of trains on the newly opened Liverpool & Manchester Railway. To move along with the times the Post Office was encouraged to explore how the speed and efficiency of mail deliveries could be improved. To that end, on 2 November 1830, the Royal Mail was entrusted to the railway for the first time. The 'railway age' had certainly arrived by 1846 when all London-based mail coaches were taken off the road and long-distance mail was consigned to rail transport. Prior to the First World War there were 130 Railway Post Offices (RPOs) carrying mail across Britain. It was not until 1928 that the designation 'Travelling Post Office (TPO)' was officially assigned to all railway mail services. From as early as 1852 mail trains used mail exchange apparatus whilst on the move, speeding up transit time considerably. There were 245 such exchange points on the railway by 1913, and this ingenious lineside system continued to be used right up until 1971.

Following the Second World War the number of TPOs timetabled to operate in Britain was reduced considerably from the pre-war figure of 77 services to just 49. Between 1959 and 1977 BR replaced its older dedicated mail vehicles at both its Wolverton and York Works, where 81 new vehicles were built (based on the Mark 1 design), and a further seventeen were converted from existing Mark 1 vehicles already in its fleet. Some of the earliest vehicles constructed still included a collection arm and net to enable mail to be exchanged without the need for stopping. The lineside mail exchange apparatus was used for the final time on 4 October 1971 when a dispatch of mail was made at Penrith from the 'North Western Night Down TPO' nearing the end of its journey between London Euston and Carlisle. There were still around forty TPOs running at this time, but thereafter mail transfers were only undertaken on passenger station platforms. BR had by this time acquired a poor reputation for its mail service delivery.

The number of TPO services remaining in 1988 was 35, but by 2003 this had dropped to just eighteen. However, mail continued to be conveyed by rail well into the 21st century despite much of the traffic having been lost to road and air competition. Leading up to the privatisation of the railways, all mail by rail operations, including TPO services, were consolidated by BR under the Rail Express Systems (RES) sectorised business unit, which aimed to focus more on the needs

In February 1995, Class 47 diesel-electric No. 47768 waits to depart with the final travelling post office train from St Pancras.

of its primary customer, the Royal Mail. Seeking to rejuvenate mail by rail, RES won government funding for a new rail distribution network, known as Railnet, using new mail distribution hubs strategically located at Wembley (The Princess Royal Distribution Centre), Warrington, Glasgow (Shieldmuir), Doncaster and Newcastle (Tyne Yard). The £150 million project also involved the commissioning of a fleet of sixteen four-car Class '325' electric multiple units, specifically designed to convey pre-sorted mail. With grant aid finally awarded, this proposal attracted Royal Mail in late 1993 to commit to the signing of a 13-year contract.

Following privatisation in 1994 all TPOs and parcels services were acquired by English Welsh & Scottish Railway (EWS) in 1996. In 2003 the Royal Mail, having to make substantial cost savings to its business, announced that it was suspending the use of rail to transport its mail. Following a phased withdrawal the final TPO services departed around the country on 9 January 2004, with the last pre-sorted mail and parcels services running in late September 2024 using the Class '325' units, sadly bringing an end to the conveyance of mail by rail after almost two centuries.

A travelling post office train collects a post bag from a lineside apparatus at Harrow on 21 June 1957.

A Royal Mail bus awaits the next train at Achnasheen station on 14 June 1963.

BRITISH RAILWAYS | 151

Class '45' diesel-electric No 45059 with the York to Shrewsbury travelling post office train at York station on 25 November 1981.

Railway accidents

Accidents have been an unfortunate reality ever since the early days of the railways. Many lives have been lost and injuries suffered as the result of collisions and derailments. Whether caused by human error, mechanical failure, environmental conditions, or a combination of factors, lessons have been learnt and measures developed in a continuous effort to reduce risk. But while railway safety in Britain continues to be a major issue in the modern era of the high-speed train, compared to other forms of land transport, rail travel is still by far the safest.

During the British Railways era there were 131 serious accidents in which a total of 631 people were killed. The first of these occurred at Winsford in Cheshire on 17 April 1948, when a stationary passenger train was run into by a following postal express, killing 24. The deadly circumstance resulted from a passenger on the first train pulling the communication cord, thus bringing the train to a standstill, then the signalman erroneously allowing the second train through even though the line was not clear.

Britain's worst peacetime railway disaster occurred at Harrow & Wealdstone station, 11 miles north of London Euston, when at 8.19 a.m. on 8 October 1952 three trains collided. Initially, an overnight Perth to Euston sleeper, hauled by 'Coronation' Class 4-6-2 No 46242 *City of Glasgow* and travelling at 50–60 mph, collided with the rear of a Tring to Euston commuter train. A third train, a Euston to Manchester express, also travelling at around 50 mph and double-headed by 'Jubilee' Class 4-6-0 No 45637 *Windward Islands* and 'Princess Royal' Class 4-6-2 No 46202 *Princess Anne*, ploughed into the wreckage created by the first two trains on the down main line. The disaster resulted in

112 people losing their lives and 340 injuries, but the casualties might have been much higher had it not been for the speedy assistance provided by detachments of the US Air Force, who were in the vicinity and applied battlefield life-saving techniques.

The Ministry of Transport report on the crash found that the driver of the Perth train had passed a caution signal and two danger signals before colliding with the local train. However, the reason for this was never established, as both the driver and fireman of the Perth train were killed in the crash, though poor visibility due to patchy fog may have been a factor. The accident accelerated the introduction of the Automatic Warning System (AWS), and British Railways agreed to a five-year plan to install the system to give drivers an in-cab audible and visual warning when approaching a signal at caution, actuated by magnets between the rails.

Of the three locomotives involved in the Harrow & Wealdstone disaster, both *Princess Anne*, which just two months earlier had been rebuilt at Crewe Works as a conventional locomotive from the experimental steam turbine 'Turbomotive', and *Windward Islands* were scrapped, but *City of Glasgow* was subsequently repaired and returned to service.

St Johns station near Lewisham was the location of the second-worst peacetime railway disaster in Britain, on 4 December 1957, where 90 people died and 173 were injured. At 6.20 p.m. on a foggy evening an electric multiple unit (EMU) from London Charing Cross had been signal-checked outside St Johns station. Despite being protected by signals behind, the rear of the halted train was crashed into at 35 mph by a delayed London Cannon Street–Ramsgate service hauled by 'Battle of Britain' 4-6-2 No 34066 *Spitfire*. The driver's position was on the left and the signals on the right-hand side, and the fireman had previously failed to notice the yellow aspect signals, only spotting the red when it was too late to halt the train in time. The collision forced the last carriage of the stationary EMU into the next two, the telescoped carriages becoming a scene of carnage. The derailed locomotive and its

The fatally damaged 'Princess' Class 4-6-2 No 46202 Princess Anne *following the Harrow & Wealdstone crash on 15 October 1952 in which 112 people were killed.*

trailing carriages dislodged the support of a viaduct, which then collapsed onto the carriages behind. The driver of a train about to cross overhead managed to stop it just in time, avoiding further tragedy.

The driver of the Ramsgate train was acquitted of manslaughter charges after two trials. Published in 1958, the Ministry of Transport report found that he had failed to slow down after passing two caution signals, so was unable to stop at the danger signal, concluding that the use of Automatic Train Control (ATC) would have prevented the collision. Although installation of the system had been agreed after the 1952 Harrow & Wealdstone rail crash, priority was being given to mainline routes controlled by semaphore signals and not colour light signals, as at St John's station.

Following the crash, No 34066 was repaired and eventually became one of the last unrebuilt Bulleid Pacifics to remain in BR service. By a strange coincidence, Lewisham had been the scene of another fatal rail disaster 100 years previously, when again a train ploughed into the rear of one that was stationary, killing eleven people.

Other serious accidents later in the BR era included one at Hither Green, South London, on 5 November 1967, when 49 people were killed and 78 injured after a train was derailed at speed due to a broken rail. On 12 December 1988 at Clapham Junction, 35 were killed and 484 injured following a three-train collision caused by faulty wiring and signalling.

The last accident before privatisation occurred at Cowden, Kent, on 15 October 1994 when two diesel-electric multiple units collided head-on in thick fog on a single-line section after a signal was passed at danger, resulting in 5 fatalities and 13 injured.

'Battle of Britain' Class 4-6-2 No 34066 Spitfire *following the crash at Hither Green on 4 December 1957 in which 90 people were killed.*

Clearing the tracks near Clapham Junction following the crash on 12 December 1988 in which 35 people were killed.

BRITISH RAILWAYS | 157

Trainspotting

Collecting locomotive numbers has been an impassionate hobby going back many decades, offering much gratification to enthusiasts of all ages. In the post-war years, hordes of male youngsters could quite commonly be seen standing at the end of busy station platforms up and down the country, or even travelling on the trains themselves, either to relocate to an alternative 'spotting' location, or just for the exhilaration of being hauled by a specifically sought-after locomotive working hard at the front of their train. Fellow passengers would look on in bemusement at these extraordinary characters leaning out of the windows in all weathers, or excitedly dashing up and down corridor coaches, craning their heads out of any available window to catch a glimpse of locomotives in engine sheds or sidings. Often dressed in a duffle coat, or in later years an anorak, and with a notebook and pencil or ballpoint pen at the ready, quite possibly a camera or binoculars around the neck, and perhaps carrying an Army surplus respirator bag, or in later years a duffle bag, containing sandwiches and a drink (preferably dandelion and burdock!); this was the archetypal trainspotter.

However, collecting the numbers of locomotives was not a new phenomenon – as a shrewd marketing ploy to promote an interest in the railways, the 'Big Four' had published books containing lists of their own locomotives before the war, but the hobby really lifted off when a young Southern Railway clerk by the name of Ian Allan recognised a niche market and in 1942 published the *ABC of Southern Locomotives*. Retailing at one shilling, and usually available at any station newspaper, magazine and book stall, the *ABC* book became such a resounding success that an entire

Trainspotters at Southampton Central station in July 1961. Rebuilt 'West Country' Class 4-6-2 No 34027 Taw Valley is the centre of attention.

series of regional spotter's *ABCs* was very soon added, followed in the 1950s by the Locoshed Book listing the 'home' depots of all BR locomotives, as well as the Locomotive Shed Directory (showing how to navigate to such installations), and a Loco Log Book within which the locomotive numbers could be neatly recorded. A monthly periodical, *Trains Illustrated*, was the icing on the cake for the enthusiast to purchase, should they have any cash to spare after buying the range of spotter's books – which were updated and published annually – and train tickets for travel to enticing and far-reaching locations to spot previously unseen and illusive locomotives.

The Ian Allan *ABC British Railways Locomotives Combined Volume* was a highly sought-after and treasured possession of any trainspotter. It was a bound consolidation of all the regional spotter's *ABC* guides. This, in the summer of 1961, cost 10s 6d (around £13 in today's money), which was a vast amount for an impoverished young schoolboy to lay out every year. A paper round or perhaps generous pocket money granted from parents was a distinct advantage! Whenever a new locomotive number was spotted, it would be neatly underlined in this prized book. But very few spotters saw every engine. Achieving that would have entailed journeys of many hundreds of miles – in 1955 BR had 19,000 steam locomotives!

To cater for this passion and to ease the woes of the trainspotter, railway societies were established countrywide, providing motor-coach tours of sheds, usually on Sundays, when many would be jam-packed with locomotives. I well remember one trip made on the weekend of 28/30 March 1964, organised by the Warwickshire Railway Society, when a trainload of sleepy trainspotters travelled overnight from Birmingham to Glasgow Central. We were then

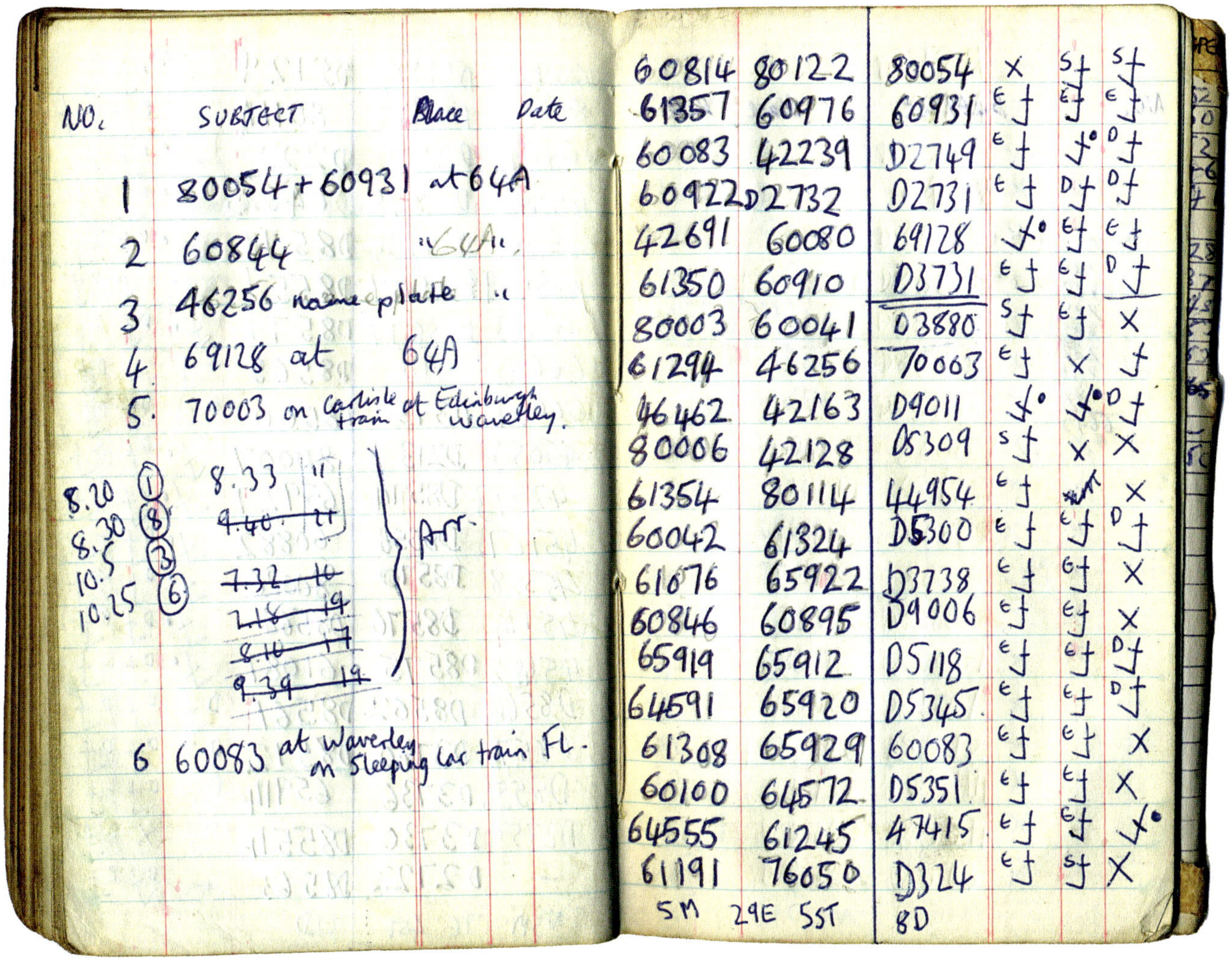

The author's trainspotting notebook following a visit to St Margarets shed (64A) in Edinburgh on 29 March 1964.

conveyed by a fleet of coaches to ten engine sheds in Glasgow and Edinburgh – in trainspotting terms, this was a 'shed bash' – in the process spotting 675 locomotives. Spotting a new number would be a 'cop'.

Shed permits were essential on such organised visits, but many trainspotters resorted to illicit means, sneaking ('bunking') around engine sheds, trying to avoid the shed foreman. Among the trainspotting fraternity, it would be frowned upon to apply for permission in advance to visit an engine shed, and frenetic trips to as many sheds as possible in one day would be made. Some sheds were considered easier to visit than others, subject to the friendliness of the shed foreman or the deviousness of the trainspotter. All manner of tricks were employed to gain access to the hallowed ground and, once inside, it could be a game of cat-and-mouse before perhaps being ejected by the foreman.

Many visits were, however, official and undertaken in a well-organised and respectful manner by the myriad of railway societies up and down the country, whose members were whisked from shed to shed by the coachload. Naturally, the trips had to be promoted in advance in a society's periodic newsletter, and the required permits obtained in sufficient time before any such trip could be contemplated. It was necessary for many of these trips to be undertaken by road, and usually on a Sunday when there were only limited or even non-existent train services available. Furthermore, there was no practical way of visiting a large number of sheds in one day, some of them being located in remote places on goods-only lines, and perhaps difficult or even impossible to reach using public transport. The Stoke Division of the LMR issued detailed conditions for visits to its engine sheds,

Trainspotters at York station behold the powerful BR-built Peppercorn Class 'A1' 4-6-2 No 60143 Sir Walter Scott on 2 August 1961.

Hordes of trainspotters at Crewe Works on 22 September 1979. Their objects of delight are Class '40' diesel-electric loco No 40187 and InterCity 125 HST Class '43' No 43132.

including the stipulation that visitors must travel by rail. It is little wonder that so many trainspotters 'bunked' sheds without permission. Prior notification even had to be given if any females wished to accompany the party! There was also a stipulation that any photographs taken were for a private collection only – this latter condition was obviously rarely enforced. Lineside photographic passes were extremely hard to come by and were issued only to the 'chosen few' responsible adults, or perhaps BR employees on a 'busman's holiday'.

Railway locomotive works such as Swindon, Eastleigh, Derby, Crewe, Doncaster and Cowlairs were also rich pickings, with guided tours normally confined to Sundays, when the workforce was absent. Annual open days such as those at Crewe, Derby and Swindon drew large flocks of spotters. Swindon Works also allowed conducted visits at a set time on a Wednesday afternoon during the school holidays, and Crewe Works accepted organised visits on a Sunday afternoon.

The hobby wasn't just confined to collecting numbers. The Branch Line Society, the Stephenson Locomotive Society, and the Locomotive Club of Great Britain, among other organisations, arranged railtours along freight-only lines or railways that were threatened with closure. Society members were often conveyed along these weed-infested bylines in outdated coaches or even brake vans hauled perhaps by a particular locomotive facing withdrawal.

Although steam haulage was fated by the early 1960s, the trainspotting passion continued unabated, with new diesel locomotives fresh out of works adding colour to the already varied scene. Even following the end of steam on BR in 1968, trainspotting continued, but in more recent years the gradual replacement of locomotive-hauled trains by uninspiring multiple units, along with safety and security regulations imposed by the railway authorities, have conspired to its decline. There are still some hardened enthusiasts out there with notebooks in their hands, but the trainspotting phenomenon of fifty or more years ago is all but a fading memory.

Trainspotters at Redhill station in the early 1960s as ex-SR 'U' Class 2-6-0 No 31790 of Guildford shed (70C) coasts through with a mineral train.

British Railways corporate design and publicity

Following Nationalisation, a new corporate identity was needed for the nascent British Railways. Between 1948 and 1956 a heraldic lion astride a locomotive wheel (nicknamed the 'unicycling lion') was used to adorn the sides of locomotives, while a sausage-shaped totem was chosen to appear on BR publicity material and station nameboards, colour-coded for each of the six regions. With some variations – the 'ferret and dartboard'

The original BR 'unicycling lion' emblem introduced in 1948.

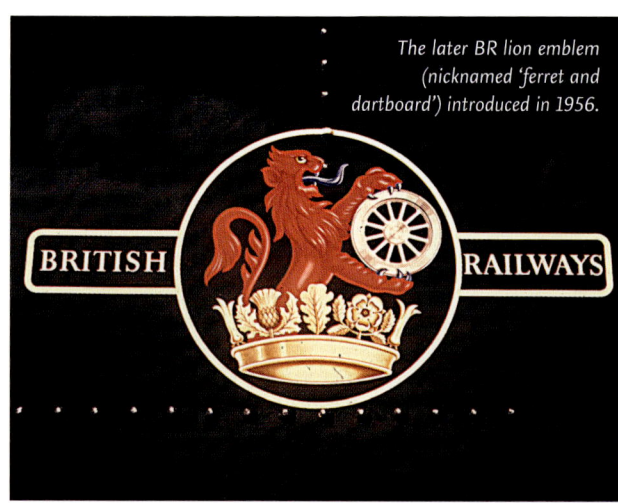

The later BR lion emblem (nicknamed 'ferret and dartboard') introduced in 1956.

The regional colour-coded station sign and 'hot dog' totem at Penrith station in 1972.

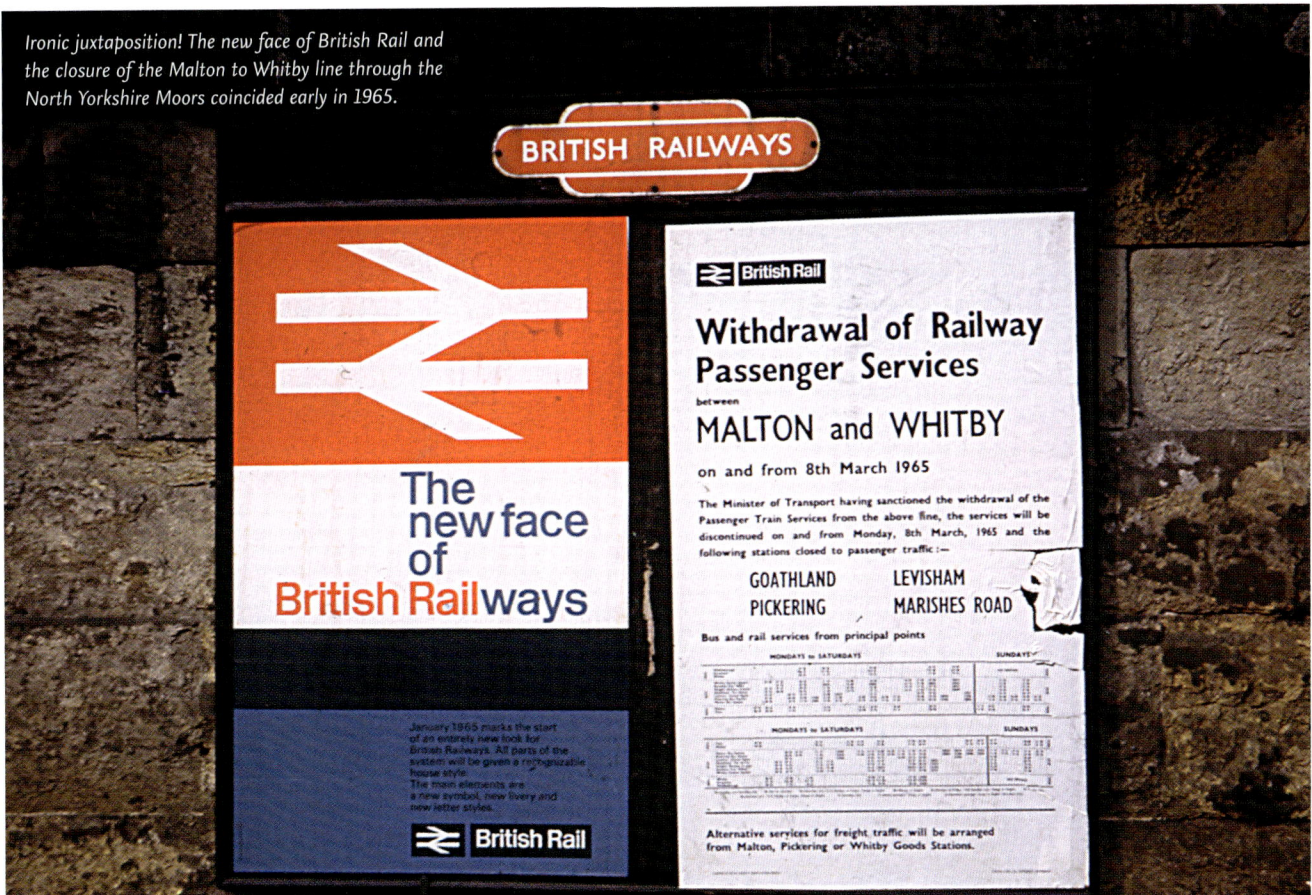

Ironic juxtaposition! The new face of British Rail and the closure of the Malton to Whitby line through the North Yorkshire Moors coincided early in 1965.

crest was used from 1956 – these remained as the BR corporate identity until the introduction of the famous double-arrow logo in 1965, nicknamed the 'arrow of indecision' at the time but subsequently proving to be one of the most enduring of logos.

By the early 1950s, as the post-war austerity period came to an end, the British Railways publicity department was in full swing producing posters, holiday guides, brochures, leaflets and regional timetables, all carrying the corporate logo. Numerous named trains, some reintroduced after the war but many brand new, received the full publicity treatment with personalised locomotive headboards and matching leaflets and restaurant car menus – the age of romantic rail travel had reappeared, at least on the surface. It was during this late-1950s and early-1960s period that British Railways commissioned the services of the famous and respected artist Terence Cuneo.

Born in 1907, Cuneo studied at Chelsea Polytechnic and the Slade School of Art, and started his career as a magazine and book illustrator. During the Second World War he worked for the *Illustrated London News* before being appointed an official war artist, producing illustrations of aircraft factories and wartime events for the War Artists' Advisory Committee, while at the same time serving as a Sapper. After the war, Cuneo was commissioned by British Railways to produce many oil paintings of its railway infrastructure and locomotives, often taking great risks when sketching on location – a highlight must have been being lashed to the top of the Forth Bridge during a gale! Cuneo's big break came when he was appointed the official artist for the coronation of Queen Elizabeth II in 1953. Following this he was in great demand, not only as an industrial and military artist but also as a railway poster artist, producing some widely acclaimed works for the British Transport Commission and British Railways. *Clapham Junction* (produced for the Southern Region) and *Royal Albert Bridge, Saltash* (produced for the Western Region) are just two of his fine works depicting life on British Railways during the late steam period. He went on to tackle the diesel and electric era, every painting having his tiny mouse trademark hidden away in the most unlikely place. Original

The Western Region's 'Royal Albert Bridge' poster was painted by Terence Cuneo in 1958.

Cuneo paintings and even his British Railways posters are highly sought after – in recent years some of his railway paintings have fetched up to £50,000. His paintings have appeared on British postage stamps, and even an InterCity train was named after him in 1990. Following Cuneo's death in 1996, a statue commemorating his life and work was unveiled on the main concourse at Waterloo station in 2004.

Looking back to the Beeching era of the 1960s, British Railways' management was wishing to divest the organisation of its anachronistic image and develop a contemporary and measurable identity. BR's design panel set up a working party, chaired by Milner Gray of its Design Research Unit, and promulgated the *Corporate Identity Manual*, which established a coherent brand and design standard for the entire organisation. It specified 'Rail Blue' and pearly grey as the standard colour scheme for all passenger rolling stock, 'Rail Alphabet' as the standard corporate typeface, and introduced the now iconic 'Double Arrow' logo formed of two interlocked arrows across two parallel lines, symbolising a double-track railway. The brand name of the organisation was shortened to 'British Rail'.

Shortly after the introduction of the InterCity 125 High Speed Train on Britain's main lines, British Rail launched the campaign 'This is the Age of the Train'. This ran between 1979 and 1984 with the aim of highlighting the social benefits of travelling by train as a modern and acceptable means of transportation for the era, rather than using the car as a matter of routine. Although a state-owned corporation, British Rail was under pressure to conduct itself more commercially. This campaign aimed to transform its image from a zestless and outdated nationalised industry into a vibrant customer-focused railway.

The uniformity of the BR branding was perpetuated until the sectorisation process was introduced in the 1980s, where selective BR operations such as InterCity, Network SouthEast, Regional Railways and Rail Express Systems began to adopt their own identities, introducing colour schemes and logos as an adaptation of the British Rail brand. As sectorisation developed as a preface to privatisation, the unified British Rail brand was dropped, except for the Double Arrow symbol, which survives to this day as a generic trademark denoting railway services across Britain.

The 'Beeching Report'

Following the Second World War the railways were in a run-down and parlous state, with nationalisation the only answer. Faced with the mammoth task of transforming the vast network into a modern and profitable concern, stringent cost-cutting became inevitable and soon gathered pace. The 1955 *Modernisation and Re-Equipment of British Railways* was an admirable attempt at launching Britain's railways into the future, but the implementation of this £1.24-billion plan was flawed – unproven and unreliable diesels were hurriedly commissioned, while modern and efficient steam locomotives, some with a mere five years of service, were being consigned to the scrapheap. By 1960

Type 2 diesel-electric D5317 (later Class '26') pauses at Galashiels station with a northbound train for Edinburgh on the last day of services on the Waverley Route, 5 January 1969.

the near-bankrupt railways were losing £67.7 million a year (an equivalent of nearly £1.6 billion today) and even though around 3,300 miles of the railway network were closed, after eight years the 'Modernisation Plan' was stopped in its tracks. The Government needed to stem the ever-increasing losses and knew that drastic action was necessary. Enter Dr Beeching.

Dr Richard Beeching, then Technical Director at ICI, the British chemical manufacturing giant, was renowned for his analytical mind and skills in solving business problems. He was appointed by the Minister of Transport, Ernest Marples, to the Stedeford Committee, set up to scrutinise modern management practices on the railways. Beeching suggested that the railways should not provide a public service but instead should be run as a profitable concern. Marples was so impressed with Beeching's ideas about how this could be achieved with appropriate cutbacks, he appointed him as chairman designate of the new British Railways Board in 1961, with a brief to restructure Britain's railway system. Early in 1963 Beeching became chairman of British Railways and within three months, on 27 March 1963, his infamous report had been published, with swingeing cutbacks looming on the horizon.

Priced at one shilling and available from Her Majesty's Stationery Office, *The Reshaping of British Railways* was a two-volume compilation of statistics, graphs, maps and analysis, becoming commonly known simply as the Beeching Report. Volume One comprised 148 pages of analysis based on statistics, with a 41-page appendix outlining lines and stations proposed for closure. Volume Two comprised thirteen comprehensive fold-out maps that had been produced to graphically illustrate the statistical information gathered for the first volume. Ranging from 'Density of Passenger Traffic' and 'Density of Freight Traffic' to 'Proposed Withdrawal of Passenger Services' and 'Proposed Modification of Passenger Train Services',

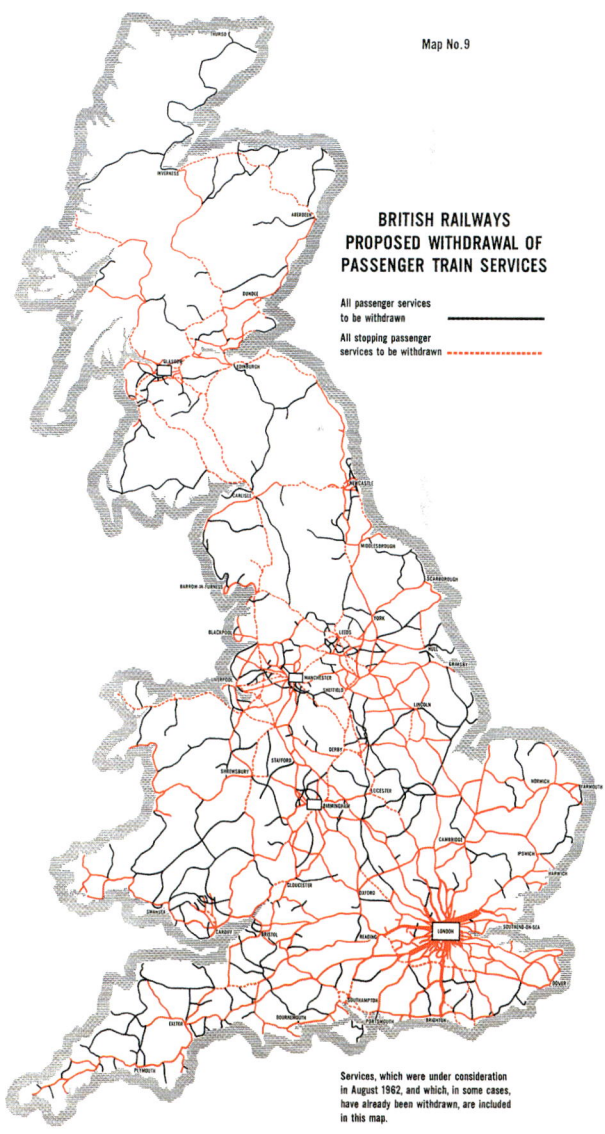

The Beeching Report map showing proposed withdrawal of British Railways' passenger services.

Dr Richard Beeching and his copy of the notorious Beeching Report published on 27 March 1963.

BRITISH RAILWAYS | 169

they broadly presented a rather gloomy picture for the railway industry. As a dissimulation of the proposed passenger service cutbacks, the final route map in the second volume outlined 'Bus Services in Britain'. Conversely, the map of 'Liner Train Routes and Terminals Under Consideration' was an all-important pointer to one of the positive outcomes of the report; the Freightliner intermodal network (using rail for the trunk haul and road transport for local collection and delivery at the terminals) is today the market leader for movement of export and import containers to and from England's 'big six' deep-sea ports. Another positive legacy of Beeching was the widespread introduction of merry-go-round (MGR) trains – so called because of their ability to receive and discharge coal while on the move – directly from collieries to power stations, a practice continuing today, albeit between port and power station conveying biomass pellets instead of coal.

In short, the report recommended the outright destruction of around 5,000 route miles of railway and the closure of over a third of the country's stations. According to the figures quoted, based on statistics gathered from merely a snapshot survey of one week's duration, 17–23 April 1961, one third of the route mileage carried only 1% of passenger and freight traffic. Thus, the fate of the railways was sealed. (A similar analysis of Britain's road network would have produced much the same outcome!)

With motorway-biased Ernest Marples as the Conservative Minister of Transport, the destruction of Britain's railways was endorsed by the Beeching Report. A change of government in October 1964 saw the slaughter progress unabated, especially in rural areas, despite an earlier pledge by the Labour Party to halt such closures if elected. By August 1968, coinciding with the withdrawal of BR's remaining standard-gauge steam fleet, another 3,500 route miles of lines had been axed. Closures, albeit at a slower rate, continued until the mid-1970s when the system stabilised to more or less its extent today. In total around 4,500 route miles, 2,300 stations and 68,000 jobs were lost. In more recent

Ex-GWR '4575' Class 2-6-2T No 5543 enters Bishops Lydeard with a train from Minehead, c.1960. This line closed on 4 January 1971 but has since been reopened as a heritage railway, the longest in England.

enlightened times, with gridlock commonplace on Britain's road network, a small number of these axed railways have been reopened, but much of what was destroyed in the frenzied destruction that came about in the wake of the Beeching Report has been lost. Even more infuriating is the fact that the 'privatised' railways of today cost more in real terms to the UK taxpayer than poor old British Railways did in 1961!

The predominantly negative conclusions of the report sparked a nationwide outcry, especially from the rural communities who were most at risk, and it was soon dubbed the Beeching 'Axe' by the press. Beeching's report claimed to have all the answers: 'most areas of the country are already served by a network of buses' and 'it appears that hardship will arise on only a very limited scale'. The consideration of hardship was the special responsibility of Transport Users' Consultative Committees, where objections to closures could be lodged. If no bus service already existed, in some cases replacement bus services had to be provided. At the end of the day, it was for the Government – having also consulted its regional economic planning councils – to decide whether a line closed or not.

Richard Beeching did not get his own way entirely, although over the next decade 4,065 route miles were closed. Subsequent political and public pressure saved the Highland lines north of Inverness, and in southwest Scotland between Ayr and Stranraer, but the January 1969 closure of the Edinburgh–Carlisle Waverley Route left the Borders with no accessible railway services.

Further south, the Settle–Carlisle Line was happily reprieved in 1989, and is now a key freight corridor in its own right, also serving as a strategic diversionary route for the West Coast Main Line. The Central Wales Line was saved in view of the region's predominantly inferior roads and lack of bus services (though cynics might also point out that it passed through a number of marginal parliamentary constituencies!). Several Cornish branch lines were also saved because of poor road connections, while in East Anglia, the East Suffolk Line from Ipswich to Lowestoft was saved through clever management cost-cutting. Other lines in East Anglia were not so lucky, including several around Kings Lynn and Peterborough that had not originally been listed for closure by Beeching – despite its criticism of Beeching while in opposition, ironically it was the 1964–70 Labour Government that relentlessly wielded the axe over and above any other subsequent governments. Fortunately, a second report by Beeching published in 1965, *The Development of the Major Railway Trunk Routes*, was not implemented, otherwise Britain's rail network would have shrunk even further.

In retrospect, many of the Beeching closures were short-sighted – network closures amounting to one third brought cost savings of just £30 million, the railways continuing to run at an enormous loss. Removing the branches starved the main lines of feeder traffic, causing an even greater loss of railway revenue. However, the arch-villain of the piece was undoubtedly Ernest Marples, then Conservative Transport Minister.

Ivatt Class '2MT' 2-6-2T No 41290 pauses at Glastonbury & Street station with a train for Highbridge in early 1966. This line from Evercreech Junction closed on 7 March that year.

Mass railway closures

The closures proposed by Dr Richard Beeching in his 1963 report were essentially endorsed and went ahead, albeit with some quite notable exceptions. During the Labour Government from October 1964, Beeching's 'Axe' was wielded unabated, even though Harold Wilson had stated before the general election that the cuts would be reversed. In the event the new Labour Government continued with the cuts due to a conflict of interest among the road and rail unions that were supporting the party, and not least because the reasons for reform were still entirely present. The result, by the mid-1970s, was the axing of over 4,000 route miles of railway, the closure of around 2,300 stations and swingeing cuts in railway staff numbers, amounting to almost 68,000. Although some regions of British Railways fared better than others, no geographical region of Britain escaped the cuts.

Western Region

In southwest England, 37 lines were closed including one that had not even been listed for closure, namely between Coleford Junction and Okehampton. This was happily fully reopened to passenger traffic in 2021, but the section west, from Okehampton to Tavistock, remains closed, preventing what could also be a strategic diversionary route avoiding the troublesome coastal lines at the Dawlish sea wall and the steep gradients via the Devon Banks southwest of Newton Abbot. Fortunately, there were five notable survivors due to the unsuitable roads for replacement bus services, namely the branch lines to St Ives, Looe, Gunnislake, Exmouth and Severn Beach. The eventual, albeit delayed, closure of the former Somerset & Dorset Joint Railway route on 7 March 1966 created a void in the lives of the people of those counties and led to an outpouring of grief among railway enthusiasts with the loss of this much-loved institution.

One of the last Beeching closures, the Haltwhistle to Alston line closed on 3 May 1976. This lonely scene of a 'hybrid' Class 108 Derby Lightweight and 101 Metropolitan-Cammell diesel multiple unit at Alston station was taken in June 1975.

The sad remains of Woolacombe & Mortehoe station in 1980. The Barnstaple to Ilfracombe line closed on 5 October 1970.

The 2 November 1964 closure notice for the Berkeley Road to Sharpness line in Gloucestershire.

In central England there was decimation with, by 1970, no fewer than 42 lines having been closed, including the former GWR main line south from Stratford-upon-Avon to Cheltenham, which had not been listed for closure.

In Wales, by 1970 27 lines had closed, leaving much of the principality devoid of rail services. The longest of these chiefly rural routes to vanish from the railway map were the three that served the county town of Brecon – the lines from Neath, Hereford and Moat Lane Junction had closed even before the publication of the Beeching Report, although curiously they were all included in the closure proposals. Two other lengthy routes that were to disappear from the timetables were between Ruabon and Barmouth, and Carmarthen and Aberystwyth, but fortunately there were two notable survivors: the Conwy Valley Line from Llandudno Junction to Blaenau Ffestiniog and the Central Wales Line from Craven Arms to Llanelli, both reprieved due to there being unsuitable roads for operating replacement bus services. The South Wales Valleys lines were decimated, although some remained open for coal and steel traffic. Four lines and

BRITISH RAILWAYS | 173

The crowded scene at Keswick station with the 12.10 diesel multiple unit from Penrith on the last day of services on 4 March 1972.

Ex-GWR '1400' Class 0-4-2T No 1453 pauses at crowded Berkeley station with the final passenger train from Sharpness on 31 October 1964.

32 new stations have since reopened within 20 miles of each other, namely Abercynon to Aberdare, Barry to Bridgend, Bridgend to Maesteg and the entire Ebbw Valley railway.

Southern Region

Southern England, despite having a higher density of population and many electrified commuter lines, did not entirely escape the cuts, with 28 lines being closed, including two that were not originally on the list. However, eight routes were actually reprieved, including Ryde Pier Head to Shanklin on the Isle of Wight and over the Romney Marsh between Ashford and Hastings. Additionally, the Romsey to Eastleigh link line via Chandler's Ford reopened in 2003.

London Midland Region

By far the most serious casualty was the former Great Central Railway main line between Sheffield and London Marylebone which, apart from a temporary reprieve for a short section, effectively closed as a through route in 1966. However, there have since been line reopenings. The Oxford to Bicester Varsity Line,

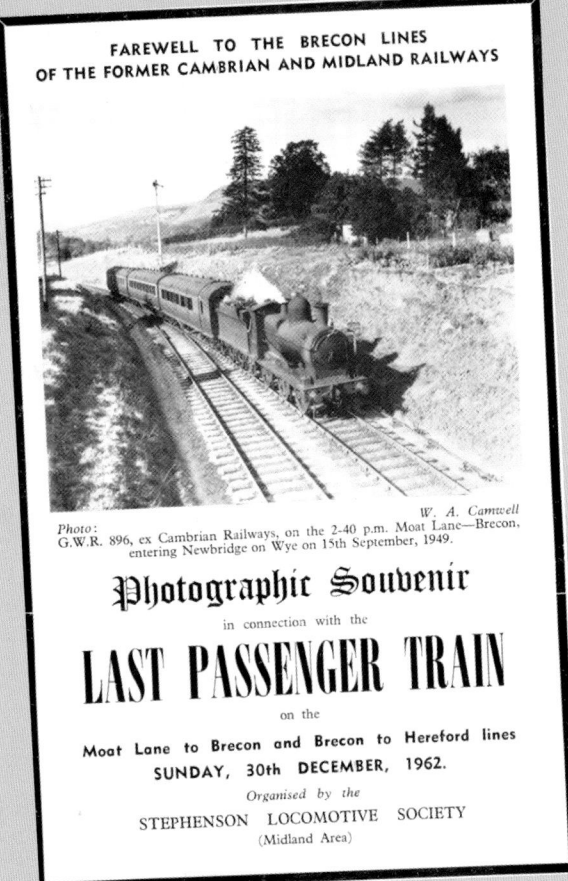

Souvenir of the last train to Brecon on 30 December 1962.

closed in 1968, reopened in 1987 as part of the wider East West Rail Project between Oxford and Cambridge. Further north, the Nottingham to Worksop route via Mansfield left the largest town in Britain without a rail link upon its closure in 1964, but the line had reopened in full as The Robin Hood Line by 1998. Dr Beeching's 'Axe' was wielded on 39 routes across the entire breadth of northern England, although there were fortunately fifteen survivors. Notable among these on the LMR were the Cumbrian Coast Line from Barrow-in-Furness to Whitehaven and the Settle–Carlisle Line, which escaped several closure threats before being reprieved by the Government in 1989.

Eastern Region

Of the 22 routes that had been closed by 1970 in eastern England, five hadn't actually been on Beeching's original list. These were concentrated in north Norfolk, with three radiating out from King's Lynn. From 5 October 1970, the East Lincolnshire Line ceased to be a through route, but remarkably the East Suffolk Line between Ipswich and Lowestoft was spared, not only through ingenious management cost-cutting but also because, by then, a section of the line served Sizewell A nuclear power station, which had been commissioned in 1966. One major route not listed for closure was the electrified Woodhead Line between Manchester and Sheffield, which was sacrificed in 1981 instead of the non-electrified Hope Valley route between the two cities.

North Eastern Region

In the northeast, not so lucky was the Starbeck to Northallerton main line via the cathedral city of Ripon, once an important ECML diversionary route, which was closed entirely in 1969. However, one of the fifteen survivors in the north of England was the highly scenic Esk Valley Line between Middlesbrough and Whitby, today shared between Grosmont and Whitby by the heritage services of the North Yorkshire Moors Railway from Pickering, this line itself originally closing throughout between Malton, Pickering and Grosmont in June 1967.

Scottish Region

Scotland did not escape the carnage, suffering no fewer than 44 route closures, including seven not originally listed by Beeching. The axing of the 98-mile Edinburgh to Carlisle Waverley Line in 1969 left the Scottish Borders as the only region in Britain without a train service, with Hawick 'cut off' between the two cities by 56 and 42 miles respectively. The reopening of the section between Edinburgh and Tweedbank in 2015 has partially addressed this deficiency. The once important 'Port Road' from Dumfries and serving ferries to Ireland from Stranraer Harbour quietly passed into the history books in 1965. There were seven lucky survivors in Scotland from the Beeching 'Axe'. These all escaped closure due to strong public and political pressure, the most notable being the long and meandering route from Inverness to Wick and Thurso, the highly scenic line between Inverness and Kyle of Lochalsh, and the Ayr to Stranraer Harbour line. Ending on a positive note, the Stirling to Alloa former main line reopened in 2008 after a 40-year gap since its closure, and has been electrified.

Crowds gathered at Hawick station to witness the last train on the Waverley Route on 5 January 1969, the 21.55 Edinburgh to St Pancras hauled by Type 4 diesel-electric D60 *Lytham St Annes*.

A new identity

In 1964 British Railways appointed the Design Research Unit, one of the leading design agencies in Britain at that time, to give it a new image. Centrally based in Derby, the agency was able to draw on the broad knowledge and expertise of railway engineering developed there in the local workforce over many decades. Coinciding with the phased withdrawal of steam traction in the 1960s, British Railways endeavoured to make an all-out effort to overhaul its corporate image and house style, renaming itself simply British Rail (although British Railways remained the company's legal name). The launch of a design consultation project in 1965 resulted in a new corporate brand and an across-the-board unique typeface designated 'Rail Alphabet'. Significantly, the new Double Arrow logo then introduced is still recognised nationally some 60 years later as station directional signage, even post-privatisation. So far-reaching was the launch of British Rail's new image, it involved the publication of a staff manual stretching to four volumes, released in stages between 1965 and 1970. The 1960s British Rail corporate identity was soon widely accepted, though was later swept aside upon the privatisation of British Rail in 1994.

The standardised livery of Rail Blue (also referred to as 'Monastral Blue') was launched in 1965, preceded

Introduced in 1965, the new double arrow emblem of British Rail was dubbed the 'arrow of indecision' and still in use today on station signs and railway advertising.

The XP64 blue livery was used on Brush Type 4 diesel-electric D1733 and a set of twelve carriages in 1964. This is how it looked on the front cover of the Ian Allan ABC of the same year.

by the experimental XP64-liveried twelve-coach demonstration train paired with Brush Type 4 (later Class '47') No D1733 painted in a slightly lighter-than-Rail-Blue prototype livery displaying the new Double Arrow logo against a flame red background beneath its four cab-side windows. These XP64 demonstration coaches featured prototype passenger facilities under consideration for the new Mark 2 fleet of vehicles just being rolled out from BR's workshops. This was quickly followed by the brand name of 'Inter-City', which was first introduced in 1966 for BR's long-distance expresses. Passenger coaches on these routes were given a new two-tone livery of Rail Blue and pearl grey with 'Inter-City' picked out in white, and there was no external lining out of carriages as there had been during the pre-Nationalisation era. Locomotives carried an all-over Rail Blue livery with safety-regulated and mandatory yellow front warning panels. Freight wagons were fitted out simply in brown or grey livery.

The introduction in 1976 of the InterCity 125 High Speed Train (HST, Class '43') on the Western Region main line between Paddington, Bristol, Cardiff and Swansea was a resounding success and HST-diagrammed services were very soon extended as far west as Carmarthen and to the southwestern tip of England at Penzance. Boasting a maximum speed of 125 mph (compared to the earlier diesels' 100 mph limit) and with greatly improved passenger comfort, these innovative and visionary trains were very soon attracting passengers back to medium- and long-distance train travel, supported by British Rail's zealous television marketing programme that encouraged customers to 'let the train take the strain'. Within three years of their introduction, the HSTs had been fully introduced on the East Coast Main Line between London King's Cross and Edinburgh, and in 1982 on the Midland Main Line out of London St Pancras. As a mark of their outstanding success, some reduced-formation HST sets remained in everyday passenger service in Scotland and the West Country around half a century after their first introduction by British Rail.

Other state railways in Europe soon followed suit with British Rail's successful inter-city brand – the West German state railway's Trans-Europe Express trains were from 1971 rebranded as such and royalties were even paid to British Rail for the use of the name for several years thereafter.

Introduced in 1976. the InterCity 125 High Speed Train Class '43' – seen here at speed near Exeter on 26 May 1985 - was a resounding success.

InterCity

As part of British Railway's post-Nationalisation policy of introducing prominent names to some of their principal express trains in the early 1950s, the Western Region was first to use the term 'Inter-City' when the name was given to a weekdays-only London Paddington, Birmingham (Snow Hill) and Wolverhampton (Low Level) 'business express' train. The service was discontinued in 1967 after the newly electrified West Coast Main Line (WCML) between London Euston and Birmingham (New Street) provided a faster service between the two major cities.

British Rail, as newly renamed in the mid-1960s, desired to abolish its outdated steam-age image. Its answer was the launch of the corporate 'Rail Blue' livery, which was swiftly followed by the brand name 'Inter-City', adopted for its principal long-distance express passenger trains. Its coaches wore the new blue and grey livery that had first been marketed by the prototype XP64-liveried demonstration train and Mark 2 passenger coaches.

The Inter-City Mark 2 coaches were British Rail's second design of carriage. The prototype corridor first-class 'FK' coach was built at British Rail Engineering Ltd's (BREL's) Swindon Works in 1963, with all carriages for the Inter-City network of services thereafter built at BREL's Derby Litchurch Lane Works, until 1975. Some of the early carriages were turned out in maroon or dark green (as on the Southern Region) but they wore the blue and grey livery for much of their lives. The Mark 2 design became the mainstay of Inter-City locomotive-hauled services, and many are still in use today with private operators, some sixty years after their first introduction into service.

The introduction of the InterCity 125 High Speed Train (HST), built by BREL between 1975 and 1982, further reinforced the Inter-City brand name. British Rail initially developed the HST in the early 1970s, considered as an interim measure, the primary Advanced Passenger Train (APT) project then under development being considered the principal way forward for the high-speed Inter-City

Poster produced by British Rail in 1977 to promote the new InterCity HST 125 services between Reading, Bath, Bristol, Cardiff and Swansea.

passenger trains of the future. As the controversial APT project faltered, HST production, based on the proven prototype Class '41' power cars and seven intermediate passenger coaches built jointly between Crewe and Derby Works in 1972, continued in earnest. The construction of the production power cars (Class '43') and intermediate Mark 3 coaches proceeded from 1974, with 95 sets being built up until 1982. They proved to be a reliable workhorse and went on to be the mainstay of principal Inter-City services in Britain up until privatisation and beyond.

Class '90' 25kV AC electric locomotive No 90006 pauses at Nuneaton station with a West Coast Main Line express on 3 July 1989.

A close-up of InterCity 125 HST Class '43' diesel No 43027 Westminster Abbey, June 1985.

On the WCML, and coinciding with BR's launch of the Inter-City brand, new high-speed services had been introduced in 1966 between London Euston, Birmingham, Manchester and Liverpool, offering a regular-interval service throughout the day. Using the Mark 2 coaches from 1974, followed by the air-conditioned Mark 3 coaches from 1975 (a variant of this was used in the HST sets), hauled by Classes '86' and '87' electric locomotives, they remained the mainstay of WCML InterCity express services until the early 2000s.

As an apparent prelude to privatisation, British Rail was divided up into different operating sectors in 1982. 'Inter-City' became 'InterCity' when the livery for both coaches and locomotives was changed to dark grey on the upper parts and light grey on the lower, separated by red and white stripes (the famous 'Swallow' logo was added in 1989). This new InterCity sector was divided into seven operating divisions: East Coast, West Coast, Midland, Great Western, Great Eastern, Cross-Country, and Gatwick Express. The sector was also responsible for sleeping car and Motorail car-carrying services. Proving to be a successful and profitable formula, British Rail within a few years was running more 100-mph services each day than any other country in the world.

Following completion of East Coast Main Line electrification in 1990, locomotive-hauled electric InterCity 225 trains (Class '91') with Mark 4 carriages entered service between London King's Cross and Edinburgh – their misleading brand name refers to their potential top speed of 225 km/h (140 mph). In fact they 'only' operate up to a maximum speed of 201 km/h (125 mph), the same as the HSTs that they replaced.

The Railways Act 1993 heralded the privatisation of Britain's railways. From 1 April 1994 British Rail was fragmented into numerous companies, with many of the new train operators taking on franchises not dissimilar to the old InterCity sector operating divisions. The term 'InterCity' soon fell into disuse, and is no longer used by train-operating companies, reflecting the absence of a single, centrally branded network of mainline services.

Class '91' 25kV AC electric loco No 91002 at rest in Leeds station with a train for Kings Cross, 15 August 1989.

The end of steam haulage

Although it had been widely accepted in both government and British Railways' management circles that steam traction would intrinsically either be cascaded around depots or entirely replaced by diesel and electric traction on a measured approach over a period of around three decades, in particular as main lines became electrified, this proved not to be the outcome. In the event the transition period was much shorter, despite BR's steam locomotive fleet amounting to about 19,000, distributed around all regions, when the 1955 Modernisation Plan was released. With swingeing withdrawals, steam traction had been virtually eliminated by the end of 1966 from all principal mainline routes in Britain, apart from the Waterloo–Bournemouth–Weymouth main line and in the northwest of England. Despite some Standard Class locomotives having seen less than ten years of service and still being in good mechanical condition, British Rail, as it had by then become, was zealously taking them out of service in their hundreds, so desperate was it to rapidly transform its corporate image.

The only pocket of resistance on the Western Region after 1965 was the 100% steam-operated Somerset & Dorset cross-country route between Bath and Bournemouth, which withstood closure until 7 March 1966, completely eliminating steam on the Western Region. On the Southern Region, steam operations remained on the London (Waterloo) to Bournemouth and Weymouth main line until the third-rail electrification programme through to Bournemouth had been completed in July 1967. This ended the sight and sound of Bulleid's Pacifics thundering through principal southern stations along the route, such as at Woking and Basingstoke, heading well-loaded passenger trains, and proved to be the swansong of mainline steam operations in Britain.

While locomotives of Great Western Railway parentage had already been ousted by Shrewsbury-allocated BR Standard Class locomotives, steam haulage continued on the Cambrian main line in Mid Wales until December 1966, when Machynlleth shed was finally closed to steam, although it took on what was to be its future role as a stabling and refuelling point for diesel multiple units. Shrewsbury depot closed in June 1967, and what was to be the last vestige of the Western Region's pannier tanks working on BR, Croes Newydd (Wrexham) shed, was closed in November 1967.

Steam traction had been eradicated as early as 1962 in East Anglia, but on other parts of the Eastern Region it took four more years before it had gone for good. While King's Cross 'Top Shed' had closed to steam in 1963, further up the East Coast Main Line at Doncaster, steam clung on to life until May 1966. Further north in the North Eastern Region, York depot, later incorporated into the National Railway Museum, lost its steam allocation in the summer of 1967 and Leeds Holbeck shed followed during the October of that year. In the industrial northeast, West Hartlepool, North

BR Standard Class '4MT' 2-6-0 No 76040 receiving attention at the Croes Newydd (Wrexham) shed coaling stage on 13 March 1967. Steam haulage ended here in November of that year.

The swan song of the ex-LNER Class 'A4' was on the Aberdeen to Glasgow via Forfar route. Here No 60024 Kingfisher is seen on that service at Gleneagles in 1965.

and South Blyth, Sunderland and Tyne Dock sheds had all already closed in September. The last two sheds to close in the North Eastern region were in the Yorkshire coal-mining areas at Royston, in November 1967, and Normanton, at the end of that year.

Steam also held on in some parts of Scotland, with Nigel Gresley's revered 'A4' Pacifics performing their swansong at the head of the Glasgow (Buchanan Street) to Aberdeen '3-hour expresses' until September 1966. At the northern end of the West Coast Main Line, The Scottish Region closed all steam sheds on 1 May 1967, except for Motherwell, which retained steam until the end of June the same year. However, Carlisle Kingmoor-based steam locos continued to work into Scotland until the end of 1967, when that shed too was finally closed to steam traction.

By New Year's Day, 1968, the end was in sight and there were just six depots remaining in Britain where steam traction was still being maintained, all of them on the London Midland Region in northwest England; Carlisle Kingmoor, Workington and Tebay had already closed to steam, and these were followed by Stockport (Edgeley) from 6 May, with Newton Heath, Patricroft and Bolton closing to steam from 1 July. This left just three, at Rose Grove, Lostock Hall and Carnforth, which were still operational for steam, but only for four more weeks, until the official last day of steam on Sunday 4 August.

Those last few months of steam operations drew enthusiasts in droves from all over Britain to witness the end of a glorious era. The end finally came on 11 August with the '15 Guinea Special', BR's last mainline passenger train to be hauled by steam. This was hauled on a return trip by a series of locomotives: Stanier 'Black Five' 4-6-0 No 45110 (Liverpool Lime St–Manchester Victoria), BR Britannia Pacific No 70013 *Oliver Cromwell* (Manchester Victoria–Carlisle via the Settle–Carlisle Line), Stanier 'Black Five' 4-6-0s Nos 44781 and 44871 (Carlisle–Manchester Victoria, also via Settle–Carlisle Line) and finally No 45110 (Manchester Victoria–Liverpool Lime St). Thousands of spectators lined the route, in addition to those who had paid today's equivalent of £280 for a ticket, and all believed that this was the final occasion that they would witness mainline steam on Britain's national network. And British Rail management were happy in the knowledge that steam traction had finally been eradicated, once and for all, marked by an official steam ban from 12 August 1968. Almost 60 years on, how wrong they were!

Of course, it mustn't be forgotten that BR continued to operate steam locomotives on its narrow-gauge Vale of Rheidol Railway in Mid Wales until 1989, when the line was finally privatised.

During the 1960s the regional BR workshops were unable to cope with the sheer number of steam locomotives requiring disposal, and consequently

Stanier Class '5MT' 4-6-0 No 45346 hauling a bulk cement train passes a long line of condemned steam locomotives at Stockport Edgeley shed on 28 October 1967.

large numbers were dragged away from depots by diesel traction, or even steam locomotives in some cases, to private contractors' sites where in most cases they would be rapidly broken up and disposed of.

Although there were eight private companies contracted by British Rail and operating on a large scale at ten locations around the country, there were many more smaller concerns up and down the country also involved in this mammoth task, and one of these was located in South Wales, at Barry Docks.

Dai Woodham's Barry scrapyard had taken its first delivery of withdrawn Western Region steam locomotives as early as 1959. Initially, the number of locomotives purchased and being delivered to the site was a manageable amount and the company was able to keep pace with the arrivals. As time progressed, with BR continuing to withdraw its steam locomotives at an ever-increasing rate, by 1968 Dai Woodham had bought no fewer than 297 steam locomotives, not only from the Western Region but also from sheds further afield on the Southern and London Midland Regions, and his two separate adjoining groups of sidings at Barry very soon became filled to bursting. This backlog came about as a result of Woodham having also bought large numbers of redundant BR goods wagons and vans. Being an easier task, the disposal of these took precedence over the breaking-up of steam locomotives, their ferrous and non-ferrous metals requiring time-consuming separation. As a result, several hundred rusting hulks were put on an extended 'death row' to patiently await their ultimate fate, with time apparently standing still for them in the short-term.

However, by the late 1960s the steam preservation movement in Britain was gaining momentum and in the end 213 of Woodham's locomotives, by then many of them rusting hulks, were sold for eventual restoration. The oldest inhabitant at Barry arrived in 1961 and was finally saved in 1986, some 25 years later. The heritage railways and mainline steam charter organisations of today are much indebted to this Welsh scrap merchant.

BR Standard Class '3MT' 2-6-2Ts No 82034 and 82031 awaits their fate at Cashmore's scrap yard in Newport, August 1967.

The scene at Dai Woodham's scrapyard in Barry on 19 July 1968. Two Ivatt Class '2MT' 2-6-0s Nos 46428 and 46447 are on the right.

The scene at Manchester Victoria station on 28 July 1968, only two weeks before the end of standard gauge steam haulage on British Rail. The resplendent locomotive is BR Standard Class '7MT' 4-6-2 No 70013 Oliver Cromwell, now preserved.

Second-generation diesel-electric locomotives

British Rail had, up until the mid-1970s, been employing a mixed bag of first-generation diesel locomotives for its freight traffic, often employing them in tandem in order for them to provide sufficient tractive effort for block train diagrams, especially for the heavier commodities such as coal in merry-go-round wagons, aggregates and iron ore. It had already become clear to British Rail planners during the early 1970s that a new Type 5 locomotive would be required to handle such heavy freight traffic. Brush Traction had previously pre-empted this potential shortfall in the BR fleet by speculatively building the prototype Type 5 HS4000 *Kestrel*, it having been evaluated on coal trains in the Midlands during the late 1960s, but the locomotive didn't go anywhere apart from beyond the Iron Curtain!

The 3,250-hp Class '56' was the first BR Type 5 second-generation freight locomotive to be built and was introduced into service in early 1977, the first 30 built in Romania suffering from poor build quality. Reliability issues with the class prompted BR to design the 3,300-hp Class '58', of modular build and following the American design practice rather than a traditionally British design, and the 50 locomotives were built at Doncaster Works from 1983.

One freight customer became so disillusioned with the reliability of the BR locomotives used for its aggregates business that it looked overseas to the General Motors Electro-Motive Division, who subsequently built five Class '59' 3,300-hp Co-Co locomotives from 1985. They proved to be the forerunner of the ubiquitous Class '66' now used in Britain following privatisation.

The final Type 5 built for BR was the Class '60', addressing BR's further need for a more capable Type 5 locomotive. After competitive tender, an order for 100 was placed with Brush Traction, the first member of this class entering revenue service in late 1990.

Electroputere LDE/BREL-built Co-Co Type 5 (Class '56') Nos 56001–56135 (▼) BR's initial answer in 1970 to the freight Type 5 was the 3,250-hp Class '56' diesel-electric, and it placed the first order for 60 Type 5 Co-Co freight locomotives. The first 30 were built by Electroputere LDE in Romania and delivered from April 1977, while 30 were being concurrently built at BREL Doncaster Works. The Romanian batch, being of inferior quality, were rectified at Doncaster. Subsequent Class '56' construction was undertaken at Doncaster, with the final 20 locomotives, delivered in 1984,

Class '56' diesel-electric locomotive No 56003 hauls a long 'merry-go-round' coal train though Doncaster station in 1986.

Class '58' diesel-electric locomotive No 58004 under construction at Doncaster Works on 5 June 1983,

Brand new Class '58' diesel-electric locomotive No 58036 at Toton TMD on 15 February 1986.

built at BREL Crewe Works. It proved to be a strong and capable locomotive, although the 135 members of the class were found to be expensive to maintain compared to other Type 5s.

BREL-built Co-Co Type 5 (Class '58') Nos 58001–58050 (▲)

Due to initial reliability issues with the Class '56's and the growing railfreight market, BR wanted an additional low-cost heavy freight locomotive type. The 3,300-hp Class '58' was of a modular design, easy to maintain and offered an export potential. Between 1983 and 1987 Doncaster Works built 50 Class '58' locomotives, and within the first two years of operation they had reportedly proved to be considerably more reliable than the Class '56's. The immediate post-privatisation period saw all Class '58's withdrawn after just 19 years of service, although 32 subsequently saw service overseas, in the Netherlands, France and Spain.

General Motors Electro-Motive Co-Co Type 5 (Class '59') Nos 59001–59005, 59101–59104, 59201–59206 (▲)

The General Motors 3,300-hp Class '59' Co-Co locomotives were built for three private operators, totalling fifteen locomotives built over a ten-year period. They were the first privately owned diesel locomotives to operate regularly on freight duties on the British main line and were also the first diesel locomotives built in the United States for the British main line. Following the initial batch built for the Mendip aggregates company Foster Yeoman in 1986, competitor ARC Southern took delivery of four Class '59/1' locomotives in 1990, and National Power six Class '59/2's in 1994–95. All are still in use today, fourteen with Freightliner and one with GB Railfreight.

Brush Co-Co Type 5 (Class '60') Nos 60001–60100 (▶)

The first two 3,100-hp Class '60' locomotives entered BR traffic in October 1990 and were immediately put to work on heavy stone traffic, replacing ailing class '56's and '58's previously entrusted to such duties, some of which were then taken out of service. Their introduction replaced the double-heading of locomotives, in particular the Class '33' diagrams in the southeast. The Class '60's also relieved the relatively new Class '58's from their 'bread-and-butter' coal diagrams. The final Class '60's were successfully delivered from Brush's Falcon Works in Loughborough during March 1993. At privatisation, all members of the class passed into EWS ownership.

Brand new Class '60' diesel-electric locomotives outside their birthplace at Brush Traction, Loughborough, September 1990.

BRITISH RAILWAYS

ARC Southern's Class '59/1' diesel-electric No 59102 Village of Chantry with an empty aggregates train at Little Bedwyn, Wiltshire, on 17 June 1991. The locomotive arrived from Canada at Newport Docks in October 1990 and entered service from Whatley Quarry a month later. The Kennet & Avon Canal can be seen on the right.

High-speed trains

By the early 1970s the age of high-speed rail travel was becoming a reality. The new Japanese Shinkansen high-speed trains ("bullet trains") were inspiring railway engineers around the world, and the French railway authority SNCF was developing its TGV (*train á grande vitesse*) prototypes. At home, the Advanced Passenger Train (APT), designed to run on the existing infrastructure of the West Coast Main Line (WCML) using a tilting mechanism, was Britain's response to the quest for speed. Following the testing of a gas-turbine prototype, six pre-production sets with electric traction were built. Beset with a multitude of problems and bad press, British Rail's controversial APT project was eventually abandoned.

British Rail was still faced with the challenge of replacing many of its early express diesel locomotives, and with widespread electrification not expected to happen for some time, due to financial constraints, a

British Rail's prototype Class '252' HST No 252001 and the experimental gas turbine prototype InterCity 'APT-E' at Swindon, whilst on test in August 1975.

Poster produced for British Rail to advertise their InterCity APT service between Glasgow, Preston and London Euston.

new generation of high-speed diesel trains was needed. And so the HST was developed by Derby's Railway Technical Centre. The prototype HST emerged in summer 1972, undertaking proving trials on the Eastern and Western Regions. So successful was the design that production orders for the Western, Eastern, London Midland and Scottish Regions were placed, with Crewe building the 197 power cars and Derby Litchurch Lane the Mark 3 intermediate passenger cars. The HSTs were reliable and became extremely popular with passengers, remaining in frontline service for decades. It proved to be the saving grace for British Rail as its answer to the high-speed train, after the troublesome and embarrassing experiences with its Advanced Passenger Train.

Despite the expensive APT project failure, design elements for the later InterCity 225, using Mark 4 coaches and Class '91' electric locomotives, became direct descendants of the APT. Upon completion of the East Coast Main Line (ECML) electrification at 25kV AC, the InterCity 225 was officially introduced into revenue-earning service in 1989. Although designed to reach speeds of 225 km/h, these have always been limited to 125 mph (201 km/h), principally due to track signalling and overhead line equipment limitations. Ongoing problems with the new Azuma units on the ECML resulted in the InterCity 225 continuing to stand in on some services between London King's Cross, Leeds and York in 2025.

Prototype InterCity 125 HST No 252001 speeds though Reading while on test in September 1975.

Advanced Passenger Train (APT-E) Nos PC1–PC2 Built by the British Rail Research Division at Derby and powered by gas turbines, the Advance Passenger Train Tilting Experimental (APT-E) unit was the progenitor of the APT (Class '370') electric 25kV AC-powered sets subsequently unveiled in June 1978. Comprising two driving power cars and two intermediate trailer cars, it made its first run on 25 July 1972 but was immediately 'blacked' by the ASLEF trade union. After some delay, the APT-E's first mainline trial was on 10 August 1975 on the Great Western Main Line, when it achieved a new British railway speed record of 152.3 mph. The train was intended exclusively for test purposes and was never used in public service. Upon completion of the trials, it was placed into the care of the National Railway Museum.

BR Class '370' Advanced Passenger Train (APT-P) Nos 37001–37007 (▼) British Rail's Advanced Passenger Train Prototype (APT-P/Class '370') tilting trains were the pre-production 25kV AC electric units. They were used on the WCML between London Euston and Glasgow Central between 1978 and 1986. The most powerful train ever to have operated in Britain, the eight traction motors fitted to the two central motor cars gave a total output of 8,000 hp. The train set a new UK rail speed record of 162.2 mph in December 1979. With ongoing technical problems, the planned APT-S 'squadron service' production units were never built and the project was quietly dropped under a cloud. All six units were withdrawn during 1985–86 and most cars were quickly scrapped out of the public gaze. A seven-car formation with non-driving motor No 370006 is preserved at Crewe Heritage Centre.

BR Class '43' InterCity 125 HST power cars Nos 43002–43198 (▶) The 2,250-hp InterCity 125 High Speed Train (HST) is widely considered to be among the most successful trains to have operated on the British railway network. Built by BREL at Crewe Works, the introduction of Inter-City 125 High Speed Train (HST) sets on the Western Region main line from London Paddington to Bristol, Cardiff and Swansea in 1976 was a great success. With a maximum speed of 125 mph (compared to earlier diesels' 100-mph limit) and vastly improved passenger comfort, they helped to boost passenger numbers on Britain's flagging railways. Within a few years the HSTs were also operating on the East Coast Main Line between London King's Cross,

Intercity Class '370' APT No 370005 on display at Wolverton Works on 9 September 2015.

Edinburgh, Aberdeen and Inverness, on the Midland main line out of London St Pancras and as far west as Swansea and Carmarthen in Wales and Penzance in Cornwall. In 2025 some reduced-formation sets were still in operation with Great Western Railway in southwest England and with Scotrail in Scotland.

BR Class '91' InterCity 225 Nos 91001–91031 (▼) British Rail's 6,300-hp Class '91' Bo-Bo express passenger electric locomotives were ordered as a component of the East Coast Main Line electrification scheme of the late 1980s, to replace most of the Class '43' InterCity 125 HSTs used on that route. A total of 31 were built by BREL at Crewe Works between 1988 and 1991, and were designated InterCity 225s, being paired with the Mark 4 coaches and a driving trailer. The Class '91' was chosen ahead of the Brush prototype six-axle 1987-built Class 89001 *Avocet* built at BREL Crewe Works, primarily because its four axles would inflict less damage on the tracks.

Five Class '43' InterCity 125 HSTs lined up at Paddington station in 1981.

Class '91' 25kV AC electric loco No 91027 at rest in Leeds station with a train for Kings Cross, 22 May 1991.

Electrification

Prior to the Second World War, the only major electrification scheme on Britain's railways was Southern Railway's third-rail network expansion between London and the south coast. Electrification resumed in the south after the war, with all lines uprated to 750V DC, including the Kent Coast routes by 1961 and the South West Main Line to Southampton and Bournemouth in 1967, and on to Weymouth in 1988. Other Southern Region lines electrified during the 1980s were to Hastings, the East Grinstead branch, and between Eastleigh and Fareham. In the north of England, the Woodhead route 1,500V DC electrification between Manchester and Sheffield was completed in 1955, but soon became obsolete as future mainline electrification in Britain was decreed as being 25kV AC.

Further electrification progress, as outlined in the 1955 Modernisation Plan, was extremely slow, with an interregnum period of dieselisation preceding many schemes, such as the London Liverpool Street and Fenchurch Street suburban lines projects of the early 1960s, and the West Coast Main Line scheme, which did not reach Glasgow until 1974. It wasn't until 1987 before the entire route to Norwich was 'switched on', with the line from Liverpool Street to Cambridge and King's Lynn being electrified in stages and not completed until 1992.

Once the stamping ground of Gresley's fine 'A4' Pacifics and their successors, the powerful 'Deltic' Class '55' diesels, the East Coast Main Line was electrified in two distinct stages – the southern end from London King's Cross to Royston was completed in 1978 but it took until 1991 before the entire route to Leeds and Edinburgh was completed following a six-year construction programme. Meanwhile, Network SouthEast had benefitted greatly from its third-rail electrification extending from Bournemouth to Weymouth, with new Class '442' 'Wessex Electric' units based on the BR Mark 3 body shell replacing the 1960s-era BR Mark 1 slam-door coaches.

Class '91' 25kV AC electric locomotive No 91005 speeds through High Dyke on the East Coast Main Line on 4 December 1992.

Class '442' third-rail 'Wessex Electric' electric multiple unit No 442422 pauses at Wareham station with a Weymouth-Waterloo train on 16 August 1991.

Class '319' dual voltage 750V DC/25kV AC Network South East electric multiple unit No 319004 at St Pancras station on a Bedford service in July 1988.

Back in London, the southern part of the Midland Main Line between St Pancras and Bedford was electrified for local services in 1983, followed soon thereafter by the introduction of dual-voltage trains on the cross-London Thameslink route in 1988, allowing passenger trains to run on the 140-mile route between Bedford and Brighton via Farringdon.

Elsewhere, two commuter lines operating out of Birmingham New Street had been electrified by 1993, while the Leeds to Skipton Airedale Line went live in 1994, and to Ilkley in 1995. The London Paddington to Heathrow electrification scheme had been completed in 1998 but it wasn't until 2020 that the Great Western Main Line electrification scheme between Paddington and Cardiff was completed, with the onward route to Swansea and the Oxford and Bristol lines being deferred indefinitely, versatile Hitachi Class '800' bi-mode InterCity Express Trains (IETs) offering a useful cost-effective solution in the meantime.

Despite the obvious long-term benefits, the electrification of Britain's railways has been carried out in a somewhat piecemeal fashion since the 1950s. This has been due to the waxing and waning of political support, as well as the drifting away of valuable experience and skillsets after completion of major schemes, thereby driving up costs, as witnessed by the contentious high-speed (HS2) project running into an obscene amount of overspend, with the original proposals being significantly curbed to just the London to Birmingham route.

Scotland has taken a more proactive approach with its 'rolling programme' by extending electrification across the Central Belt as well as on to Stirling. Alloa and Dunblane. This will be followed by an extension to Perth. In England, the long-overdue North Trans-Pennine electrification scheme between Leeds and Manchester and on to York is finally progressing after years of procrastination, and the long-awaited completion of the Crossrail scheme in London, now named the Elizabeth Line, was finally opened in May 2022, more than £4 billion over budget.

Despite this recent progress, there are still many important routes that have yet to be electrified. Notable among these are the Midland Main Line between Kettering, Nottingham, Derby and Sheffield, the North Wales Coast route between Crewe and Holyhead, Edinburgh to Aberdeen, and all routes to the southwest of England.

Class '308' 25kV AC electric multiple unit No 308152 on the Wharfedale Line near Guisley in the winter of 1994.

Passenger and freight sectorisation

The regions of British Rail were replaced by business sectors in 1982, a move that was considered to be a prelude to privatisation and heralding the end of BR's 'Rail Blue era'. On the passenger side, three new sectors were created. The express passenger services were already under the control of InterCity. Network SouthEast operated commuter services in London as well as further afield on selected routes through its various subdivisions. The government-subsidised Provincial (named Regional Railways from 1989) took control of all remaining regional passenger services, while Passenger Transport Executives managed the local services in the metropolitan counties.

The Network SouthEast sector, with its new distinctive livery of red, white and blue, covered an extensive area stretching from the Midlands to eastern England, the Thames Valley to the south coast and as far west as Exeter via Salisbury. A major replacement programme for its ageing rolling stock coupled with further third-rail electrification and the introduction of the popular Network Railcard under the business-savvy BR Sector Director Chris Green, previously the Scotrail manager, all contributed to its later success.

The Regional Railways sector was considered to be the 'poor relation' within British Rail and was forced to soldier on with outmoded locomotives and rolling stock as well as run-down first-generation diesel multiple units on its vast sprawling network that stretched from the Midlands to East Anglia and Wales, and to northern England and Scotland. The rolling stock question was gradually addressed by the introduction of new bus-type four-wheel 'Pacer' units between 1984

Very smart Class '73' electro-diesel No 73142 Broadlands at Victoria station with a Gatwick Express service on 14 June 1985.

In Network SouthEast livery, Ryde Rail Class '486' No 486031 at Ryde St Johns station on the Isle of Wight's electric third-rail line between Ryde Pierhead and Shanklin, September 1989.

Regional Railways' Class '150' diesel multiple unit No 150102 at Lincoln station on 21 June 1986.

Regional Railways' Class '31' diesel-electric locomotives Nos 31410 and 31421 at Liverpool Lime Street station on 19 March 1993.

and 1987 and the more comfortable 'Sprinter' diesel multiple units between 1987 and 1989 – these 'Sprinter' units are still in widespread use on the network today. Simply by its geographical nature, Regional Railways was never going to be a profitable concern, relying on government subsidies of over four times its annual revenue to keep its trains running, especially on the rural lines. The cost of rail travel across the network doubled in real terms during the period between 1979 and 1994. On a positive note, no rail closures occurred following the creation of Regional Railways despite some obvious loss-making candidates on routes such as in the far north of Scotland and in Mid Wales.

The Railfreight sector was also created in 1982, and a new corporate identity came about with locomotives and rolling stock being finished in 'Railfreight Grey'. A new two-tone grey colour scheme, some with a red lower-body stripe, was applied to locomotives, which were also embellished with individual colourful sector symbols and imaginative diamond-shaped depot plaques. Locomotives and wagons were dedicated to specific business customer commodities and, in 1987, were grouped into five freight subsectors: Railfreight (responsible for all freight operations and later subdivided into train operations), Trainload Freight, Railfreight Distribution (non-trainload freight), Speedlink (a wagonload air-braked wagon service), Freightliner (intermodal traffic), and Rail Express Systems (Travelling Post Offices, mail and parcels traffic).

The period from 1994 leading up to privatisation witnessed continued freight reorganisation and the emergence of private enterprise, with shadow freight franchises being created. Transrail Freight had the largest sphere of operations that encompassed the north and west of England, Wales and Scotland, also developing a wagonload service branded 'Enterprise'. Mainline Freight was confined to the southeast, East Anglia and East Midlands. Loadhaul operated in the northeast, Yorkshire and Humberside, and Railfreight Distribution managed the Freightliner and Channel Tunnel traffic.

English Welsh & Scottish Railway eventually acquired and merged five of the six freight companies sold during the process of privatisation of British Rail, with Freightliner sold on as a management buyout.

Class '33' diesel-electric locomotives Nos 33026 Seafire and 33030 in the 'Dutch' Civil Engineer's livery approach Crediton station with a ballast train from Meldon Quarry to Tonbridge on 29 January 1993.

Railfreight Class '58' diesel-electric locomotive No 58005 passes through Clay Cross with a 'merry-go-round' coal train in 1987.

BRITISH RAILWAYS | 207

Railway preservation

When published, the Beeching Report was essentially an analysis of the economic status of the British Railways system, and Dr Richard Beeching's recommendations were implemented from a need to take heed of the transport requirements of society, whilst creating a more viable and cost-efficient railway network. From the ashes of the consequent wholesale route closures rose the phoenix of the extensive railway preservation movement that exists today, although as early as 1951 writer Tom Rolt and a group of enthusiasts had led the way by saving from closure the narrow-gauge former slate-carrying Talyllyn Railway in Wales. With railway closures gathering pace around Britain, in 1960 the Bluebell Railway in Sussex was to become the first heritage standard-gauge steam-operated passenger-carrying railway in the world offering a public service. Beeching had unwittingly initiated an upsurge in the heritage steam railway movement, with many railway preservation societies emerging during the 1960s and 1970s. The pioneering Talyllyn and Bluebell Railways, and indeed many others subsequently established, prevail today, notwithstanding many challenges that they have faced along the way, and continue to face, both commercially and politically.

From those early beginnings, the preservation movement has gone from strength to strength, with today more than 130 heritage railways covering 560 miles of track and operating 460 stations, in addition to numerous railway centres and museums located around Britain. All of these lines, most of them victims of Dr Beeching's 'Axe' back in the 1960s, have been brought back to life by dedicated enthusiasts – all are tourist attractions in their own right and major contributors to their local economies. While many

Talyllyn Railway 0-4-2ST No 1 Talyllyn *approaches Brynglas halt on 1 September 1991. Built by Fletcher, Jennings in 1864, it is still in service.*

of Britain's preserved railways remain isolated from the national rail network, some benefit from having physical connections, allowing the through-working of charter trains and visiting locomotives from other parts of Britain. Also, a vast network of closed railway lines across Britain's landscape have seen a new lease of life as footpaths and cycleways, many of these routes running through some of the most beautiful scenery and adding enormous value to the country's leisure sector.

The railway preservation movement has benefitted greatly from the Welsh scrap merchant Dai Woodham (see page 186), who failed to cut up so many steam locomotives that he had purchased from BR for scrap in the 1960s. After languishing at Barry for many years, over 200 of these locomotives were bought by preservationists for use on the increasing number of heritage railways being established. After years of painstaking restoration work, many of these locomotives are now at work, not only on our heritage railways but also on mainline charter operations around the country. A remarkable achievement by the A1 Steam Locomotive Trust was the building of the brand-new 'A1' Class 4-6-2 No 60163 *Tornado*, which emerged from Darlington Locomotive Works in 2008. A culmination of eighteen years of exacting work at a cost of £3 million, this superb machine has not only put in many fine performances on the main line, but also draws enormous crowds wherever it travels. At the other end of the scale, GWR Steam Railmotor No 93, originally condemned in 1934, has with Heritage Lottery funding been restored to full working order using many new fabricated parts. Granted mainline certification, it saw service on Network Rail's Liskeard–Looe branch line in Cornwall in November 2012.

New-build Class 'P2' 2-8-2 No 2007 Prince of Wales *under construction at Darlington Works on 11 June 2019.*

New-build Peppercorn Class 'A1' 4-6-2 No 60163 Tornado at its birthplace of Darlington on 11 May 2019.

Following the success of *Tornado*, three 'new-build' steam locomotives have since been completed and are now working on our heritage railways, namely GWR 'Saint' 4-6-0 No 2999 *Lady of Legend*, GWR 'Grange' 4-6-0 No 6880 *Betton Grange* and Marsh 'H2' Atlantic 4-4-2 No 32424 *Beachy Head*. Also, currently under construction are GWR 'County' 4-6-0 No 1014 *County of Glamorgan*, LMS 'Patriot' 4-6-0 No 45551 *The Unknown Warrior*, BR Standard '2MT' 2-6-2T No 84030 and the mighty LNER 'P2' 2-8-2 No 2007 *Prince of Wales*, with many more in the planning stages. Diesel traction is also not being overlooked, with the new-build BR Class '23' 'Baby Deltic' D5910 progressing well at the Barrow Hill Roundhouse, and Britain's first mainline diesel locomotive, LMS No 10000, being recreated by the Ivatt Diesel Recreation Society.

New-build GWR railmotor No 93 puffs along the banks of the East Looe River at Terras Bridge with a train from Looe to Liskeard, 11 November 2012.

New-build GWR 'Saint' class 4-6-0 No 2999 Lady of Legend at Baron Street depot on the East Lancashire Railway, 11 March 2023.

New-build Class 'H2' 4-4-2 No 32424 Beachy Head approaching Horsted Keynes on the Bluebell Railway, 18 November 2024.

The death of British Rail

As Margaret Thatcher's Conservative Government approached the end of its fourth year, Britain's railways were in a sorry state. Declining passenger numbers and recurrent labour disputes were contributing to annual losses approaching £1 billion. A government-commissioned report into the state of British Rail and its future viability was published in January 1983. Regarded by some as the 'Second Beeching Report', Sir David Serpell's report proposed various options to reduce BR's deficit, a worst case scenario being the closure of over 80% of Britain's railways, with just three main routes radiating out from London remaining, namely the West Coast Main Line, the East Coast Main Line as far as Newcastle, and the former GWR route to Bristol and Cardiff. Other less stringent options would have still seen wholesale rail closures, and even the Government was unconvinced. Happily, Serpell's proposals were quietly sidestepped and over the next decade British Rail's fortunes, thanks to investment in the infrastructure and new rolling stock, gradually improved.

By the early 1990s British Rail was on track for a brighter future but this final chapter in the history of Britain's nationalised railways was effectively drawing to a close. Although selling off nationalised assets into private ownership had been an important component of Thatcher's policies during the 1980s, the privatisation of railways had initially been considered a step too far. Despite the relatively minor sell-offs of the railway engineering workshops, British Transport Hotels and Sealink, along with the restructuring of railway operations into business

Great Western Class '43' InterCity 125 HST speeds alongside the Kennet & Avon Canal at Little Bedwyn, near Hungerford with an express for the West Country on 14 February 1998.

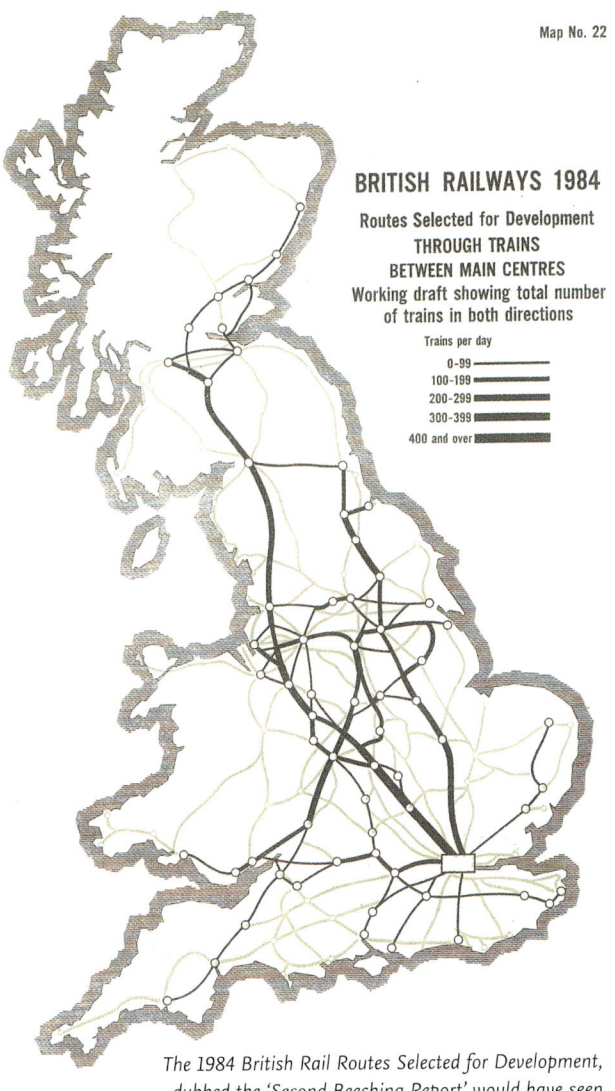

The 1984 British Rail Routes Selected for Development, dubbed the 'Second Beeching Report' would have seen the further decimation of Britain's railways.

locomotive fleet, its multiple units and coaches, were handed over to three rolling stock leasing companies (ROSCOs).

The 25 train-operating companies (TOCs) were awarded fixed-term leases to run services on specific routes – in effect they owned virtually nothing, hiring both locomotives and rolling stock from the ROSCOs, paying Railtrack for the use of the track and infrastructure, and contracting out train maintenance, cleaning and on-board catering.

While privatisation of Britain's railways officially came into being on 1 April 1994, the full effects took a number of years to filter through. There were also further changes to come: under a new Labour Government, the Strategic Rail Authority (SRA) was established under the Transport Act 2000, as a non-departmental public body designed to provide strategic direction to the privatised rail industry. Following the passing of the Railways Act 2005, the SRA was wound up in December 2006, its duties being divided between the Government's Department for Transport, Network Rail (the successor to Railtrack) and the Office of Rail Regulation (ORR). Some powers were also devolved to the then Scottish Executive, the Welsh Assembly and the Greater London Authority. The Scottish Government now has complete control of the internal Scottish rail network through its arm's-length company, ScotRail Trains Ltd.

The most controversial element of the original 1993 Act was the story of Railtrack, one of the saddest affairs of the rail privatisation saga. Following the Ladbroke Grove accident of 1999, in which 31 people were killed and 523 injured, the company was severely criticised for its railway infrastructure maintenance and safety record. With the relationship between Railtrack and the Rail Regulator falling apart, the next major accident, at Hatfield in 2000, was the final straw. Repairs and compensation for the accident, coupled with spiralling costs for rebuilding the West Coast Main Line, led the company to go cap in hand to the Government. Some of the taxpayer bailout was then used to pay a £137-million dividend to its shareholders! Unsurprisingly, Railtrack was declared bankrupt in 2001. While Railtrack was in administration, the Government was forced to pay out a further £3.5 billion in order to keep the railways running. The Railtrack story ends in October 2002,

sectors, it wasn't until the passing of the Railways Act in 1993 that the 45-year-old state industry was to be finally hived off.

Under this controversial Act, British Rail was separated into over a hundred separate companies. The Office of the Rail Regulator was set up to regulate all of the main elements of the industry, with the Director of Passenger Rail Franchising responsible for awarding franchises to 25 passenger train operators. Railtrack took over the track, signalling and stations and it, in turn, let out most of the stations to the newly franchised passenger train operators, also contracting out the maintenance and renewal of its infrastructure. Freight services were sold off to two freight-operating companies (FOCs) – English Welsh & Scottish Railway, and Freightliner – while the entire British Rail

Mainline's Class '60' diesel-electric No 60076 conveying 'HEA' hopper wagons with sinter for Scunthorpe Steelworks passing South Bank Coke Ovens, Middlesbrough, on 5 June 2000.

when its assets were bought by the newly formed not-for-profit government-created company, Network Rail. In 2022/23 Network Rail's workforce was around 40,000, with a revenue from the passenger and freight train operating companies of around £10 billion.

A great deal of debate has taken place about the overall impact of rail privatisation. Supporters argue for vastly improved customer service, while opponents respond that quality remains variable around the network. While many cheaper advance fares are available, standard fares are considered to be amongst the highest in Europe. And though passenger numbers have grown substantially, sceptics attribute this as much to a period of good economic growth along with ever-increasing road congestion.

The more straightforward privatisation of the rail freight business, with no franchise arrangements, has seen significant growth. Although coal traffic has been a recent loss, this has been balanced by an increase in imported biomass from ports and containerised fast-moving consumer goods.

Reaching an overall conclusion can therefore be difficult, but as Christian Wolmar notes in *Fire & Steam: How the Railways Transformed Britain* (2008):

> *The biggest irony, and indeed failure, of privatisation was that far from reducing the cost of the railway to taxpayers, it soared to unprecedented heights. Privatisation also brought with it a lack of transparency about the financial affairs of the railways, making comparisons difficult, but a reasonable estimate of the cost to taxpayers since the creation of Network Rail stands at around £5 bn annually.*

The cost of British Rail to the taxpayer during the last complete year of public ownership in 1994 was £1.6 billion, which was equivalent to £2 billion when Christian Wolmar made his point.

The scene of the rail crash near Hatfield in 2000. This serious incident was the final straw for Railtrack, which was declared bankrupt a year later.

English Welsh & Scottish Railway's Class '56' diesel-electric No 56081 passes Redcar Steelworks with empty potash hoppers for loading at Boulby Mine on 14 March 2001. This wondrous scene has disappeared forever as the steelworks closed in 2015.

Index

'15 Guinea Special' 185
'1500' Class 0-6-OPT 21
'1600' Class 0-6-OPT 21–2
'2251' Class 0-6-9 21
'5700' Class 0-6-OPT 21, 22

'A1' Class 4-6-2 20, 209, 210
A1 Steam Locomotive Trust 25, 209
A1A-A1A locomotives 63, 82, 103, 118
'A3' Class 4-6-2 24, 58
'A4' Class 60, 130
'A4' Pacifics 35, 185, 200
ABB Transportation 120
ABC of Southern Locomotives 158–9
AC Cars 94
accidents 154–6, 215
Advanced Passenger Train (APT) 180, 196, 197, 198
Allan, Ian 158–9
Amalgamated Society of Railway Servants of England, Ireland, Scotland & Wales (ASRS) 92
Andrew Barclay Sons & Co 69
ARC Southern 192
Arlington Fleet Services Ltd 36
Armstrong Whitworth 68
Asea Brown Boveri (ABB) 34, 38
Ashburton 16
Ashford Works 22, 32, 36, 47, 58, 63, 65, 73, 116
Associated Electrical Industries 90, 118
Associated Society of Locomotive Engineers and Firemen (ASLEF) 92, 93, 198
'Austerity' locomotives 42
Automatic Train Control (ATC) 156
Automatic Warning System (AWS) 155

Barclay, Andrew 71
Bass, Michael Thomas 92
'Battle of Britain' 4-6-2 20, 22, 155
Beeching, Dr Richard 16, 31, 77, 123, 125, 140, 145, 167, 169, 171–2, 176, 208
'Beeching Axe' 13, 47, 106, 171, 172, 176, 208
Beeching Report (*The Reshaping of British Railways*) 6–7, 77, 97, 123–5, 140, 145, 168–76
Belgian Maritime Transport Authority 135
Beyer, Peacock & Co 81, 118
    Type 3 B-B 'Hymek' BR Class '35' 76, 106
'Big Four' 9, 12, 16, 20, 29, 32, 38, 42, 58, 61, 68, 75, 102, 122, 126, 134, 137, 148, 158
    see also Great Western Railway; London & North Eastern Railway; London, Midland & Scottish Railway; Southern Railway
biomass 170, 216
Birmingham RC&W Company 94, 118, 132
    Bo-Bo Type 2 BR Class '26' 82
    Bo-Bo Type 2 BR Class '27' 82
    Bo-Bo Type 3 BR Class '33' 84

Lion D0260 (prototype) 88, 89–90
Blue Pullmans 100–1, 133
'Blue Train' electric multiple units (later Class '303') 77, 113
Bluebell Railway 208
Bond, Roland 58
'Bournemouth Belle' 133
BR Class '01'–'13' shunters 68, 69–71, 73, 76
BR Class '43' InterCity 125 HST power cars 101, 104, 167, 179, 180, 182, 198–9
BR Class '70'–'91' electric locomotives Co-Co 116–120, 182, 197
BR Class '91' InterCity 225 182, 197, 199
BR Class '92' Co-Co 120
BR Class '99' 134
BR Class '370' Advanced Passenger Train (APT-P) 198
BR Standard Class 23–4, 32, 34–6, 42–7, 58, 184
    '2MT' 2-6-2T 24, 47, 210
    '3MT' 2-6-0 45–6
    '4MT' 2-6-0 23, 45
    '4MT' 4-6-0 45
    '5' 4-6-0 61
    '5MT' 4-6-0 45
    '6MT' 'Clan' Pacific 4-6-2 34, 44
    '7MT' Britannia 4-6-2 34, 42–4, 60
    '8P' 4-6-2 No 71000 44
    '9F' 2-10-0 47
BR Swindon Works B-B Type 4 'Warship' Class BR Class '42' 103
BR Swindon Works C-C Type 4 'Western' BR Class '52' 104
BR Swindon Works Type 1 0-6-0 BR Class '14' 106
BR-built 1Co-Co1 Sulzer Type 4 'Peak' BR Class '44' 85
BR-built 1Co-Co1 Sulzer Type 4 'Peak' BR Class '45' 85
BR-built 1Co-Co1 Sulzer Type 4 'Peak' BR Class '46' 85
BR-built Sulzer Bo-Bo Type 2 BR Class '24' 81
BR-built Sulzer Bo-Bo Type 2 BR Class '25' 81–2
Branch Line Society, The 161
Branch Lines Committee 140
'Brighton Belle' 133
Brighton Railway Works 22, 23, 32, 36, 46, 63, 73
Bristol Bath Road depot 23, 89
'Bristol Pullman' 133
Bristol/Eastern Coach Works 94
Britannia Pacifics 185
'7MT' 44
British Leyland 97
British Pullman Car Company 100–1, 132
British Rail Engineering LTD (BREL) 34, 36–9, 97, 119–20, 180, 190–2, 198–9

BREL-built Co-Co Type 5 (Class '58') 190, 192
British Rail Research Division 198
British Railways Act, 1968 31
British Railways Board (BRB) 12, 19, 31, 169
British Railways (BR) 6–7
    birth 6, 7, 8–9
    corporate design 164–7
    death 7, 214–16
    image 178–9
    logo 135, 165, 167, 178–9, 182
    losses 6, 19, 74, 93, 214
    nadir 7
    publicity 164–7
    regions 12–13
    renamed British Rail 178–9
    see also Modernisation Plan, 1955
British Thomson-Houston Company Bo-Bo Type 1 Br Class '15' 81
British Transport Commission (BTC) 9, 12, 16, 29, 42, 74, 100, 102–3, 165
    abolition 31
    Branch Lines Committee 6, 16–19
    Hotels Executive 31
    Railway Executive 29
British Transport Hotels Ltd (BTH) 31, 214
British Transport Ships 134
Brown, Boveri & Cie 63
Brush 85
    A1A-A1A Type 2 and 3 BR Classes '30' & '31' 82
    Class '50' 89
    Class '53' 89
    Co-Co Type 5 (Class '60') 190, 192
    D0280 *Falcon* (prototype) 86, 88, 89
    HS4000 *Kestrel* (prototype) 88, 90, 190
    prototype six-axle 1987-built Class 89001 Avocet 199
    Type 2 76, 82
    Type 4 (Class '47') 34, 55, 80, 86, 88, 89, 90, 128, 132, 179
    Type 5 88, 90, 190
Brush Traction 80, 86, 88, 90, 117, 120, 190
Brush/BR-built Co-Co Type 4 BR Class '47' 86
Bulleid, Oliver 20, 22, 32, 35, 42, 63, 65, 116
Bulleid diesel-electrics 63
Bulleid Pacifics 20, 156, 184
    'West Country' Class 4-6-2 35, 61

Caledonian Railway 38–9
'Calendonian Sleeper' 117, 119, 120, 137
Callander and Oban Railway 138
Cambrian Railways 20, 38
camping coaches 148–9
'Car-Sleeper' service 139
Carlisle 13, 44, 53
'Castle' Class 4-6-0 20, 58, 130
Central Wales Line 171, 172

220 | BRITISH RAILWAYS

Channel Tunnel 36, 120, 206
'Cheltenham Flyer' 130
Clapham Junction crash 156
Clayton
    Bo-Bo Type 1 Br Class '17' 81
    Class '17' 82
    Type 1 80
Clayton Equipment Company 80, 81
Co-Co locomotives 63, 65, 84–7, 116, 120, 190–2
coal 9, 25, 62–3, 93, 125, 170, 190, 216
    Yorkshire 58, 60
Collett, Charles 21
Collett 21
    'Castle' Class 4-6-0 20
    'Hall' Class 4-6-0 61
'Condor' freight services 83, 123, 125
Conservative Governments 31, 75–6, 93, 171, 214
'Continental Car Sleeper' service 139
Conwy Valley Line 173
'Cornish Riviera Limited' 130
'Coronation' Class 60, 154
'Coronation' Pacifics 63
Corporate Identity Manual 167
corridor coaches 130
Corridor Firsts/Seconds 128
Cowden crash 156
Cowlairs Works 38, 94, 161
Cox, Ernest 58
'Crab' Class 2-6-0 36
Cravens Railway Carriage & Wagon Co 94, 126
Crewe Works 23–4, 32–4, 42, 44, 47, 68, 81, 85–6, 104, 116, 120, 145, 161, 180, 192, 198–9
Crewe-Chester line 34
Cross-Country 182
Crossrail (Elizabeth Line) 202
Cumbrian Coast Line 176
Cuneo, Terence 165–7

D. Wickham & Co 94
Darlington Works 23–5, 36, 46–7, 68, 71, 73, 81, 209
Dean, William 22
Department for Transport 215
Derby Litchurch Lane Works 34, 180, 197
Derby Works 23, 32, 34, 45, 46, 63, 68, 81, 85, 94, 126, 128, 137, 161, 180
Design Research Unit 167, 178
Deutsche Bundesbahn 102
'Devon Belle' 133
Dick Kerr Works 88
diesel engine sheds 108–9, 159–61, 184
diesel engines 200, 210
    early 62–5, 74–5, 76, 100, 132
    high-speed 196–7
    prototypes 88–90
    see also specific trains
diesel multiple units (DMUs) 82, 94–7
    'Derby Lightweight' 94
    'Sprinter' 97, 206
diesel shunters 68–73
diesel-electric locomotives 32, 34–5, 39, 42, 62–3, 68, 71, 73, 76
    first-generation 80–7

second-generation 190–2
    Type 1 80–1
    Type 2 81–4
    Type 3 84–5
    Type 4 85–7, 88, 90
    Type 5 87, 88, 90
diesel-hydraulic locomotives 102–6
District Marine Superintendents 134
Doncaster Works 23–5, 32, 34–6, 45–6, 65, 68–9, 116–17, 119, 126, 161, 190, 192
Double Arrow logo 135, 165, 167, 178, 179
Drewry Car Company 69
Drummond, Dugald 38, 39

E26000 (prototype) 116, 117
East Coast Main Line (ECML) 13, 24, 58, 76, 87–8, 90, 120, 176, 179, 182, 184, 197–200, 214
East Suffolk Line 16, 171
East West Rail Project 176
Eastern Counties Railway 36
Eastern Region 12–13, 24–5, 37, 69, 73, 76, 81–3, 86, 89, 90, 133, 136, 139, 176, 184, 197
Eastleigh Works 22, 32, 35–6, 71, 73, 97, 116, 126, 128, 161
Edinburgh to Carlisle Waverly Line 176
Edinburgh & Glasgow Railway 38
electric locomotives 110–20
    early 62–5, 74–5, 76–7, 100
electric multiple units (EMUs) 116–20, 155–6
Electric Train Heating (ETH) 82
electrification 110–13, 118, 196–7, 199–202, 204
Electroputere 190 LDE/BREL-built Co-Co Type 5 (Class '56') 190–2
Elizabeth II 165
EM1 locos 65, 116
EM2 locos 116
English Electric 63, 73, 80, 82, 88, 116, 118
    0-6-0 diesel shunters 68
    1Co-Co1 Type 4 BR Class '40' 86
    Bo-Bo Type 1 Br Class '20' 80
    Bo-Bo Type 2 BR Class '23' 'Baby Deltic' 80, 83, 210
    BR Class '50' 88
    Co-Co 4 BR Class '50' 86–7
    Co-Co Type 3 BR Class '37' 84–5
    Co-Co Type 5 'Deltic' BR Class '55' 87
    DP1 *Deltic* 87, 88
    DP2 (prototype) 90
    GT3 88, 89
    Type 1 (Class '20') 80
    Type 3 (Class '37') 80
    Type 4 76, 132
    Type 5 Class '55' 'Deltic' 76, 83, 88, 132, 200
English Welsh & Scottish Railway (EWS) 119–20, 151, 192, 206, 215
'Enterprise' service 206
Esk Valley Line 176

Fairburn, Charles 23, 42
Fairburn Class '4MT' 2-6-4T 23
Falcon Works 82, 86, 89, 192
ferries 134–5, 138
First Great Western 139

First World War 8, 9, 29
'FK' coach 180
'Flying Scotsman' 35, 132
Foster Yeoman 192
Fowler, Henry 23
Fowler, John 68
freight services 7, 9, 19, 75, 83, 122–5, 171, 179, 190, 204–6, 215
freight-operating companies (FOCs) 215
Freightliner 119, 120, 125, 170, 192, 206, 215
French National Railways (SNCF) 135, 196

gas turbine locomotives 62–5, 88–90, 196
Gatwick Express 116, 182
GB Railfreight 120, 192
    Class '73' 116–17
GEC 73, 119
    Stockton Works 63
Geddes, Sir Eric 9
General Motors Electro-Motive Division 190
General Motors Electro-Motive Type 5 (Class '59') 190, 192
General Railway Workers' Union of Railwaymen 93
general utility vehicles (GUVs) 139
George, Henry 23
Glasgow & South Western Railway 39
Glasgow to Aberdeen '3-hour expresses' 185
Gloucester Railway Carriage & Wagon Co 94, 126
'Golden Arrow' 133
Gorton Locomotive Works 36, 65, 111, 116–17
Grand Junction Railway 32
'Grange' Class 20
Gray, Milner 167
Great Central Railway 13, 36, 122, 175
Great Eastern Main Line 13, 77, 81, 119, 120
Great Eastern Railway 13, 36, 182
Great North of Scotland Railway 39
Great Northern Railway 13, 34, 148
Great Western Main Line (GWML) 198, 202
Great Western Railway (GWR) 6, 8–9, 13, 20–2, 25, 36, 38, 45, 47, 58, 60, 62–3, 68, 88, 92, 130, 136, 138–9, 145, 148, 173, 182, 184, 199, 214
    GWR 'Grange' 4-6-0 No 6880 *Betton Grange* 210
    GWR 'Saint' 4-6-0 No 2999 *Lady of Legend* 210
    GWR Steam Railmotor No 93 209
Great Western Royal Hotel 29, 31
Greater London Authority 215
Green, Chris 204
Gresley, Nigel 20, 24, 25, 65, 130, 185, 200
Gresley Pacifics 34–5, 200

'Hall' Class 21
'Harrogate Sunday Pullman' 133
Harrow & Wealdstone disaster 154–5, 156
Hatfield disaster 215
Hawker Siddeley 90
Hawksworth, Frederick 21
Hawksworth 21, 22
    'County' Class 4-6-0 20
Hawthorn Leslie 0-6-0 diesel-electric shunter 68
Heritage Lottery 209
high-speed (HS2) project 202

high-speed trains 7, 101, 167, 179–80, 182, 196–9
Highland Railway 39
Hilton London Paddington 31
Hitachi Class '800' bi-mode Intercity Express Trains (IETs) 202
Hither Green crash 156
Holmes, Matthew 38
Horwich Works 23, 36, 38, 45, 68, 71, 73
hotels, railway 29–31
hovercraft services 135
Hudswell, Clarke & Co 0-4-0 diesel-mechanical shunter 68
'Hull Pullman' 133
'hump method' 122
Hunslet Engine Company 22, 69
Hunslet-Barclay 97

Ideal Stocks Committee 123
Inman, Lord 31
Inter-City 179–80, 182
InterCity 7, 139, 167, 179, 180–2, 204
    BR Class '91' Intercity 225 182, 197, 199
    Intercity 125 High Speed Train (HST) Class '43' 101, 104, 167, 179, 180, 182, 198–9
    'InterCity Sleepers' 137
International Union of Railways 63
Inverness & Nairn Railway 39
Inverurie Works 39
Isle of Wight 12, 47, 69–71, 111, 134–5, 175
Ivatt, H. G. 23–4, 42, 63
'Ivatt Atlantics' 34–5
Ivatt Class 23–4, 36, 45–7
    '2MT' 2-6-0 24
    '2MT' 2-6-2T 23
    '4MT' 2-6-0 23
    'Coronation' Class 4-6-2 23–4
Ivatt Diesel Recreation Society 63, 210

'Jubilee' Class 34, 154

Kilmarnock Works 39
'King' Class 4-6-0 60, 63, 106
King's Cross 'Top Shed' 184
Knapp, Jimmy 92

labour disputes 92–3
Labour Governments 6, 9, 171, 172, 215
Labour Party 92, 170
Ladbroke Grove accident 215
Laker, Freddie 145
Lancing Carriage Works 36
'Leader' Class 0-6-0+0-6-0T 22
Leeds Holbeck shed 184
'Light Pacifics' 22
line closures 6–7, 13, 16–19, 47, 77, 97, 106, 123–5, 140, 145, 168–76, 208
Liverpool & Manchester Railway 150
Loadhaul 206
Lochgorm Works 39
Loco Log Book 159
Locomotive Club of Great Britain 161
Locomotive Exchanges 42, 58–61
    mixed traffic 61

Locomotive Shed Directory 159
Locoshed Book 159
London & Birmingham Railway 29, 37, 50
London & North Eastern Railway (LNER) 9, 13, 24–5, 29, 34, 36–9, 58, 60–1, 65, 68, 111, 116–17, 122, 130, 148, 210
London & North Western Railway (LNWR) 8, 32–4, 37, 42
London & South Western Railway (LSWR) 35, 47, 58, 122
London, Brighton & South Coast Railway 32, 36, 132
London, Midland & Scottish Railway (LMS) 9, 13, 23, 25, 29, 34–6, 39, 42, 45–7, 58, 61–3, 68, 76, 80–1, 85, 86, 148, 210
London Midland Region (LMR) 12–13, 16, 23–4, 35, 37, 47, 63, 76, 81–2, 89, 100–1, 133, 136, 160–1, 175–6, 176, 185–6, 197
London, Tilbury and Southend line 13
London Transport 12, 111
London Transport Executive 12

Machynlleth shed 184
Mainline Freight 206
'Manchester Pullman' 101, 132–3
Manchester, Sheffield & Lincolnshire Railway 36
'Manor' Class 4-6-0 20
Mark 1 trailer units (4TC) 77, 111, 126–8, 136–7, 150, 200
Mark 2 trailer units 128, 179, 180, 182
Mark 3 trailer units 128, 137, 180, 182, 197, 200
Mark 4 trailer units 182, 197, 199
Marples, Ernest 169, 170, 171
marshalling yards 122–5
'Master Cutler, The' 133
Maunsell, Richard 68, 73
McIntosh, John 39
'Merchant Navy' Class 4-6-2 20, 22, 60
'merry-go-round' (MGR) trains 125, 170
Methven, Sir Harry 31
Metro-Vick Type 2 80
Metropolitan-Cammell Carriage & Wagon Co 94, 97, 100, 128, 132
Metropolitan-Vickers Co-Bo Type 2 BR Class '28' 83
Metropolitan-Vickers Electrical Co. 63, 80, 118
Midland & Great Northern Joint Railway 19, 140
Midland & South Western Junction Railway 19
Midland Main Line 13, 63, 179, 182, 202
'Midland Pullman' 133
Midland Railway 34, 50, 122
    Locomotive Works 34
Midland Region 45, 84
milk 140
Ministry of Transport 155, 156
mixed traffic 4-6-0 20
'Modernisation Plan', 1955 6, 12, 19, 32, 36–7, 47, 74–7, 80–2, 84–5, 88, 93–4, 100, 102, 108–11, 113, 116, 123–5, 169, 184, 200
'Modified Hall' Class 4-6-0 21
motive power depots (MPDs) 50–5
Motorail 138–9, 182

named trains 130–3
National Coal Board 21, 73
National Power 192
National Rail Strike, 1955 6, 93
National Traction Plan 83
National Union of Rail, Maritime and Transport Workers (RMT) 92
National Union of Railwaymen (NUR) 92
Nationalisation 6, 9, 12, 16, 20, 22–5, 32, 34–9, 42, 53, 58, 62–3, 68, 88, 97, 116, 120, 123, 140, 145, 164
Network Rail 38, 215–16
Network Rail Liskeard–Looe branch line 209
Network Railcard 204
Network SouthEast 97, 120, 128, 167, 200, 204
'Night Riviera' sleeper 137, 139
No 10800 (prototype) 81
No E26000 (prototype) 65
North British Locomotive Company 25, 76, 80, 119
    A1A-A1A Type 4 'Warship' BR Class '41' 103
    B-B Type 2 BR Class '22' 104
    B-B Type 4 'Warship' BR Class '43' 103–4
    Bo-Bo Type 1 Br Class '16' 81
    Bo-Bo Type 2 BR Classes '21' & '29' 83
North Clyde Line 113, 120
North Eastern Railway (NER) 13, 25, 34, 37, 50
North Eastern Region 12–13, 24–5, 45, 46, 47, 73, 133, 136, 176, 184–5
North Road Darlington Works 25
North Trans-Pennine electrification 202
North Yorkshire Moors Railway 176
Northern Ireland Railways 37

'Ocean Liner Expresses' 133
Office of Rail Regulation (ORR) 215
Oswestry Works 38
Oxford to Bicester Varsity Line 175–6

'Pacer' units 204–6
Park Royal Vehicles 94
Parliament 7, 8, 9
passenger sectorisation 204–6
Passenger Transport Executives 204
Penrith 19, 53
Peppercorn, Arthur 24
Peppercorn Class
    'A1' 4-6-2 24–5
    'A2' 4-6-2 25
    'K1' 2-6-0 25
Pickersgill, William 39
Pilot Scheme 81, 82, 83, 85, 104
Pressed Steel Company 94
'Princess Coronation' Pacifics 34, 42, 53
'Princess Royal' Class 4-6-2 34, 154
privatisation 7, 182, 192, 204, 206, 214–16
Provincial (later Regional Railways) 204
Pullmans 128, 130, 132, 136, 149
    see also Blue Pullmans

'Queen of Scots' 133

'Race to the North', 1888 58
'Rail Alphabet' typeface 178

Rail Blue (Monastral Blue) 167, 178–9, 180, 203
Rail Express Systems (RES) 150–1, 167, 206
Railfreight 206
'Railfreight Grey' 206
Railnet 151
Railtrack 215–16
Railway Executive 9, 12, 42, 58
'railway mania' 8
railway preservation 186, 208–10
Railway Technical Centre 197
railway works 32–9
   see also specific works
Railways Acts
   1921 9
   1993 7, 182, 215
   2005 215
Railways Division 12
Ravenglass & Ersdale Railway 149
Regional Railways 120, 167, 204–6
Reid, William 38
Riddles, Robert 23, 42, 44–7, 58
road transport 19
Robert Stephenson & Hawthorns 22, 80, 86
Robertson, Sir Brian 74
Robin Hood Line 176
rolling stock 20, 204–6
rolling stock leasing companies (ROSCOs) 215
Rolt, Tom 208
Royal Mail 139, 150–1
   Class '325' 120
rural branch lines 140
Ruston & Hornsby 71

St Johns disaster 155–6
St Rollox Works 38–9
ScotRail 139, 204, 215
Scottish Executive 215
Scottish Region 12–13, 35, 39, 45–6, 69, 71, 80–1, 83, 136, 176, 185, 197
Sea Containers 135
Sealink 134–5, 214
seaside branch lines 144–7
'Second Beeching Report' 214
Second World War 9, 20, 22, 29, 32, 34, 42, 63, 65, 73, 110, 111, 116–17, 131, 148, 150, 168
semi-roundhouses 50
Serpell, Sir David 214
Settle–Carlisle Line 88, 171, 176, 185
Severn Tunnel Junction 138–9
'shed bashing' 53
Shinkansen high-speed trains ('bullet trains') 196
Shipping and International Services Division 135
Shrewsbury 20, 184
'Silver Jubilee' 130
sleeping car trains 136–7, 182
Somerset & Dorset Joint Railway 12, 47, 172, 184
South Eastern Railway (SER) 58
'South Wales Pullman, The' 133
South Wales Valleys lines 173–5
South West Main Line 110, 200
Southern Railway (SR) 9, 32, 36, 58, 61, 62, 63–5, 68, 73, 80, 85, 110, 116, 158, 200

Southern Region 12–13, 22–4, 35, 37, 45–7, 58, 63, 77, 81, 84, 86, 97, 110–11, 116, 120, 128, 133, 136, 148, 175, 184, 186, 200
speed records 130
Speedlink 206
SR Class 'D3/12' 350-hp 0-6-0 diesel-electric shunter 68
SR slab-fronted diesel-electric locos 73
Stanier, William 23
Stanier 23–4, 32, 34, 42
   2-6-4T 23
   Class '5' 4-6-0 ('Black Five') 20, 23, 25, 36, 45, 61, 185
   Class '5MT' 4-6-0 23
   'Princess Coronation' 34, 42, 54
   'Royal Scot' Class 4-6-0 58–60, 63
'Star' Class 20, 42
steam locomotives 6, 16, 20–5, 32, 34–9, 42–7, 50, 53, 55, 60–3, 62, 68, 74, 76, 88, 100, 130–2, 161, 184–6, 208–10
steam sheds 184–5
Stena Line 135
Stephenson Locomotive Society 161
Stockton & Darlington Railway 34
Strategic Rail Authority (SRA) 215
Stratford Works 36, 53–5, 69, 81
Swallow logo 182
Swindon Works 20–2, 24, 32, 36–7, 42, 45–7, 68–9, 76, 89, 94, 103–4, 106, 126, 161, 180

Talyllyn Railway 208
taxpayers, cost of British Railways to 19, 75, 80, 171, 215–16
'Tees-Tyne Pullman' 133
Thameslink 202
'Thanet Belle' 133
Thatcher, Margaret 214
Thompson, Edward 24
Thompson Class 'B1' 4-6-0 25, 61
Thrall 38
tilting trains 196, 198
TOPS classification 68, 89, 97, 118–19, 134
Tourist Second Opens 128
traction maintenance depots (TMDs) 108–9
train á grande vitesse (TGV) 196
train-operating companies (TOCs) 215
Trainload Freight 206
Trains Illustrated (periodical) 159
trainspotting 158–61
Trans-Europe Express 179
trans-Pennine line 19
Transport Acts
1947 9
1962 12, 19
2000 215
Transport Consultative Committees 19, 171
Transrail Freight 206
Travelling Post Office (TPO) 128, 150–1, 206
Type 2 'Baby Warships' 76
Type 2 (Scottish Region) 80
Type 4 'Peaks' 76, 90
Type 4 'Warships' 76
Type 5 190–2

unions 6, 92–3
United Pointsmen and Signalmen's Society 93
Urie, Robert 35

Vale of Rheidol Railway 185
Virgin Rail Group 119, 120
Vulcan Foundry 80, 86, 90, 116, 118

W. G. Bagnall 22
Wabtec 35
Waggon & Maschinebau 94
War Department 42, 58, 73
Ward, Thomas, scrapyard 89
Warwickshire Railway Society 159
Waterloo-Bournemouth-Weymouth line 184
Welsh Assembly 215
West Coast Main Line (WCML) 13, 35, 63, 77, 86, 88–90, 111–13, 118–20, 171, 180, 182, 185, 196, 198, 200, 214–15
'West Country' and 'Battle of Britain' Class 4-6-2 22
'West Country' and 'Battle of Britain' light Pacifics 20
Western Region (WR) 12–13, 16, 20–3, 36, 63, 76, 80, 82, 84, 87, 100–4, 106, 118, 128, 133, 136, 149, 172–5, 179–80, 184, 186, 197–8
'White Rose, The' 133
Whittle, Sir Frank 62
Wilson, Harold 172
Winsford, Cheshire 154
'Withered Arm, The' 12
Wolmar, Christian 216
Wolverton Works 37, 126, 150
Woodham, Dai, Barry scrapyard 22, 44, 45, 186, 209
Woodhead Line 36, 111, 116, 117, 120, 176
Woodhead Tunnel 6, 65, 111
Worsdell, Wilson 25
Worsdell Class 'J72' 0-6-0T 25

XP64-liveried demonstration train 128, 179, 180

York Works 37–8, 126, 150
Yorkshire Engine Company 22, 69, 81
'Yorkshire Pullman' 133

Zeeland Steamship Company 135

Endpaper captions

Front: Classic shot of work-stained BR Standard Class '9F' 2-10-0 No 92216 hauling a long train of mineral wagons sometime in the early 1960s.

Rear: Class '47' diesel-electric No 47811 passes Cockwood Harbour with an InterCity express on 26 March 1994.

Photograph acknowledgements

t = top; b = bottom; l = left; r = right; m = middle

Alamy: front jacket cover (Clive Jones/Alamy Stock Photo); front endpaper (Allan Cash Picture Library/Alamy Stock Photo); rear endpaper (Anthony Kay/Archive/Alamy Stock Photo); 217 (PA Images/Alamy Stock Photo)

Ben Ashworth: 173bl

Casserley, Henry: 17t; 22br

Cuneo Fine Arts/Getty Images: PLC cover

Colour-Rail: 4/5 (M Beckett); 16tr; 16bl; 17b; 18t; 18b (T B Owen); 19br; 20b (T B Owen); 21tr (T B Owen); 23 (J Harrison); 24b (G H Hunt); 29 (S R Lillie); 30t (D L Dott); 33b; 38 (T B Owen); 39; 40/41 (T B Owen); 43b; 44tr (P Chancellor); 44b; 45t (G Parry Collection); 45bl; 47tr (D C Ovenden); 47b; 51t; 52t (T B Owen); 53 (Charlie Cross); 59t; 59b; 60 (T B Owen); 61; 62 (B Perryman); 65; 74b; 75; 36; 84t (B J Swain); 85ml (F Hornby); 88 (A. Cox); 89tr; 89b; 90t; 90mr (G Devine Collection); 91t; 91b (P J Hughes); 93tl (T B Owen); 93b (G H Hunt); 94; 96t; 96b (R Patterson); 101; 102; 103ml (T B Owen); 103b (T B Owen); 104t; 104br (David Lawrence); 105t; 105b (F Hornby); 106/107 (Roger Kay); 109b (R Hunter); 110 (C J B Sanderson); 111 (K C H Fairey); 112/113 (John E Henderson); 122 (P R Binks); 124b (G H Hunt); 126 (David A Lawrence); 127t; 127b; 128/129t (J Rodgers); 128/129b; 130 (R Green); 134 (A Price); 135; 137b (B Perryman); 138b; 139; 149 (F Hornby); 141t (J Spencer Gilks Collection); 141b; 142/143; 144b; 145 (C Hogg); 147b (T B Owen); 148 (T B Owen); 151b (G Goodall); 154/155 (F Hornby); 160 (R Yale); 164ml; 164mr; 164b; 165 (David A Lawrence); 170; 173t (I Thomas); 178b; 179; 181t (G Parry Collection); 181b (T B Owen); 182/183 (John E Henderson); 184 (R Siviter); 190 (P J Hughes); 191t; 192/193 (T B Owen); 194/195 (Edward Ward); 197b (G W Parry); 199m (I Thomas); 199b; 200 (Edward Ward); 201t (D Pye); 201b (T B Owen); 202/203; 205t (T B Owen); 205b; 206 (E Stocker); 207b; 214 (B Perryman)

Gordon Edgar Collection: 6/7; 8; 12; 21b; 22bl; 24m; 25 (A E Durrant); 26/27 (Alan Orchard); 31; 35b; 43t; 46tr; 46b; 48/49; 50; 51b; 52b; 54/55; 56/57 (D F Witts); 66/67; 71 (Charlie Cross); 77; 81; 82tl (Charlie Cross); 82tr (Charlie Cross); 82ml (Charlie Cross); 83; 85tl (Charlie Cross); 86 (Charlie Cross); 87b 97 (Graham Roose); 98/99; 108ml (A E Durrant); 116m; 117br; 118b; 120tl; 120br; 121t (Roy Burt); 124b; 158; 162/163; 185 (Alan Orchard); 186 (Eric F Bentley); 187t (Charlie Cross); 187b; 188/189

Gordon Edgar: 33t; 35t; 37; 68; 69; 70t; 70b; 72t; 72b; 73; 78/79; 80; 84bl; 85tl; 87tr; 95t; 95b; 108b; 109m; 117t; 118ml; 119t; 121b; 123t; 136; 150; 152/153; 161; 172; 191b; 198; 204; 207t; 208; 209; 210t; 210b; 211;

212/213; 216; 218/219

Mike Esau: 146t

John Goss: 168; 174; 175; 177

Julian Holland: 10/11; 14/15; 32; 74tr; 125tr; 131tr; 137tr; 138tr; 159; 169br; 176; 215

Gavin Morrison: 131b; 171

G R Mortimer: 133

Science Museum Group: 9; 19bl; 92; 100; 114/115; 125b; 133; 144tr; 149; 151tr; 154/155; 156bl; 166/167; 169bl; 180; 196; 197tl

Shutterstock: 6tl; 28; 30; 178t

Unknown: 64t; 64b; 178tr

With thanks to Gordon Edgar for research assistance and advice.